Outlaws in the
Promised Land

Outlaws in the Promised Land

MEXICAN IMMIGRANT WORKERS AND AMERICA'S FUTURE

James D. Cockcroft

GROVE PRESS, INC./New York

For my best friend Hedda Garza—
may the great love always be ours.

First Grove Press Edition 1986
First Printing 1986
ISBN: 0-394-54592-3
Library of Congress Catalog Card Number: 84-73206

First Evergreen Edition 1986
First Printing 1986
ISBN: 0-394-62365-7
Library of Congress Catalog Card Number: 84-73206

Library of Congress Cataloging-in-Publication Data

Cockcroft, James D.
   Outlaws in the promised land.

   1. Alien labor, Mexican—United States.   2. Alien
labor, Mexican—United States—Forecasting.   3. United
States—Emigration and immigration—law and legis-
lation.   I. Title.
HD8081.M6C63   1986   3316'2'72073   84-73206
ISBN 0-394-54592-3
ISBN 0-394-62365-7 (1st Evergreen ed.   : pbk.)

Printed in the United States of America

GROVE PRESS, INC., 196 West Houston Street, New York, N.Y. 10014

5   4   3   2   1

CONTENTS

ACKNOWLEDGMENTS

This book is, indirectly, a product of many minds and hands whose labors I can never adequately repay. To do so, I would have to locate and thank all those migrant workers in the United States, Mexico, and elsewhere (Lagos, Teheran, Berlin, etc.) who, in their many forms of expression and education, illuminated for me the intricacies of what has become a worldwide confluence of migratory streams bearing the hopes, sufferings, and future of much of humanity.

Many of these hardworking men, women, and children helped "educate the educators"—colleagues and students who participated in research teams I directed from 1980 to 1983 on the subject of international labor migration in the Sociology Departments of the Universität Bielefeld (West Germany), the Universidad Autónoma Metropolitana (UAM)–Azcapotzalco (Mexico City), and Rutgers University (New Brunswick, New Jersey), and in the Department of Mexican American Studies at San Diego State University in California. To these students and colleagues I am also greatly indebted.

Team research conducted with a dozen faculty members and graduate students at the UAM-Azcapotzalco produced much of the material on the migrants' experiences that informs these pages. Hundreds of questionnaires were administered to migrant workers and their families in central and western Mexico (the greater Bajío region, so-called food basket of Mexico).

Typical of the "participatory" character of our research was the in-depth work we conducted with the residents of La Purísima, Michoa-

9

cán, an agrarian community located next to the state capital of Morelia midway between the metropolises of Guadalajara and Mexico City. Some of the schoolchildren of the town helped administer the questionnaires to their relatives and neighbors. Both the drafting and the final wording of the questionnaires were accomplished collectively by our research team and the migrant workers and their families.*

We achieved this cooperative method of work because of two shared assumptions. The first is that knowledge, a product of continuous human exchange, is meaningless in the absence of action—and vice-versa. The second is that any educational activity is necessarily subjective; therefore, the task of the people conducting it becomes one of defining specific goals and designing appropriate methods for achieving them.

From the outset, our research team promised the residents of La Purísima only what we could deliver: a more or less regular consultation and cooperation with them; delivery of information available to us but as yet unknown by them; and, in the absence of a budget to pay anyone a decent wage, a commitment to acknowledge the residents' help and to deliver to them copies of a book synthesizing our (and their) findings on their community—and offering additional information on the larger national and international context of their lives.

Many were the townspeople who informed us after receipt of the book—*Trabajadores de Michoacán*—that ours was the first outside group to "keep its promises." The book—in effect *their* book—has since become a useful tool in their and others' work with local, regional, and national authorities and/or groups to demand social reforms and to improve their lives. Since this was our goal all along, we could not have been more satisfied.

For funding assistance, I would like to thank the Ford Foundation in Mexico City for its seed grant for the same project, the Fulbright Program for its grant on my behalf, and the UAM-Azcapotzalco for use of its facilities during 1980–81, when much of the Mexican research was conducted.

Once again, I would like to thank the people of La Purísima, Michoacán, for their hospitality and generous help. I also would like to

---

*A complex, exciting, and rewarding way to gain knowledge and contribute to social change, "participatory research" has in recent years become the subject of much attention and controversy. For an excellent collection of materials illustrating the participatory approach and dealing with some of the experiences in the Bajío region, consult Jorge Fuentes Morua, ed., *La organización de los campesinos y los problemas de la investigación participativa* (Morelia: imisac, 1983), and articles by members of the UAM-Azcapotzalco Migration Research Team in *Revista 'A'* 4:8 ("Migración y problemas fronterizos," January–April 1983).

thank the members of the UAM-Azcapotzalco Migration Research Team—especially José Antonio Alonso, Martha Loyo Camacho, Nora Pérez Rayón, Javier Rodríguez Piña, and Paz Trigueros—for their invaluable participation in the fieldwork research. I particularly wish to acknowledge for their cooperation at critical moments of the research and for their contributions to my own intellectual development Herman Baca of the Committee for Chicano Rights; sociologists Jorge Bustamante, Maximiliano Iglesias, and Martín de la Rosa; and migrant worker Isauro Reyes, whose testimony composes Chapter 1.

Words cannot adequately express my debt to free-lance writer Hedda Garza, whose keen insights, usually original and always based on hardheaded common sense and an eclectic knowledge of history, helped advance my understanding of many of the issues raised here. She also provided invaluable editorial assistance in early drafts of the chapters, in proofreading, and in providing a highly useful analytical index. Her friendship, companionship, and love sustain me in every way.

Finally, I would like to acknowledge the professional skills of Grove Press editor Lisa Rosset and free-lance copy editor Joy Johannesen. Their editing of the manuscript unquestionably added to the book's clarity, simplicity, and cohesion—no small accomplishment, given the complexity of the subjects raised. To Rachel Salazar and all the hardworking people at Grove go many thanks as well. Naturally, the final responsibility for the contents of this book is mine.

—James D. Cockcroft

Friends Lake, Feb. 7, 1986

INTRODUCTION

▼

"The crops are all in and the peaches are rotting.
The oranges are stacked in their creosote dumps.
They're flying them back to that Mexico border
To pay all their wages to wade back again.

We died in your hills and we died on your deserts.
We died in your valleys. We died on your plains.
We died 'neath your trees and we died in your bushes.
Both sides of that river we died just the same.

Is this the best way we can grow our big orchards?
Is this the best way we can grow our good fruit?
To fall like dry leaves and rot on the topsoil,
And be known by no name except deportee."
—"Deportee," lyrics by Woody Guthrie

"There can be no economic revival in ghettos when the
most violent among us are allowed to roam free. It is
time we restored domestic tranquility. And we mean to
do just that."
—President Ronald Reagan,
State of the Union Address,
February 6, 1985

Today, a growing proportion of America's labor force is immigrant labor from south of the border. Six out of ten immigrants without legal documents residing in the United States are Mexicans. Contrary to popular belief, the Mexicans do not stay long, and they do not take more than an occasional job away from Americans, most of whom would never work under the oppressive conditions offered.

Yet there is heard in the land a public outcry—orchestrated by influential politicians and powerful segments of the mass media—to "regain control of our borders" and to "restore domestic tranquility." Racism is on the rise; not since the mass deportations of Mexicans during "Operation Wetback" more than three decades ago has there erupted such a hue and cry against this nation's Mexicans and Latinos.

Constructing a tall and sturdy fence along the US-Mexican border, as the Carter administration tried to do in the late 1970s, is an insult to human intelligence and an outrage against human dignity—as well as an impractical folly. Mexican immigrant workers, who for generations have risked life and limb to enter the United States to help harvest the nation's crops, build its railroads, and service its industries, have jokingly dubbed the only partially completed steel-mesh fence "the tortilla curtain," so porous is the almost 2,000-mile-long border separating the two nations.

Ordinarily, however, Americans do not hear the knowledgeable voices of these Mexican immigrants. One of them, Isauro Reyes, speaks to us in this book's opening chapter. It is time that we open our ears to such voices and heed what is being said, for, as we shall learn, the destiny of these men, women, and children is inexorably intertwined with our own.

Isauro Reyes has traveled to the United States often, as have most of his neighbors in the rural hamlet of La Purísima, Michoacán, in west-central Mexico. Readers should keep in mind that La Purísima is better off than most of the hometowns of Mexican immigrant workers. And yet the conditions of life there suggest the reasons why so many Mexicans seek temporary employment every year *en el norte*—in the United States.

La Purísima is an agricultural village of about 2,000 people. Most of the families are *ejidatarios*, owners of parcels of communal lands known as *ejidos*. Besides growing sorghum and other commercial crops, the *ejidatarios* operate a thriving pig farm of 700 animals, financed by Banco Rural (Banrural), and they are planning a poultry industry as well. Whether *ejidatarios*, small farmers, or dayworkers (*jornaleros*), most of La Purísima's families are hopelessly in debt, usually to the nation's main source of agrarian credit, the government-run Banrural. As one group of the town's *ejidatarios* explained to this author in 1980,

> Banrural is our *patron* [boss]. We're the workers and we don't even get a wage or have a labor union. We feel more exploited by the Bank than if we were officially its employees. Our earnings in the field are far inferior to what we would earn if we worked for the Bank.

La Purísima's dayworkers are even worse off. Having no tractors, fertilizers, or irrigated land, most of them migrate to Mexico City to seek employment in construction, or to other parts of the Mexican countryside to "follow the harvest trail." In other Michoacán villages, such as the more impoverished Tlazazalco many miles west of La Purísima, peasants are trying to organize a new system of obtaining credits and supplies independent of Banrural, based on a nascent coalition of towns and *ejidos*.

Most of La Purísima's residents have never finished grade school, and a third do not know how to read or write. On the average, the town's farmers and workers earn less than a dollar a day, even though a warm climate and irrigation allow two harvests a year. Little wonder, then, that more than half of the hundreds of people interviewed in 1980–81 by this author and the Universidad Autónoma Metropolitana–Azcapotzalco Migration Research Team stated that they had at least one relative living outside the village (California ranked first, Greater Mexico City second, and Texas third).

For more than 150 years many Mexicans residing in the United States—above all migrant workers like those from La Purísima—have been treated as though they were "outlaws in the promised land." This book's title is meant to reflect the irony of such treatment even as the same Mexicans have been avidly sought by employers anxious to take advantage of their inexpensive labor power.

"Outlaws" is not meant here in the pejorative sense of "bandits," although it is well known that many Americans stereotype Mexicans that way. Rather, it is meant in the literal sense of "outside the law," a category that employers find especially attractive because it entails literally *no rights whatsoever for the workers involved*.

A laborer without rights is an employer's dream come true. And the Mexican migrant workers have the added advantage, from an employer's point of view, of being easily importable and deportable as long as they are defined as outside the law. As we shall see, America's employers call the tune when it comes to letting Mexican laborers in or kicking them out, and they do their level best to keep the border doors revolving at a rhythm that suits their needs.

Yet for two consecutive administrations, one Democratic and the other Republican, there has been urged upon the US Congress legisla-tion like the Simpson-Mazzoli bill that would place large numbers of Mexican workers inside the law instead of outside it—with, as Chapter 8 explains, numerous restrictions on their rights. If employers benefit from keeping Mexicans outside the law, then why do so many of them now welcome legalizing the migrants' status? Just as significantly, if both the Carter and Reagan presidencies so vigorously sought such a change in the Mexicans' legal status, then why did the Simpson-Maz-zoli bill repeatedly fail to pass?

Indeed, just what is the controversy raging around Simpson-Maz-zoli and the Mexican immigrant workers all about anyway? And why has it surfaced now and not earlier?

This book reveals that the controversy is deeply embedded in the character of the current economic crisis (see Chapter 5), as well as in earlier events in history. The diverse contradictions characterizing the recruitment and deportation of millions of Mexicans since the turn of the century, and especially since the legal importation of Mexican la-borers during the so-called bracero period (1942–64), are still very much with us. Past history and current realities, then, explain why the contradictions reappear so starkly in bills like Simpson-Mazzoli now coming before the Congress (see Appendix IV).

In the pages that follow, we will attempt to answer such compli-cated questions as the following:

· If the purpose is to "regain control" of the border with Mexico, then why does legislation like Simpson-Mazzoli include an open-ended "guest worker" program that places no limits on the number of Mexi-cans entering the United States?

· If "illegals" (note the emotive similarity of the word to "outlaws") are to be punished, then why are they being given amnesty?

· If employers of Mexican "illegals" are to be fined or jailed, then why do so many of them support or accept the legislation?

· If there is no provision for some kind of national ID card, then why do critics insist on saying that there is one?

· If the rights of minorities and immigrant workers are to be protected by the legislation, then why do Latino and black organizations oppose it?

· Why do AFL-CIO spokesmen and leading politicians like Walter Mondale and Ronald Reagan support this legislation one day and oppose it the next?

· Why do some conservatives condemn the legislation as "rewarding criminals" while others champion it in the name of preserving the linguistic and racial "balance" of the American people?

When, in the fall of 1984, the Simpson-Mazzoli bill met its most recent of many deaths, proponents of "regaining control of our borders" and using cheap Mexican immigrant labor suffered only a legislative defeat, not an economic one. In terms of everyday economic reality, nothing changed.

In fact, in January 1985 the Immigration and Naturalization Service (INS) announced it would attempt to change the rules so that the main labor item guaranteed by Simpson-Mazzoli—easy importation of Mexican workers—could be implemented more easily. INS officials explained that they wanted to keep the issue of Mexican immigrant labor out of the legislative arena (where defeats of Simpson-Mazzoli made it difficult to deal with, in any case) by handling it through regulations. Once the new rules are published in the Federal Register, giving people a chance to comment, the INS can issue the final rules, which will have the force of law.

According to the INS's new proposed rules, farmers no longer will have to search for American workers if the Agriculture Department declares perishable crops to be in danger. Nor will they have to provide housing to temporary foreign workers; a cash housing allowance will suffice. Moreover, employers will no longer have to show that qualified American workers are not available. They will no longer have to provide any minimum period of employment for the foreign workers, who will be allowed to stay in the United States for twenty days after the job ends to search for work elsewhere. The implications, spelled out in this book, are clear: for employers, it is "open season" on Mexican immigrant workers and American labor unions, permitting virtually unchecked exploitation of foreign workers and seriously undermining union efforts to organize not just farm laborers but industrial and service workers as well (see Chapters 7 and 9).

The proposed INS rules confirm and accentuate the urgency of the ultimate question raised in these pages: can American democracy survive when it condemns so many millions of honest, hardworking people to the ranks of "outlaws" ("illegals," "aliens"), stripping them of every fundamental human and labor right? American democracy may be facing its most difficult hour since the McCarthy era. The historic cancer of American racism, symbolized by the continuing physical attacks on, even murders of, Mexican immigrant workers and the recent vote in Greater Miami's Dade County to eliminate bilingual education, threatens to erode the entire social system's uncertain stability. America's future rides on the fate of Mexican and other immigrant workers in far more ways than the economic and social ones emphasized here.

1

An Immigrant Worker Speaks

A village spokesman whose father and grandfather migrated to the United States before him, Isauro Reyes is a *ranchero* (small farmer) from La Purísima, Michoacán. Fifty-six years of age, father and grandfather of an immense family, he owns a ten-acre parcel of land on an irrigated *ejido* (community land guaranteed by agrarian reform law) that he has worked since a boy. Slump-shouldered, short, his face criss-crossed with crow's-feet wrinkles, he speaks with calm passion, his hands often waving for emphasis, his deep-set brown eyes sparkling.

I first went to the United States in 1954, as a *bracero* [legally contracted immigrant worker]; I signed a contract. The first of the bracero contract signups were held in 1942 and 1943 in Mexico City, Toluca, Uruápan, Irapuato, and another community, another *rancho* [cluster of small farms] this side of Toluca—I can't recollect its name. In all those places there were contract centers.

Eventually the *coyoteada* [system of paid guides for migrants entering the United States] came along. It began when some men got in good with employers there at the contract signup centers and, as I understand it, the word spread that there was an easy way to make some money by charging every bracero who wanted to go north a certain fee. And that's what happened; they started making us pay. Back then they charged five hundred, sometimes as much as a thousand pesos. If the *coyote* got your card for you and you went with a group

19

that he took to the border, he charged fifteen hundred pesos. There are *padres* living right around here who were clever enough to get in on that. There's one in Tejaro, another in Vandacareo, who sent a ton of folks on the bracero trail. They made bundles of money; with a lot of willing workers, you can collect many thousands of pesos. They sent folks northward with those people who were at the contract office. It went like this:

"*Padre*, I want to go to the north."

"Yes, but you need such-and-such an amount."

"Yeah, okay, here's your money."

"Then on such-and-such a day you be there."

Almost every week a group was taken to the north, so those *coyote padres* got rich solely from the trade in braceros. Over here in Morelia there's a guy, his name is Jesús Tudillo, who was the runner for that *padre* from Tejaro, running braceros. That son of a gun is living in a really first-class setup after retiring from his service for that Tejaro *padre* as an operator of the bracero trail. He robbed what would be like two hundred thousand pesos today, and in addition he's got himself a high-class piece of real estate over in Morelia.

After closing some of the contract centers around here, they moved them closer to the border, to Hermosillo, Monterrey, Nuevo León, Reynosa, Ciudad Juárez, Chihuahua, and as far north as Mexicali. After that you had to go far away just to try to get a contract. So it was that I had to go to Mexicali to contract myself out the first time. In those days, since I have always been on good terms with the government and at that time it was with the mayor, I would hear from the mayor each time the list arrived laying out the number and kinds of workhands needed. And I myself would call together the *compañeros* of my community here, right here in La Purísima, and I would go to the mayor.

"You just got the list, right?"

"Yes."

"Okay, then, there'll be coming so many from each *rancho*."

Says he, "No, man, let me conduct this business."

"No, no, what do you mean, let you conduct this business, if he has already sent you the list that says exactly how many workers are needed?"

He said, "Okay, Isauro, you're right. But what about me?"

"Your reward is carrying out your responsibility," I told him.

That was how I handled things. That was back in '54.

I had already been in Texas—Edinburg, Texas—as an "illegal," and that was no good. I got out of there. The work was the worst, picking tomatoes. No way. I earned four, maybe five pesos a day. No, I packed my bag. I arrived here and waited for the bracero list. The list sent me all the way to the border in Mexicali. I was assigned to lettuce up there in the Imperial Valley in California.

Ay, what an exhausting job, to go along an endless row like from here to my first house, the thatched hut down below near those fields, hoeing, cultivating, weeding. We used *el cortito* [banned as inhumane by California governor Jerry Brown in 1975], a six-inch short-handled hoe, and bent over like this, all the way stooped over, to make for pure weedless lettuce. A mountain of weeds piling up like this, to leave just one plant cultivated. In the evenings I would unbend myself and see my face flabby with fat and my hands swollen because all the blood had rushed downward. I lasted six months in that valley—from the start of the cultivation to the end of the harvest.

Later, in '55, I left again and got sent to Coachella, California, picking tomatoes, chile peppers, and artichokes. And there I threw myself into it for another six months. I returned home that same year, got my things together once more, and went to Orange County to pick oranges. I was there forty-five days, but one thing: you made very little, you know? They doled out just enough for you to survive. So I returned again, no sooner arriving and working my land a few days, arranging the labor to keep it producing, than leaving again.

In '56 I contracted myself out again. I was in California three months picking peaches and cherries. I returned, and later there was another list, and I left for Alamo, Texas, to pick grapefruits for forty-five days. With all these trips I made enough to dress and feed my family and still have a little left over. So I said to my woman, "Here, take this money and make a down-payment on a tractor and have the boys see that the tractor does that labor." Then I went back for another forty-five days in Alamo, Texas, picking grapefruits.

It was the same in 1957. They continued to give out just enough work to keep people going, so I signed up and my lot was to pick cotton in Texas. I lived there two months, returned home, and then left for Pecos, Texas, also for cotton, and lasted three months. There went another three months. Then I came back and left again in '58, and I was in Amarillo, Texas, also cotton, another three months. Then home again, sign up again, and it was Lobos, Texas—cotton again.

I was making just enough to let the boys finish primary school and to dress and feed the family. There was not enough left over for anything else; I used the income and credit from my land parcel here to begin building this house. Later, I managed to save up some more dollars from working in the north to finish the house.

In '59 I signed up and went to Michigan—no, Arkansas, and from Arkansas I traveled to Michigan. In Arkansas it was cotton, and in Michigan cucumbers. That was the year I made it all the way to Canada. The bus driver lost his way and took us into Canada. The Canadians also transported braceros in those days from here in Mexico, and they paid them better. The money's worth the same in Canada as in the United States, but there they paid you more. But because we were traveling under a contract to work in the United States, we were not allowed to stay in Canada. It always said where you were going in the contract: "You are going to the county of Michigan" or "to the county of Texas." For example, if McAllen, Texas, is the municipality or district, the contract said, "You are going to the county of McAllen."

It seemed like they treated us contracted workers better then the *mojados* ["wetbacks" or "illegals"], because they provided us with cooks paid for by the company; so they fed us well. But in 1960, the last year that I went as a bracero, they made us pay the cook or, if we preferred, board ourselves. Actually, they had been checking the cooks' wages off from our pay all along. So we began to provide the lunches and dinners ourselves, and it came out cheaper than paying for the company cook, so we made a little bit more money. We did everything—we cooked, washed, ironed, and did all the housework. We arrived from a day's work to work again—but hard, man—patting and flipping tortillas, preparing supper, preparing fried beans for the next day, cooking the meat—in a word, we did everything.

In cotton they paid us by the quintal—a quintal is a hundred pounds—at two-fifty a quintal. In cotton we worked from sunup to sundown days and days and a half; at times, though, like during the harvest, it rains a lot, and we didn't work a full day every day. If we worked a full day we made around ten dollars, four and a half quintals—four hundred or four hundred and fifty pounds. There were a few who could pick up to five hundred pounds, and they saved up a few more cents. They could pick more because they had very agile hands. To pick cotton you have to lift up—pick not like this but like this—and get to the dry part here in the middle. Then, you and your workmates are lining up like this, all the way up to your waist in cotton, and you are grabbing with this finger while the other is right behind picking. And someone else is right behind you, and then the next guy, right?

We worked very hard back then and spent just enough to sustain ourselves. Everything here in La Purísima was very poor. If there are houses here, they were made with pure American money that was earned over there. In those days this was a sad and miserable place.

When you pick cucumbers, you wear sacks in front of your belt, sacks of this size, see? That leaves you with room to move your feet, and so you're moving along like this picking cucumbers. You get five dollars a quintal for the most tender cucumber. And for a cucumber already full-grown like this they paid you two-fifty, and for one like this, super-big, a dollar a quintal. Well, it didn't come out so bad for us. And later it was done by groups, and if the group didn't move, you didn't make anything.

Once I was working with a group of nine—four working hard and five not so hard. Five weren't putting out, you know what I mean? So I spoke to an American about it. He was one of the more decent ones, a schoolteacher, you know? And so with the little bit of English I knew I told him that it did not suit the four of us to be saddled with the other five who moved so slowly and that we couldn't put up with their making money off our backs.

"No," I said, "it would be very good next week to cut us four off from them to work alone."

Now, yeah, now with those lazy bums off our backs we made as much as ten, fifteen bucks a day, because now we worked and we harvested more. But it wasn't much more. Rarely did anyone from our country have the luck to land a good job. Maybe an occasional guy earned forty, fifty dollars a day, but when there were other better jobs I never got the chance to land one. I was stuck in pure agriculture and fruits; but there were a few who worked as cooks and earned top dollar.

That's how we did it, that was how it was during the days of contracting out. As an "illegal" I went no more than twice. Once was here to Texas. There the law grabbed us right away, I didn't last more than eight days. There were still contract centers, but I left and went to pick cotton in Tamaulipas, and from there I slid over the border, nineteen hundred and . . . oh, somewhere around 1950. I lasted some days at that, three months, but I lasted only eight days in the United States, and the other months I finished off here along the border, along the Río Bravo picking cotton.

That Río Bravo is a very dangerous critter. In those days it gobbled up a lot of people. We would cross it in a launch that was known as a *patero* [duckboat]—a launch that was no less than two meters long. A *coyote* would charge us two, three dollars to get across to the other side. As soon as we were across, we would follow him to where we were going to work. That time I went as a *mojado* and not as a bracero because at first I was going to the border of Tamaulipas, I was not heading for the north, but once there we began to get together with the others. Someone would say, "Look, let's cross over, what the hell, let's try our luck," and you would say, "Sure, let's get movin'."

We went. I already knew that during those years, from '50 on back, they were producing a lot of cotton, and it was good cotton, so the money was good. That's why I went there. And throughout the 1950s there were a whole lot of people picking cotton from here northward to the border; I went as far as Baja California to pick cotton. I went by bus as far as Sinaloa. Then from Sinaloa I followed the trail picking cotton on farms all the way to Baja. Once the harvest ended in Sinaloa, it began in Sonora; then when it finished in Sonora, it began in Baja California; and that's how my life went in the 1950s.

All of those trips were under legal contracts. I didn't go there as contraband, as an "illegal" again, until about a year ago [1980]—this coming March it will be a year. I went from here to Tijuana, Baja California. I went because of my son—the one that's studying. I was, quite frankly, completely exhausted and worn out from having to work so hard to come up with the money to support my children.

Look, I know our *ejido* is better off than most around here—we have tractors, fertilizers, and above all, we have irrigation. But truth to tell, we're hopelessly indebted to the government bank. Banco Rural is our *patrón*, our boss. We're the workers, and we don't even get a wage or have a labor union. Let me tell you something: we feel more exploited by the bank than if we were officially its employees. Our earnings from farming are far less than what we'd get if we were bank employees. Why do you suppose that we have to migrate? We can't make it as farmers, that's why. We're always in debt.

Why, I remember back in 1948, 1949, the Banco Rural sent in the *federales* [army troops] to collect our debts, soldiers with guns. And at that time I was president of the *ejido*, so I said to the bank inspector, "I'm very sorry, my peasants are not bandits that you have to control with the *federales*. We are honest, hardworking peasants. We are producers, not bandits that you have to send the *federales* to collect our investments, the loans from the bank. I cannot accept this from you, I'm very sorry, but you are going to have to withdraw these troops." And he had to withdraw them.

Look, I was paying a thousand pesos a month last year just for this one boy's education. Then . . . this one, my studious son, he came along and said to me, "Papa, you know what? I'm enthusiastic about studying, but I see you are so worn out with so many others here to take care of and giving me a thousand pesos a month. The situation is too rough, so I think I should quit school for a while. I want to study, it's true," he says, "but what do I gain if you are so run-down and don't have enough? I'd be better off stealing."

"You don't have to steal," I said. "I've never stolen in my whole life. I'm at the end of my rope now, but I will never be a thief, never."

"But what are you going to do then?" he asked me. "The *mixtamal* [a type of cornmeal used to make tortillas] is being prepared now, and that's all there is to eat."

When the *mixtamal* is mashed, it comes out to four servings a day—more like three and a half a day, you hear me?

"Father," he says, "you are very fatigued, you are going to wear yourself out, and for what? So I'm interested in studying, but with you like this, with you so beaten down, it's better that I don't study."

"No, son, go on studying, I must continue the struggle."

He said, again, "You are very tired. You know what? Let's see if we can't go and get a little help up there in the north, man."

I realized by now that I could not stop him, so I said, "Yeah, okay."

But to myself I said, "I'll take this boy of mine along so that he can see that it's no picnic. He'll find out that up there it's work every day and the jobs are backbreaking hard."

I told him, "Okay, then, get yourself ready and we're leaving on such-and-such a day."

We left here on the twentieth of March. It cost us seven hundred and twenty-five pesos to get from Morelia to Tijuana. And we arrived at that Hotel Mecacha, and there I located a friend of mine. He's a *coyote* from around here, from the lakeshore on the other side. "Listen, Esteban," I told him, "I know that you can get people over to the other side. Well, I have my son here."

"Of course, man," he said. "You'll go tonight. Even my son is going. Just don't take off and leave the boy alone. How far are you going?"

"Well, I'm going as far as Harbor City—there I've got a few nephews. I'll see you there and pay you then."

"Fine, you'll leave tonight."

That's how it happened. In Harbor City, near Los Angeles, me and my boy got work right away, and it lasted for a week and a half. We worked in *la yarda* [home gardening and yard work] and in construction, digging foundations for houses. Then there wasn't any more work for us because there were so many "illegals" looking for work and the ones who had sponsors were the ones who got work.

So I said to another *compañero*, "Hey, here it's going to be real tough, man. In the old days when we used to come here under contract there was a lot of work here, but with all the contraband there are lots of people and very little work."

"Yeah," he told me, "I'm heading for Chicago. I'm going to telephone right now."

He had a nephew in Chicago. So he phoned Chicago and asked his nephew to send him money for the trip. He already had been over there in Chicago. He had luck with the phone call and came over to say goodbye.

"Hey," says he, "I'm leaving. And you, are you staying?"

"Well, yeah, so long as I can't muster the money to get me a flight there."

"Look," he says, "I know where your cousins live, and you could call them right now and ask them for the fare."

"Good, if you know then ask your nephew over the phone."

Yes, they gave him the phone number, and I called my cousins. I told them, "Here I am in California. Can you help me get there?"

"Yes, of course."

I told him, "Guess what, I'm with my young son."

Says he, "Look, for the present we are going to send you three hundred dollars. You get here, and later we'll send for the boy."

That's what happened. They sent me the money, and I went to Chicago. All together I lasted for two months and twenty days without work—one month ten days in California and one month ten days in Chicago. There just were no jobs. I finally got one because my employer was a friend of mine from around here who had become a labor contractor in Chicago for the *gringos*. I had once helped him in the *polilla* ["gathering chickens," or the business of rounding up and guiding immigrant workers] so that he could become a labor contractor, and over there he developed into one of those real hot-tempered ones. In Chicago we found we could be mutually helpful again. I got him people, I did all the tasks for him, managed all the work in everything for him—machines and *yardas* and statues, working with the ruler and level and hammer and wire. Well, I did all the labor for him.

The job was putting up statues in luxurious gardens. In the gardens we put in Buches trees, that's what they're called. Those trees have spines so that people don't dare trespass into the perfect shining gardens. *Yardas* is the grass that covers a huge area—the lawn. Over there all the Americans use these huge spaces for nothing but lawns—yards, pure grass. Well, that's American taste. It's the luxury of the house. That's the work we did.

But that friend . . . I didn't want to drink, and right there the trouble started. In a short time we parted, and then I met with my cousins and they told me, "It's alright, look, if we don't find another job for you, we'll struggle to see if we can't accommodate you here."

Nothing would work out for me! I spent two weeks again without work, and there wasn't any work anywhere, and I said to them, "You know what, cousins? I'm very well off here. I don't go without shoes, and I have loose change to spend, but what am I gaining here? And what of my sons back home? They have to eat, and they can't without getting something from me. I'm sure they're going through hard times there, so I think it's better if I return home."

Then the oldest said, "You're right, cousin, we understand what you're saying. Already you see how my brother has driven his car to every nook and cranny of the city to find work—and I myself went with him—and there are no jobs anywhere."

I said to him, "Look, I think we might find work, but if I stay here any longer, what's my family going to do? Supplies are running out down there. It's better that I leave."

Then I telephoned a guy who had stayed in Michigan. They had operated on that guy there. I said to him, "Listen, do you have work there? I've had a problem here with this so-and-so I was working for."

He told me, "Look, I'll try to help you, but I've been operated on, and I'm not on the job now. We'll see if my boss comes by, and if he does, I'll talk to him."

Yeah, he spoke to him, but he didn't have anything.

"Okay," I said to him, "now we know there's nothing, so I'm going to leave."

"I wanted to see you this last time," he said, and his voice had a nasal sound. He was very ill from the operation. They operated on his gall bladder. But I had to tell him, "I'm very sorry, Alfredo, no, I'm going to leave."

"Look," says he, "if you're going home tell my people that I've had an operation so that it doesn't take them by surprise, because I am very ill. I believe they want to fly me there, the *gringo* is personally going to take me there, but I don't know, the doctor will decide it."

I stuck around Chicago for three more days and phoned Alfredo again, and he told me, "Look, I think they're going to send me home now. It looks like I'm going to get better."

Then—that same day I had to leave for Mexico—I said to him, "Good, then, that's all I wanted to know. Now I'm going. I'm leaving today."

He and the other boys gave me messages and things to bring to their families. I was taking back about three thousand dollars for them and a heap of clothes like this, big and thick. For another guy I was carrying a trunk like this of nothing but clothes, and in addition I had mine too, so I arrived burdened down with cargo. I traveled by bus from Chicago to Laredo. In Laredo I took a taxi to get to the bus terminal to grab a bus for here, and then direct to Morelia!

My son had stayed in California and then had come home. I had sent money to him in California for his travel to Chicago, but he hadn't expected the money and had come home because things were going so badly in Los Angeles, which I had already realized was the case. So when I saw that he had arrived before me, I told him it was good that he came home.

The townspeople who go to the United States, those who believe in law and responsibility, go to work as "illegals" in order to send money to their families and maybe also to buy a few cows and build a house. They are the responsible ones. The irresponsible ones are those who don't spend their money in the United States but return to their lands in Mexico to drink or to go to Morelia to spend their money on foolish pleasures. In addition, right there in Chicago and in California and over here in Houston, well, people from right here in our own town and other neighboring towns over there are just plain lost. They have stopped working just to drink. They don't even have much clothing. I saw it all in Chicago. I have relatives there, and a few are living lost lives. They work only for their daily booze. The young cousin I stayed with was out drinking every day, and he left me alone there. He'd go out and arrive the next day, and he would always come back drunk.

I said to him, "Red"—because, you see, he was blond—"listen, Red, you are not doing well. No, cousin, you're doing poorly. If you continue your life this way you'd better get out of here and go to Mexico, because you're not even helping your mother." She's the one that has nothing, over the hill there. "You'd better go back to Mexico."

He became half serious. "No," says he, "for me it's the same here or there."

I told him, "No, it's not the same, because there you don't have money for booze and here you do." Then I said to him, "But more than that, if you keep this up, it doesn't matter to me if I cut myself off from you from here on out."

Even if you do that, they just get angry because you won't drink with them. After that I went to see other friends and relatives. I visited everyone, but mostly people from my community. And so many of them had become nothing but drunks that I said to them, "Go back to your lands, you have your mothers, your fathers, and . . . better you go back there to work, for what do you have here? You spend every penny; neither your parents nor you put it to good use. So better you return to your country."

"You're right," they said. "We're going back."

But they've stayed on there. Even youth and older men with obligations and responsibilities, a lot of them are boozing it up too. But for the community here, I don't consider it bad that the people go work in the United States. Those who used to go as braceros were beginning to build their houses with the money they made there. Now anyone who goes there "illegally" also has become accustomed to getting around in the United States. In fact, now the people who like going to the United States are no longer content to stay here. A guy works for the first time there, and in a little while he says, "In such-and-such a month I'm going north," and they go. Then they don't like it here because over there are other pleasures and some money.

A single guy going without work for four, five months over there is one thing, but to go that long without work and have family responsibility back here in your own country is to be irresponsible and neglectful of your family. There are thousands, there are millions of Mexicans over there in the United States who do that to their families, millions who don't come back, who stay over there. Many are married, and their women and children are suffering back here. I see that as wrong. It is distressing to think of those people forgetting their country, forgetting their relatives, their children, their wives, with no more cause than their own irresponsibility. By the thousands I have seen them there in the United States, including this last time that I went.

Then there are others like the one who lives opposite the house down there where we were before, the one who has those cattle over there. He's the one who goes north just to get money and return here and strut around every day drinking and showing off, every day, pretentious. . . . They bring bad habits, they come back dressed in fancy clothes, first-class, they become self-centered. That's not good. They discredit their country with that—going to the United States to bring back money and flaunt it here in Mexico, going around dressed up in fancy clothes. The ones who bring back money and act with reserve, invest it well, put it in the bank to work, to live with their children, with their wives, they're the good ones.

When we used to go under contract, many also stayed, but we had a little more security then because the American government was responsible for us. It was responsible when some problem occurred. As a bracero you go at government expense; as an "illegal" you don't.

Even as an "illegal," though, the American government worries when some Mexican over there dies. It's a question of conscience or obligation or responsibility. What do I know? But with responsibility in the hands of the American and Mexican governments, I say it's better because there's a subsidy, they pay for things after you die. If someone dies, they help the wife and kids. Above all when they are little they help out until they reach whatever age the law sets, like eighteen for girls and twenty for boys. The family gets aid until the children are that old. Even with "illegals," if the illegal is working for a boss who carries insurance and he dies over there, then the government obligates the boss to help the relatives and send the body here, to our country.

It's like with that guy who died in California. He was driving a tractor, and he had a heart attack, and he fell from the tractor. A big double tractor tire, but one of those huge ones, crushed him. Then, in accord with the United States government rules or the insurance or whatever, the boss was obligated to send the body to his house here in the country, just over there in the *rancho*. And every month they're sending his wife something like three hundred or four hundred dollars a month for the little kids. The kids are small. She's got two by her husband who died over there.

So the difference is that when we went there under contract the government itself covered the death expenses, and now for the "illegals" the employer sometimes does. The government used to pay the costs of the coffin, its transfer to the relative, or certain sums of money were given right away to the widow. Alright, look, they used to give her up to five or ten thousand dollars right after the death. But then figure how much they'll be giving to these people over the years, let's say fifteen years at least. How much money are they going to give this here Magdalena? In fifteen years, let's say it's a hundred and seventy dollars monthly for fifteen years, well, it's a heap of dollars, a tidy sum, that's for sure.

Just the other day I was talking with Faustino about the "illegals" in Chicago. They're getting a hundred and seventy dollars a week when they're out of work, those that are in the factories, just the factory guys. You see, there's an office they have, it must be by government agreement with the factory, and that office gives them the money. But earlier, when they're working there in the factory, part of their paychecks is being kept out for taxes, and then, when they're out of work, it's paid to them, they give it to them. It's a kind of unemployment insurance that the *gringos* have. We don't have anything like that here in Mexico. Of course, most "illegals" don't have the necessary documents to collect on it, though.

There's this guy, he's still over there, his name is Fernando Gómez, and his wife was left behind to put their children through school here. A few of their children are already teachers, and others are about to become apprentice engineers and lawyers, because he was supporting them from over there in the United States. Between him and his wife the two of them helped their children reach those professions. I was in his house one day after he had been laid off from work, and he told me, "Here we are not even working, and there are the hundred and seventy dollars a week. We don't even have to go to get it; they send us the check here." He had some forged documents, I guess, because otherwise he couldn't collect.

Well, that's good what the government does over there, I say, but let's consider the field work. The agricultural worker gets nothing if he doesn't work. Only the factory worker does, and I guess that's alright.

This whole generation has gone "illegally" over there. Kids, small boys go there and in a few months grow by leaps and bounds. That's for sure, those foods in the United States make them grow and fatten up. I believe it's the food, no?—because they get mighty plump over there. I have a nephew here who came back from there but really fat. All of them come back fat from the United States, remade.

But, well, what I'm saying is that they are irresponsible, and sometimes, no, sometimes it's as if all we want to do is discredit our country. We have people so boozed up that they go around preaching English here, the little that is taught over there. I say to them, "No, man, you mustn't preach English here. That's not right. Speak your own language. When you go to the United States, English is necessary and Spanish is not. But here in our country, you have to speak our language."

For me, living here is preferable to living in the United States, although the food is better over there. But you live better here because in the United States it's the way it is in Mexico City. In the capital you have to work hard every day, and if you're late to work they fire you quickly. In the United States it's the same. If you don't complete every bit of the job they push you out—above all if you're in a factory. That doesn't happen in the fields, but then again field work is harder. In the factory you don't work as hard, but you have to be on time. Here in the capital a few days ago they fired a guy from my community, there in the subway construction project. He showed up late quite a few times and was told by the guy in charge there, "What's the use, you're late a lot, and we don't want even one lateness."

It's the same in the United States. You're fired at a factory if you're late a lot. On top of that, in order to live there you have to spend more money. If you want to dress like others in the United States, then you have to buy more clothes. Clothes are cheaper over there, but you need more. Also, you have to send money to your family all the time. For me, it's better here.

Yes, I like the United States, but to go work there now—I think not. You exhaust yourself there, and if you don't please a boss in the field you get fired too. I can do all the field jobs now, and in a few days' time I can learn a new factory job too. But I don't like being ordered around or being criticized. And it's very hard in the fields just now too, because with so many "illegals," there's real bargaining down of the wages— pure *yarda* "illegals." Just now there's farmwork only in California and in part of Michigan, but in Chicago it's only *yarda*, depending on the contractor to bring you your *yarda* business. No, it's better I retire now, that's why I came back. It's not for me to be in the United States. . . .

I believe that a new bracero or "guest worker" contract would be in part good and in part bad. Mostly it would be bad, and here's why. If once again there were contracts our country would be left without agriculture, without the land being worked, because there would be no producers. And if there were any producers at all, those that stayed here or had money would work halfheartedly. Moreover, in order to go to the United States, the peasant will say, "I'll even sell my parcel or rent it out for three or four years." When you have ten acres, at least for every six months you can get fifty thousand pesos renting it out, but managing your parcel well you can make around a hundred thousand pesos every six months.

Then we'll be hearing the criticisms of the *hacendado* [owner of the *hacienda* before it was returned to the peasants during the 1930s in ten-acre parcels] who still has some pieces of the *hacienda*. He'll say—and I've grown familiar with how the *hacendado* speaks—"Look at that, will you, there are those big-balled bums"—and we always knew they talk about us that way—"for what purpose did they want the land? For what? To abandon it? Is that why the government took our land from us?"

Renting out our parcels, abandoning our land, that's how we discredit our government once there are new contracts for going to the United States. And that's what happened the last time. Perhaps we were more protected then, going to the United States contracted, but in some places we deserved to be discredited because we no longer were working the land, we no longer produced but instead went to the United States to work. And telling it like it is for a change, we wasted money and . . . because we Mexicans are sometimes so messed up, some of us earned money and headed for the bar, the *cantina*, and let's go buy clothes, and that woman over there . . . well, now, I say no to that.

A heap of millions of Mexican people are over there in the United States, since the contract times becoming today's "illegals." I believe that Los Angeles has more millions of Mexicans than Chicago and Houston, because Chicago and Houston are strictly industry while there in California you have agriculture, so there they have a heap of millions of Mexicans.

We Mexicans, Salvadorans, Guatemalans, I say we're all looking for no more than a way to earn some money. I don't know how to explain to you that they will never be able to prevent entry into the United States from our country, whether it's the Río Bravo or—but what a river that Bravo is. Why, it's gobbled up a lot of Mexicans. People challenge that Río Bravo; even women, single girls, have died there in that Río Bravo, because that Río Bravo, its water goes like this, in a swirl, all of it like a whirlpool like this, see. They figure it runs as smooth and straight as our irrigation channels here, but it doesn't. The water goes like this in a pure whirlpool, and wherever a whirlpool grabs a person, it grabs him and he doesn't get out, it takes him down under. You have to enter the river like this to cross it, but you'll get out miles away, because if you try to get out like this the water will envelop you and drag you down to the bottom. No, you have to get out like this, and you mustn't swim strongly, you must swim relaxed, because if you don't you'll tire, and the water grabs you and it brings you all the way to the bottom.

Then too you have to look out for an animal that's called—it's a fish, this fish is called . . . maybe shark . . . no, not that—it has a beak like so, but it's a fish, and served as a meal it's very tasty, but I don't remember its name. It catches you like this and bites you in the stomach and empties your guts. That fish is evil. There in that town of Río Bravo—that's how they call the town—I say there they catch a lot of that fish, and it's very delicious, but it's a hazard in the river's depths. That little animal is dangerous.

I traversed those borders a lot. The only one I don't know is—and it's near this side of the South Pacific—is Nogales, Arizona. I never crossed over there to get to the United States, but from there to here I've crossed all the borders, and I know all of them. I also know all of the places from here in Mexico to the border. I know all of them. And sometimes I think about them, and it's like I'm seeing them now as clear as day, those places I frequented in the United States. I remember the very places I was at, I remember where I was, in what field, and when I went to the United States, like this last time when I went with those guys, I said to them, and especially to my son, "Look, I was in that town . . ." And later when I went to Chicago, I said to my cousins, "Look, I passed here, and I was there in Michigan." I remember everything as if I were walking right now there in the United States. It's good you recorded all this.

But for myself, I say, I'm not in agreement with the idea of there being more contracts. Mexico went backwards in those days. The day our governments make that agreement, Mexican agriculture will end.

2

The Role of Mexican Immigrants in US Economic Growth

*"America is so rich and fat, because it has eaten
the tragedy of millions of immigrants."*
—Michael Gold, *Jews Without Money*, 1930

When Isauro Reyes's peasant grandfather first migrated from Michoacán at the turn of the century, the *hacienda* was paying him thirty-one cents a day; a day's supply of corn cost thirty-two cents. Although by comparison factory and railroad workers were better off than *hacienda* peons, the Mexican labor force as a whole was travailing under abominable conditions. Wealthy families in commerce, mining, agriculture, and industry, usually of pure Spanish blood or of foreign extraction, lorded it over Mexico's oppressed Indians and *castas* (mixed races).

Many workers resided in miserable barracks provided by employers and were tied by debts to the company store (*tienda de raya*). All were subject to sudden layoffs and replacement by an immense reserve army of labor queuing up at factory gates, mineshafts, and other labor recruitment centers for a day's work. Sons and daughters of peasants increasingly migrated to the cities in desperate quest of a means of survival. Up to a third of urban women were employed as domestic servants. Real wages had remained constant for decades, malnutrition continued widespread, and the average life expectancy was little more than thirty years.

The more imaginative, strong, and able naturally strove to improve their lot, usually by means of organizing mutual aid societies (*mu-*

tualismo), labor unions, or political movements. At the local and regional levels, peasants had launched periodic armed rebellions throughout the nineteenth century. By 1880 thousands of Mexico's workers had banded together in such organizations as the Great Circle of Workers, the Great Confederation of Workers, and the Workers' Congress. Most of their demands centered on elimination of backward conditions like the company store, fines, night work, fifteen-hour workdays, and child labor. They and the more militant labor unions and political movements that followed them launched some 250 strikes between 1880 and 1910, during the "Porfiriato" (1876–1911), the extremely repressive dictatorship of army brigadier general Porfirio Díaz.

For their efforts, many peasants and workers suffered whipping, rape, imprisonment, or massacre by federal troops. However, their long experience of popular resistance led ultimately to the 1910–17 armed uprising against wealthy elites and foreign interests known as the Mexican Revolution.

During the final decades of the nineteenth century, news spread throughout Mexico of US employers avidly seeking inexpensive labor. As a result, Mexican laborers in growing numbers became a significant force in the economic and social life of the United States. They picked crops, tended cattle, felled trees, mined ores, laid rails, and entered the unskilled ranks of American industrial labor, contributing vitally to the incredible economic growth of the United States from 1890 to 1920, particularly in the Southwest, today's burgeoning economic heartland. As had some of their fathers before them, they introduced the word *huelga* to the American labor scene, in many instances before the word "strike" had ever been uttered.

Ever since then, generations of Mexican workers have responded to the needs of a US economy that has never, despite fluctuations, ceased requiring Mexican labor on an increasing scale. In recent years, in spite of politically intolerable unemployment rates of 8 percent and up, the US demand for immigrant labor has not only persisted but expanded. Moreover, projected US population figures (see Chapter 5) indicate a growing scarcity of labor power in those sectors most in need of semi-skilled or unskilled labor, which translates into a further expansion of the market for Mexican "unqualified" labor in coming decades.

A century ago it was the labor of Mexican and other first- and second-generation immigrants from around the world that helped make the United States a rich country. "Robber-baron" capitalists with

Anglo-Saxon names like Morgan and Rockefeller grew rich off immigrant labor and proceeded to augment their wealth and try to impose their capitalist values upon the peoples of the less-industrialized regions of the world. On the eve of World War I, President Woodrow Wilson announced that "within the last year or two we have . . . ceased to be a debtor nation and have become a creditor nation. . . . We have got to finance the world in some important degree, and those who finance the world must understand it and rule it with their spirits and with their minds."[1]

Ever since the United States invaded Mexico in 1846 and seized half its territory, the Mexican people had been experiencing this self-righteously aggressive approach firsthand. In 1914 US troops occupied Veracruz, and in 1916 General John J. Pershing's forces invaded Mexico from the north. European great powers also invaded the country periodically (an average of once every six years between 1823 and 1861). Because of this history of repeated acts of aggression, recent Mexican governments have forged a foreign policy based on "nonintervention in the internal affairs of other nations and the right of self-determination"—a doctrine Mexico uses today in its negotiations with the United States on the crucial issues of war in Central America and Mexican immigration (see Chapter 6).

Many of the roots of current immigration debates, labor struggles, and Mexico-US relations can be found in the history of Mexican migration to the United States from 1848 to the present. By reviewing the diverse ways in which generations of Mexican laborers have contributed to the economic growth of the United States, this chapter and the one that follows offer a historical framework for understanding the role Mexican immigrant workers are being called upon to play today and the one they likely will assume in ever greater numbers for at least the next thirty years.

The role played by Mexican immigrants is both economic and political. Economically, they offer themselves for hire in the US on a temporary basis, leaving and returning to Mexico in a rhythmic flow. They also provide the Mexican government and wealthy classes a convenient "escape valve" for the social pressures of widespread underemployment and poverty.

Ever since the post–Civil War phase of US economic transition from a free-market economy allowing widespread competition among small and medium-sized firms to one dominated by giant banks and industries requiring foreign expansion for their prosperity, Mexican laborers have formed a reserve army of labor only periodically visible. Their presence, availability for employment, or use as strikebreakers (scabs) or labor pool additions has served, in effect, to hold down the average wage level of American labor, to intimidate labor unions, and in general to help maintain labor discipline. Initially useful too in supplementing or even replacing earlier immigrant labor pools (in 1882 US immigration law "excluded" the Chinese, and in 1907 it restricted Japanese immigration), Mexicans soon became the only significant foreign labor pool that could not be replaced or excluded no matter what attempts were made.

Mexican labor proved fundamental for the development, survival, or growth of much of US agribusiness, as well as for the garment and electronics industries, select sectors of heavy industry such as automotive and steel, and the restaurant, hotel, and other service industries. Today, the substantial presence of Mexicans in an ever-expanding and ever more international reserve army of labor facilitates economic recovery and potential expansion for industry as a whole. Not surprisingly, during the relative economic stagnation of this post–Vietnam War era, employers in heavy and medium industry and its ancillary [...] rily on the inexpensive and easily [...] ey step up their offensive against [...] 7). The 1980 Census shows that [...] in the US labor force are now in manufacturing.

[...] the American economy, as is usually [...] workers actually subsidize it. The [...] , and clothing these laborers have been borne largely [...] themselves and by state programs inside Mexico. For more than [...] ury US employers have been aware [...] vides them. As the *New York Jour-* [...] 6, "Men, like cows, are expensive to raise, and a gift of other [...] gladly received. And a man can be [...] v!"[2] Moreover, generations of Mexican immigrant workers have [...] nost of their meager dollar earnings on American products, further abetting US economic growth.

Because of the harsh conditions of most of their work, Mexican immigrants use up their productive capacities relatively early in life and are then replaced by younger migrants. Pesticides poison the waters fieldworkers drink and the air they breathe, causing untold harm

[handwritten note in margin:] WHY IS IT THAT MEXICANS POURING FOR SPECIAL IN THE U.S. LABOR HELPED THE FLOW CONTINUE?

to their health, birth defects in their children, and sometimes death. An indeterminate number of Mexican immigrant workers—by official estimates of both governments, at least 400 a year, but probably far, far more—are killed or disabled in the course of their travels and labors. In just five weeks during the late summer of 1985, the Yuma County sheriff's office reported finding in southern Arizona's desert ten bloated corpses of "suspected aliens" not far from the sun-bleached bones of dozens of other victims of the hazardous crossing. The seemingly endless supply of Mexican immigrant workers has been maintained at a high human cost.

Economically, socially, and politically, the distinct languages, customs, and appearances of Mexican Indian and mestizo (Indo-white) immigrant workers have both enhanced America's human diversity and aroused its racism, serving to reinforce and deepen the divisive animosities plaguing the multiracial, multinational American working class.

Labor leaders themselves have sometimes been at the forefront of American racism. American Federation of Labor (AFL) president Samuel Gompers, for example, often told union members and the press that Mexicans had an inferior capacity to produce. Supposed men of reason like the widely read author T. Lothrop Stoddard periodically added their voices to this racist brew. In 1920 Stoddard asserted that Mexicans were culturally inferior and were undesirable immigrants because they were "born communist." The House Judiciary Committee on Immigration and Naturalization in the early 1920s took most seriously the testimony of its eugenics consultant, Dr. Harry N. Laughlin, who intoned, "We in this country have been so imbued with the idea of democracy, or the equality of all men, that we have left out of consideration the matter of blood or natural born hereditary mental and moral differences." The doctor warned that "no man who breeds pedigreed plants and animals can afford to neglect this thing." A 1930 book titled *The Alien in Our Midst* offered articles championing white supremacy and claiming to demonstrate "scientifically" that Mexicans are racially inferior.[3]

Such nativist views are as virulent today as in the past and extend into the highest offices of the land. Former CIA director William Colby, for example, raising the specter of a "Spanish-speaking Quebec in the US Southwest," claimed in 1978 that Mexican immigration represented a greater future threat to the United States than did the Soviet Union.[4]

Politically, Mexican immigrant workers have served employers, the US government, labor leaders, politicians, and journalists as a convenient and increasingly needed scapegoat for economic hard times. "They're taking our jobs!" is the cry the powers-that-be love to hear from American workers—and indeed, much of the mass media parrots this distortion.

In general, these workers have rarely displaced US workers. Mexican "illegals" have always belonged to a labor market with special rules that are unacceptable to most American workers. Current immigration law (US Congress, 8 USC, Section 1324) permits an employer to hire "undocumented aliens" at the same time that it allows "undocumented aliens" to be deported. Thus, under what in fact is a labor law disguised as an immigration law, Mexican migrant laborers are placed in a defenseless position. Substandard wages and harsh work conditions make their jobs suitable only for workers in the highly vulnerable and exploitable condition specific to that subclass known as "the undocumented."

This is true even when legal provision is made for "sanctions" against employers hiring "illegals." California law has had such sanctions for a long time, but to no noticeable effect. As emigrant workers from Michoacán informed this writer in 1981, "The employers themselves tell us, 'Come, don't stop coming, you are the ones who get the job done. The people here don't want to work—if you don't come, we'll lose everything.' " Employers want and demand easily disciplined "illegal" immigrant labor for specific jobs at substandard wages.

Because of racism and cultural realities, employers make black Americans the "last hired and first fired"—preferring a young immigrant worker who knows no English, will accept lower pay, and will be too frightened to talk back. Less than half of the workers who pick and process the food that ends up on Americans' tables receive the minimum wage; more than a third of them are under 17 years of age. Many are Mexican.

Even though Mexican migrants usually accept jobs Americans will not touch or employers will not offer to the working poor, it is not true that certain jobs are inherently bad or low-wage while other jobs are good or high-wage. The "good" jobs become good because of labor's organizing and fighting to improve them. Indeed, immigrant workers, including Mexicans, were at the forefront of the first campaigns to launch sustained movements for industrial labor unionism in America.

While in the short run the presence of large numbers of "illegals" does constitute a drag on labor's wages and ability to organize, Mexican immigrants do not cause unemployment. Most unemployed Americans did not lose their jobs to temporary Mexican immigrants. In fact, according to the US Labor Department, in the eight Southwest and Midwest labor market areas that experienced the greatest increase in the Mexican immigrant labor force from 1968 to 1977, the unemployment rate was notably *lower* than the national average. As for areas of high unemployment, when the Reagan administration launched "Operation Jobs" in May 1982, rounding up and detaining 5,635 "illegals" of whom 87 percent were Mexican, there were few job applicants for the newly vacated positions. Most of the detainees were released and back at their workplaces in a matter of days.

The facts notwithstanding, a recurring feature of the US economic crises (periods of depression or recession) of 1907–8, 1920–22, 1929–34, 1937–39, 1947–49, 1953–54, 1969, 1973–75, and 1979–83 has been the attribution of many of their symptoms—especially high unemployment—to the presence of Mexican migrant workers. In most of these crises, labor union spokesmen, particularly in the AFL and later the AFL-CIO, claimed that Mexican immigration was an important cause of unemployment and demanded mass deportations and/or sealing of the border with Mexico. While their diagnosis of the cause and their prescription for the remedy were unrelated to the actual causes and potential cures of the crises, they served, intentionally or not, to divert attention from the true problems facing American workers.

Periodic factory raids, neighborhood roundups, and mass deportations of Mexicans reinforce their scapegoat role and the racism that accompanies it. They serve to strike fear in the hearts of Latino immigrants. "Yes, we would go out [for recreation] from time to time, but we always lived tense with fear," commented Michoacán's emigrants. "Where the *migra* [INS] usually grabbed us was at work." Factory raids deepen this fear while helping employers to get rid of labor militants or avoid paying migrants for the last week of work.

Roundups of Mexican "illegals" also serve to arouse fear in US workers. As a highly visible expression of the state's power to invade workplace or neighborhood, these public anti-Mexican raids, far from reassuring other workers who witness them, intimidate all workers. They may make an occasional worker feel lucky he or she is not dark-skinned or "without documents," but they clearly have a chilling effect on any act of labor resistance, be it unionizing, striking, or simply slowing down production or requesting a restroom break. In fact, it is well known that INS roundups of Mexicans are often directed at those very workplaces or neighborhoods where the presence of labor agitators, Mexican or not, has been discovered, or where a union organizing drive is underway. They are fundamentally antilabor acts carried out under the guise of "defending the jobs of Americans."

Yet the very outcry for "regaining control of our own borders" that rationalizes such acts often muffles the equally strong clamoring of employers to increase the Mexican immigrant labor pool so that production and growth can continue or be renewed. It is a gross oversimplification to state that mass deportations of "illegals" only accompany times of economic slowdown in which these workers are no longer needed. Indeed, during all periods of economic crisis in the twentieth century for which there are even rough statistical estimates, the high numbers of Mexican deportees have been outstripped by the numbers of Mexican immigrant workers allowed to enter or remain in the country.

Paradoxically, deportation and importation of Mexicans occur simultaneously and for identical reasons: to provide scapegoats for society's economic problems; to guarantee a large surplus of workers in the labor pool in order to meet production needs or to hold the general wage level down; to deter other workers from seeking better wages or work conditions by implying that they can always be replaced; and to make things difficult for potential labor organizers while assuring a pool of potential scabs. In sum, the deportation-importation of Mexicans serves to keep workers intimidated, divided, and confused.

This "revolving door" strategy of employers is also played out in the political arena. It is, in fact, at the very heart of contemporary debates on immigration policy and law. When it comes to the politics of immigration, other questions—even those of political refuge or amnesty—fade by comparison. Whether the issue be quotas, amnesty, deportation, legalization of some resident migrants, or restriction of others, US employers' growing need for abundant, easily exploited Mexican laborers relentlessly imposes itself, however much cloaked by other passing features of US immigration law and policy. This is the inexorable force responsible for the many variants of a "guest worker" program put forward in the US Congress and for the occasional decrees by the executive branch of government that allow more Mexicans to enter the country temporarily. Today, as yesterday, the main determinant of Mexican immigration into the United States is employer demand, *not* worker supply.

The "revolving door" for Mexican immigrant labor has a long and sordid history rooted in the different patterns of economic growth experienced by the two nations, in employer needs, and in Mexican labor's extreme exploitability. Examination of these historical roots peels away the layers of illusion and confusion that so often surround any discussion of Mexican immigrant workers.

Historical Roots of the Migratory Flow

Mexico's late start in industrialization, compared with that of the United States, and its continued reliance on intense exploitation of cheap labor instead of complete technological transformation led to growing US influence over its economy and fostered the extreme vulnerability of its peasants and workers to "superexploitation." Superexploitation (what Isauro's grandfather experienced when he earned thirty-one cents a day but paid out thirty-two for his corn ration) is the payment of labor power below its value or below what it takes for a laborer to sustain himself. In more recent times, the vulnerability of Mexico's labor is evident in the fact that not until 1968 did the Mexican worker's real wage recover its 1939 level. The intervening years witnessed Mexico's greatest industrialization since the late nineteenth century and the United States' massive importation of Mexican labor under the bilateral bracero program of 1942–64 (examined in the next chapter).

Although both nations undertook capitalist development during the nineteenth century, they started at different moments from different population bases and followed distinct paths. Their unequal rates of development led to the gradual integration of their two economies on unequal terms and to periodic wars or diplomatic conflicts between their governments. In addition, while the United States expanded by means of warfare and plunder (Indian Wars, Mexican War, Spanish-American War), Mexico suffered a hundred years of military invasion, pillage, and impoverishment (an average of one invasion every ten years between 1821 and 1920).

Gaining its independence from European colonialism nearly half a century before Mexico, the United States enjoyed a big head start over its southern neighbor in the production and trade of goods. The colonialism it experienced under British rule differed notably from that imposed upon Mexico by Spain. Britain, after all, was the world's premier industrial pathbreaker, dominating trade and production throughout much of the Western Hemisphere until 1850; by comparison Spain was an agrocommercial backwater. Consequently, British rule in the American colonies readily allowed for early capitalist forms emphasizing increased productivity and commerce through "free" wage labor and mechanization, at least north of the Mason-Dixon Line. On the other hand, Spanish colonialism relied almost entirely on the intense exploitation of cheap, often indebted labor for economic production in its colonies. (Both colonialisms utilized slavery, of course, although by 1810 there were fewer than 10,000 black slaves in Mexico.)

No matter what the system of production, significant economic growth cannot be expected to occur anywhere in the absence of an adequate labor supply. Here too the United States enjoyed a huge advantage over Mexico. Casualties among the US laboring population in the wars with Britain were minimal compared to those suffered by Mexico in its more sanguinary independence wars forty years later (1811–21), when more than half a million people, or a tenth of Mexico's population, perished. Subsequent decades of war, high infant mortality, and shortened life spans caused by malnutrition, disease, or overwork further limited Mexico's labor supply.

In fact, for most of the nineteenth century Mexico's population grew scarcely at all—from about 6 million in 1810 to only 8.7 million in 1874. It finally began to show signs of sustained growth in subsequent decades, reaching 15 million in 1918 (after the loss of another tenth of the population during the 1910–17 revolutionary upheaval). In 1930 the Mexican population was still only 16.6 million, nearly an eighth of it having emigrated to the United States during the prior three decades. Meanwhile, the US population, augmented by a half-million births a year and by European, Asiatic, and Latin American immigration, grew from 13 million in 1813 to 50 million in 1880 to 100 million in 1918 to 123 million in 1930. This meant that from the mid-1870s on, the United States had a rough equivalent of *seven times* the number of laborers Mexico had—an awesome amount of raw labor power able to fuel a mighty industrialization.

After US mercantile capitalism emerged relatively unscathed from the wars against Britain, it greedily cast its eyes toward its neighbors. Thomas Jefferson had envisioned the future course of US economic and military expansionism when he said in 1786, "Our confederacy must be viewed as the nest, from which all America, North and South, is to be peopled."[5] The doctrine of "manifest destiny" proclaimed that it was the destiny of the United States to occupy the entire North American continent.

By 1799, of thirty foreign commercial ships landing at Veracruz, Mexico, twenty-five were of US registry. By 1805, with US government support, Wilkinson's "Mexican Association" was arming itself to "free" Mexico from Spanish rule. In 1823 President James Monroe instructed American ambassador to Mexico Joel Robert Poinsett, a notorious meddler in Mexico's internal affairs who viewed Mexicans as "ignorant and debauched," to explore the possibility of incorporating northeastern Mexico (today's Texas) into the United States.[6] Armed expeditions into Texas became the order of the day, leading to Texas's secession from Mexico in 1836 and its annexation by the United States in 1845.

Then, in April 1846, President James K. Polk claimed Mexican soldiers had killed Americans on US soil. Congressman Abraham Lincoln asked Polk to indicate just where this incident had occurred, but he received no precise answer. The battle had in fact taken place well inside Mexican territory, near the Rio Grande, about 150 miles south of the Texas-Mexico border (the Nueces River). The United States used the incident as a pretext for declaring war. The Mexican War, ended by the Treaty of Guadalupe Hidalgo in 1848, ultimately brought under US control almost half of Mexico's territory, along with the valuable gold, copper, water, and other resources of today's Southwest.

Although often overlooked in US history books, one of the earliest American immigrant revolts against class, racial, and religious oppression took place during this war. In the 1830s a tide of violent nativist attacks against immigrants had begun sweeping the United States, targeting especially the Irish and Germans. When large numbers of young immigrant workers were drafted to fight in the war against Mexico, there occurred wave upon wave of desertions—9,207 by war's end. More than 200 immigrant draftees organized themselves into what became known as the Saint Patrick's Battalion, led by a redheaded Irishman, John Riley (although the Irish were not a majority in the battalion). Many of the battalion members who took up arms against the US Army under Protestant general Winfield Scott viewed the Mexican Catholics as "brothers," victims like themselves of prejudice and power. Seventy-five of those not killed in battle were captured, summarily tried, and hung, adding to the war's extremely high casualty rate (an estimated 50,000 Mexican dead and 13,000 American dead).

The war and its consequences proved to be a historic watershed for Mexican labor's increased role in US economic growth. Some 100,000

Mexicans in the conquered territories became, in effect, additional labor power for US capital. Backed by the US Army and Cavalry, as well as by the Texas Rangers, Arizona Rangers, and other local militias, American railmen, miners, industrialists, ranchers, farmers, and land tycoons systematically violated provisions of the Treaty of Guadalupe Hidalgo guaranteeing the property and civil rights of those Mexicans who chose to remain in what was now the United States rather than abandon their homes. In the following few decades, US citizens of Mexican descent lost some twenty million acres. In addition, many lost their lives in heroic but vain acts of armed resistance against this lawless and violent pillage. Most Americans showed nothing but racist disdain for the Mexicans' culture and language, respect for which had also been guaranteed by the Treaty of Guadalupe Hidalgo (an often overlooked legal basis for continuing contemporary programs in bilingual education in the face of threats to eliminate them). Poor white immigrants from other nations, or their second-generation offspring, were similarly robbed or abused in the United States, although not subjected to the widespread burnings and lynchings suffered by Mexicans.[7]

Meanwhile, nascent industrialism in Mexico was held in check by big landholders (*hacendados*), miners, and exporters who in late colonial times had grown accustomed to amassing wealth and power by trading mineral and agricultural products for European manufactured goods. By 1824 the high rate of importation of cotton textiles (which represented 30 percent of all imported manufactures through Veracruz) was undermining Mexico's own textile industry, which at the time accounted for a quarter of the nation's manufacturing enterprises. Mexico's foreign debts, war debts, and budgetary and balance-of-payments deficits were used by European and increasingly by US capital to gain influence over the nation's economy. Soon foreign bondholders had a virtual stranglehold on the Mexican economy. Advocating "free trade" for their manufactured goods, foreign capitalists sided with the *hacendados*, mine owners, and exporters against emergent Mexican industrial interests.

By 1870 England and the United States accounted for about 70 percent of Mexico's trade, and Mexico's foreign debt had soared to new highs. Currency devaluations and inflation, then as today, benefited merchants and large-scale property owners at the expense of those whose labor produced most of the wealth, depriving artisans, workers, and peasants of a sizable portion not only of their meager real income but also of their property. Here, then, was another historic source of Mexican labor's vulnerability.

When the civil wars of the 1840s and 1850s led to anticlerical legislation by Benito Juárez's Liberals, Mexico's wealthy elites saw a golden opportunity to strip the peasantry of almost all its lands. Article 27 of the Liberals' 1857 constitution forebade "corporately held property," an implicit reference not only to church estates but also to village and *ejido* lands owned communally by Indian and mestizo peasants. Under protection of the new constitution, *hacendados*, government bureaucrats, merchants, moneylenders, land speculators, and even some *rancheros* (small-scale private farmers) legally purchased or confiscated millions of acres of communal lands during the subsequent decades. This expropriation in turn generated a desperate "free" labor force unattached to the land, anxious to migrate to areas offering survival wages both in the interior of Mexico and north of the border.

French troops occupied and ruled much of Mexico from 1862 to 1867, until Juárez's Liberals succeeded in expelling them. The Mexicans' modern-style guerrilla war against 40,000 French troops, which cost the nation another 50,000 lives, left Mexico once more bankrupt and in debt, but with one striking difference: there now existed an expanded, fast-growing "free" wage labor force, much of it landless and destitute. By 1910 the census showed 80 percent of the population dependent on agricultural wages working for 20,000 landholders, and 96.6 percent of rural households holding no land whatsoever. From the ranks of the landless peasantry came the inexpensive labor power for the capitalist development of both Mexico and, through emigration, the United States. This double use of Mexico's growing "free" labor pool went hand in hand with the growing integration of the two nations' economies (examined in Chapter 4).

During the final decades of the nineteenth century, when Mexican real wages held constant or declined and population figures began to rise sharply, almost doubling, American employers turned from Chinese to Mexican immigrant workers on a significant scale. The Chinese labor force had been largely depleted. Many Chinese had collapsed from overwork in the virtual slave gangs that laid the nation's railroads. Some had been lynched by angry nativist mobs. By the 1880s there were not nearly enough Chinese laborers even to keep the country's railroads running, much less to meet the needs of rapidly expanding capital.

nportation of Chinese workers to reseen problem when many of acist and nativist outcry for their usion Act of May 6, 1882, which geoning labor union movement, o the use of Chinese "coolies" as ss during the second half of the ng contract labor. Exempt from mporarily residing in the US"— of Mexican nationals. So it was pool right at its doorstep—the se, Mexican nationals did not bring their families; they could readily return home or, if necessary, be deported.

In the 1870s and 1880s US capital interests were given right-of-way and handsome cash subsidies by the Mexican government in the construction of more than 19,000 kilometers of railway, which relied largely on the wage labor of Indians displaced from their ancestral lands. The new railroad grid linked the rich mining areas of northern and central Mexico to key Gulf ports, Texas border towns, and industrial centers like Chicago and Pittsburgh. This revolution in transportation facilitated the movement of migrant workers from Mexico's interior northward, along with the exchange of valuable Mexican raw materials for US manufactured goods.

The movement of Mexicans to the United States went into full swing, as shown by the steady rise in population figures for Mexicans residing in the United States. Indeed, from 1880 to 1920, while the US population doubled in size, the Mexican population residing in the United States, fueled by growing waves of Mexican migrants, multiplied ninefold (Table 1). Even allowing for a wide margin of error in what are, after all, crude population estimates, the trend is unmistakable. The migration of Mexicans during the first third of the twentieth century shifted an estimated one-eighth of Mexico's population north of the border—one of the largest mass movements of a people in human history.

Initial impetus for this migratory flow had been provided by the California Gold Rush and by the movement of people in Sonora, Sinaloa, and other northern Mexican states to and from the former Mexican territories of the US Southwest after 1848. By end-century Mexican migrants from northern, central, and even southern Mexico were labor-

TABLE 1
Trends in Mexican Migratory Flow & Population in US

Year	Estimated Mexican Migrants	Estimated Mexicans in US
1880	NA	68,000
1890	NA	78,000
1900	50,000*	104,000
1910	400,000 [1910–20]	222,000
1920	1,000,000 [1920–30]	600,000
1930	640,000 [1930 alone]	1,430,000
1940	25,000* [1931–40]	2,500,000
1960	3,500,000† [1950–60]	3,400,000
1970	93,000* [1978 alone]	4,500,000
1980	3,000,000‡ [1970–80]	9,000,000

NA = not available
*INS figure for legal admissions only
†Braceros only
‡Author's estimate based on various compilations of data, the most scientific of which is Manuel García y Griego and Leobardo F. Estrada, "Research on the Magnitude of Mexican Undocumented Immigration to the US: A Summary," in Antonio Ríos-Bustamante, ed., *Mexican Immigrant Workers in the US* (Los Angeles: UCLA Chicano Studies Research Center, 1981).

Sources: INS data; US and Mexican censuses; author's averaging of available data and most common estimates.

ing in a wide range of productive activities throughout the Southwest and parts of the Northwest and Midwest as well. They were engaged mostly in agriculture, but also in railway construction and maintenance, mining, forestry, and some industry. They earned from fifty cents to two dollars or more a day at a time when a dollar was worth two pesos in Mexico, or from five to twelve times their usual wage back home. The modern-day practice among peasants and workers of flipping a coin to decide between going to Mexico City or the border to get some *lana* (money) dates from this time: "*Vámonos al norte, pues!*" ("Let's go north, then!")

The number of migrants was augmented by the technological revolution taking place in traditional Mexican economic activities. For example, in the silver mines, source of most of Mexico's foreign exchange, steam power was replaced by electricity, air compression drilling was introduced, the cyanide and electrolysis processes were instituted, and manganese largely replaced mercury as the transforming agent for silver. These innovations made possible the tapping of immense piles of tailings for additional silver and the processing of far greater amounts of silver-bearing minerals in a single day. Moreover, much of the labor force could be laid off, particularly among the 40 percent employed as carriers and the 25 percent employed as pickmen. In agriculture, Mexico's second-leading foreign exchange earner, hydraulic pumps, electric motors, reapers, tractors, and combines began to dominate production, further economizing on labor and paving the way for what Porfirio Díaz's minister of agriculture described in 1910 as Mexico's "capitalist agriculture" farmed by a "rural proletariat."[8]

In Mexico's north, farming that relied on wage laborers was profitably commercialized. Sinaloa became a major exporter of *garbanzos* (chickpeas) and other vegetables to the US market. Throughout the north, a rising spiral of prices chased by wages proved to be a magnet for internal migration, placing Mexico's "labor pool" that much closer to the US border.

Not surprisingly, in post–Civil War America, US employers in the newly robust industrial and modern agricultural sectors began routinely sending labor recruiters to the Mexican border. McCormick's reaper and the refrigerated freight car, among other inventions, had long since helped convert family homestead farming into a large-scale commercial enterprise. By 1889 one-sixth of California's farms were producing more than two-thirds of the state's crops (by value). Meanwhile, America's great smokestack industries were transforming the urban landscape. Railroads crisscrossed the nation, increasing trade and production manyfold.

US business's expanded demand for more inexpensive immigrant labor was the main cause of the sudden escalation of the Mexican migratory flow northward. As the US commissioner general of immigration reported in 1910, "The principal reason underlying this increase is the extensive industrial development now taking place in the southwestern part of the United States." Labor recruitment agencies, the commissioner observed, were reaping "an enormous profit."[9] Thus, far more than Mexican poverty or the Mexican Revolution of 1917, US demand for labor brought about the mass migration of Mexicans northward. In the absence of this demand, Mexican workers could have achieved nothing by emigrating to the United States. Moreover, according to INS figures for 1912–20, political asylum from the violence of the Mexican Revolution was granted to only 8,000 Mexicans, most of whom were not from the working class or peasantry. Mexico's revolutionary turmoil made only a small contribution to the mainstream of the migratory flow initiated years earlier.

US demand for temporary Mexican immigrant labor was further spurred by the outbreak of World War I. As a large sector of the US male labor force went off to fight in the trenches of Europe, demand skyrocketed for alternative sources of labor to keep the wheels of the economy spinning and to produce for the war effort.

As a result of the combined efforts of the multinational US working class and Mexican and other immigrants willing to work long hours for a pittance, US economic growth from 1880 to 1930 became legendary. Mexicans flooded the booming construction sites of much of the Southwest and Midwest. The main railway routes knitting the US home market into a cohesive whole and connecting it to Mexico were completed. Citrus and cotton agroindustries sprang up along the shores of rivers in California, Arizona, and Texas. Cattle ranching expanded in Texas, Kansas, and elsewhere. Sugarbeet production in Colorado and Kansas increased fourfold in the first decade of the new century, and the railroad yards and slaughterhouses of Kansas City, Chicago, and Milwaukee echoed with the Spanish accents heard in Mexico's northern regional hubs of Hermosillo, Torreón, and San Luis Potosí.

In mining and forestry, the production of lumber, copper, and coal on the mountain slopes of Arizona, Colorado, and New Mexico increased enormously. Arizona gold discoveries in 1867–68, followed by increases in silver and copper mining, led to vastly augmented production by cheap Mexican labor. Often, Mexican workers in US-owned mines in Cananea (Sonora) or US rail subsidiaries in northern Mexico were transferred by their employers to corresponding operations in the United States. Meanwhile, steel magnates and other industrial employers began hiring Mexicans, sometimes using Mexican and other immigrants to break strikes. In such ways American employers in diverse sectors accumulated profits from the labor of Mexican immigrants.

State Policies, Labor Resistance, and the "Revolving Door"

Because of internal political squabbles and frequent foreign military interventions, Mexico did not firmly establish itself as a national state until after the victory over the French in 1867. From its first days of independence from Spain in 1821 to the establishment of the 1857 constitution, which was to last sixty years, the young nation experienced more than fifty separate governments. Consequently, the Mexican state was unable to carry out a consistent foreign policy regarding Mexicans residing in the United States until the late nineteenth century.

Exchanges between various Mexican governments and the United States on the issue of maltreatment of Mexicans by Americans occurred frequently throughout the nineteenth century, and continue to do so today. The Mexicans periodically issued formal protests against US violations of the 1848 Treaty of Guadalupe Hidalgo, particularly with regard to property losses, burnings, and lynchings suffered by Mexican expatriates. As late as 1923, Mexico pressed compensation claims covering losses incurred since 1848 by Mexicans residing in Texas. These claims were far outweighed, however, by US claims for losses suffered by its citizens during the Mexican Revolution of 1910–17. In 1941 Mexico agreed to pay $40 million as an agreed difference between the claims, and the matter was declared closed.

Permanent and temporary Mexican residents in the United States have always been known in Mexico as the *México de afuera* (Mexico abroad). Although complicated by questions of borders, patriotism, language, class, and citizenship (Mexicans born abroad are considered Mexican citizens), the popular feeling of sympathy, or at least curiosity, among Mexico's 75 million people for the *México de afuera* has strong historical roots. Juárez's Liberals set up consulates and *juntas patrióticas* in the US Southwest, rallying considerable support among Mexicans there for the Liberals' nationalistic, anticlerical cause. In the northeastern state of Tamaulipas, Mexican Texans fought under the so-called Red Robber of the Rio Grande, General Juan N. Cortina, who opposed both the French imperialists and the Texas confederates on either side of the Rio Bravo. Indeed, many US-citizen "Mexicanos" went to Mexico to fight the French. Then, in 1865–66, Juárez's anti-French army recruited some 3,000 Union veterans of the American Civil War with offers of good pay and land bonuses.[10]

Throughout the nineteenth century, a Spanish-language press flourished in the US Southwest. The dictatorship of Porfirio Díaz (1876–1911) repressed journalists in Mexico, but Liberal and radical exiles kept publishing their broadsides from the United States. Díaz's government tried in vain to counter the democratic sentiments of the exile press by subsidizing rival newspapers. Most of the stateside Mexican newspapers focused both on the daily life of the *colonia mexicana* (Mexican community) and on matters internal to Mexico. The many points of view of the different political and class groupings in the Mexican community often appeared in the pages of this Spanish-language press.

Inside Mexico the state sought through the official press to adopt a nationalist position on the issue of emigrants to the United States. In 1906, for example, newspaper articles stated, "Good workers never have to leave their country" or "You have a homeland, don't trade it in for a warehouse of slavetraders."[11] But whenever there was an economic crisis in the United States—as during 1907–8, when a Wall Street panic sent shockwaves throughout the Mexican economy, causing unemployment to surpass 50 percent—the official Mexican press encouraged emigration. The government often followed suit, as in 1909, when the Díaz dictatorship established a precedent for the bilateral bracero program of 1942–64 by signing a treaty with the US government that called for the contracting of 1,000 Mexicans to work the sugarbeet fields of southern California.

Nevertheless, the northward migratory flow of Mexican workers represented an embarrassment for the Díaz dictatorship, which was proclaiming an era of peace and prosperity under its iron-fisted rule. "Order and Progress" was its slogan. But if there was prosperity and progress, then why did so many Mexicans emigrate? And if there was peace and order, then why were there so many strikes, riots, or revolts by migrants on both sides of the border? The outlawed Partido Liberal Mexicano (PLM), backbone of Mexico's vigorous, combative, and violently repressed "Precursor Movement" to the 1910 Revolution, recruited many of its members or sympathizers from among migrant workers. It defended their rights in its program issued from St. Louis, Missouri, July 1, 1906, which announced, "The dictatorship has brought about the depopulation of Mexico. Thousands of our fellow countrymen have had to cross the border in flight from pillage and tyranny. . . . For those Mexicans residing abroad who so solicit, the [future revolutionary] Government will provide repatriation, pay the transportation costs of the trip, and give them land they may cultivate."[12]

In 1906 the PLM turned itself into a political-military organization led largely by anarchists. It coordinated the many armed revolts inside Mexico in 1906 and 1908, contributed key battlefield victories to the anti-Díaz 1910 Revolution, and went on to occupy and govern much of northern Baja California in 1911, after which it faded in importance. Much of the 1906 PLM program, however, was incorporated into the 1917 Mexican constitution, Article 123 of which prohibited unregulated hiring of Mexican citizens for employment abroad.

As early as 1906, President Díaz's friend Rafael de Zayas Enríquez had investigated the PLM. "Make no mistake about it," he warned Díaz, "the present movement is not isolated, nor is it confined to the working class." He went on to say that in the absence of the government's "looking after the people," there would soon occur "a deluge that inundates."[13]

The PLM drew considerable support not only inside Mexico—where in 1906 its outlawed newspaper, *Regeneración*, was reaching 30,000 readers, mostly workers—but also from Mexican communities in the United States. In a multitude of ways, these US-based communities backed the 1910 Revolution. The US government, Pinkertons, and detectives from the Furlong Secret Service Company systematically harassed Mexican revolutionaries, especially PLM militants and sympathizers, beating and jailing them or keeping them on the run as "illegal" immigrants, as well as opening their mail and coordinating intelligence operations with the Mexican government. Mexicans in the US joined PLM-sponsored unions, attended PLM rallies, and packed the courtrooms where PLM militants were put on trial. In addition, PLM militants cooperated with and drew support from American trade union radicals like the "Wobblies," or Industrial Workers of the World (IWW), founded in 1905 and based mainly among unskilled and semiskilled immigrant workers. The PLM also enjoyed the backing of America's Socialists, led by Eugene Debs. But Debs gradually came to view the PLM as too anarchistic, withdrew his support in 1911, and turned instead to the "democratic" successor to Díaz, Francisco I. Madero (assassinated in 1913 as a result of a plot hatched in the American embassy in Mexico City).[14]

From the time of its inception, the PLM organized Mexicans on both sides of the border in an escalating series of crippling strikes, including the 1903 strike by 1,000 Mexican and Japanese sugarbeet field workers in Ventura, California; the 1906 Anaconda strike in the copper mines of Cananea, Sonora, which was crushed with the aid of US troops; related mining strikes in both countries (many Mexicans perished during the shooting of strikers and burning of women and children in their tents at Ludlow, Colorado, when IWW-led miners protested Rockefeller's notorious exploitation); the textile and rail strikes of 1906 and 1908 in Mexico; and the 1910 strike by Mexican trolley workers in Los Angeles, California.

PLM members and Mexican immigrant workers supported American labor's cause throughout the Southwest. In 1907, in the mining community of Morenci, Arizona, PLM member Praxedis Guerrero and others founded the Unión de Obreros Libres (Union of Free Workers), whose striking workers in 1983–85 were still fighting Phelps Dodge and the National Guard in much the same way their predecessors had at the time of their union's founding. In response to labor troubles in California, especially the Gas Works strike of 1910, the PLM joined in the creation of the California State Federation of Labor. The PLM-backed Gas Works strikers, 90 percent of whom were Mexican, won wage hikes through their actions. Mexican immigrant workers joined the IWW's Agricultural Workers Organization (AWO) for the 1915 harvest. Many of them remained active thereafter, in spite of a "criminal syndicalism" law in California and other states that made IWW members in effect "outlaws." Countless anonymous Mexican immigrant workers who formed the backbone of the IWW in the Southwest were gunned down by law enforcement personnel and employers' hired goons during the 1916–24 period. Of the IWW's total annual dues income from 1916 to 1924, between one-third and one-half came from the AWO. In 1917 Mexican-influenced strikes were still going strong. That year workers won a more favorable contract with Spreckles Sugar, and some 9,000 Mexicans struck the copper companies in southern Arizona.[15]

Revolutionary factions other than the PLM in Mexico also cultivated support among the *colonia mexicana*. In 1915 forces in Los Angeles supportive of the moderate Constitutionalist Venustiano Carranza organized the Constitutionalist Union of Mexican Workers, the precedent for subsequent Mexican consulate efforts to counter radical tendencies in labor, whether leftist or rightist. From 1915 to 1917 followers of the Plan de San Diego launched what in effect became an international effort on behalf of revolutionaries inside Mexico. Although its origins remain unclear, its impact was devastating in south Texas, where Mexican residents engaged in armed uprisings against "anglo" ranchers and merchants. Thousands of US troops and the Texas Rangers quelled the rebellion, killing hundreds of Mexicans and driving them from their lands.

The Mexican Revolution of 1910–17 considerably loosened, without necessarily breaking, the traditional bonds that tied peasants and workers to the *haciendas*, mines, and mills of rural Mexico. The years of pitched battle between contending factions of the Revolution, in which millions were killed or wounded, further contributed to people's willingness to migrate northward. A large number of deaths resulted from inadequate medical care and sanitation, as well as from invoking the death penalty for captured soldiers, a precedent established in 1913 by Carranza, landholder-capitalist and former governor during the Díaz regime. Carranza's Constitutionalists eventually—with US diplomatic and military support—won the civil war against the popular armies of more radical revolutionaries like Emiliano Zapata and Francisco "Pancho" Villa.

Faced with a manpower shortage during World War I, the United States removed all barriers to Mexican entry in 1917–18, including laws banning contract labor. Despite the fact that the 1917 Immigration Act called for immigrants to pay an eight-dollar head tax and pass a literacy test, more than a third of a million Mexicans crossed into the United States in the next six years. Yet this movement was by no means one-way.

In 1919 the famous "Red scare" sponsored by Attorney General A. Mitchell Palmer led to the violent deportation of hundreds of "aliens," "anarchists," and "communists," a number of whom were Mexicans. The key targets of the Palmer Raids, as they were known, were southern European and Latin American labor organizers influential in the unionization of America's working class during the prior two decades. The vast majority of those arrested were innocent of any wrongdoing, though some of them did, of course, exercise their democratic right to express left-wing philosophies.

The Palmer Raids coincided with the return of American workers from the European battlefields of World War I. The need for immigrant labor was momentarily reduced. When US unemployment rose to alarming heights during the recession of 1920–22, the policy of the "revolving door" for Mexican immigrant workers began in earnest. The US government allowed mass deportations of Mexicans, not because they were believed to have been "born communist" (although that view was encouraged[16]), but because they were allegedly "the cause" of unemployment. Nevertheless, as the figures in Table 1 reveal, the size of the Mexican labor pool did not diminish—in fact, it grew. Various sectors of the economy still required cheap immigrant labor, and all sectors benefited from an abundant "reserve army of labor" with which to break strikes, control wages, and maintain labor discipline.

The calculated nature of the "revolving door" policy on the part of many employers was illustrated by the actions of the Cotton Growers Association. As a condition of its recruitment of labor during the temporary admission program of World War I, it promised to pay for the repatriation of some 13,000 Mexican workers if they were subsequently laid off. Of course, association members knew that the immigrants, once dismissed, would have no choice but to head back home, with or without their help. During the 1920–22 recession, when the workers were laid off, the association balked at keeping its promise. In the face of pressure by organized labor and the Mexican government, the cotton growers finally reached a settlement, but they did not honor it. The burden of paying for the repatriation of many of these workers fell on the Mexican government.

But with economic conditions in Mexico so unpromising, a repatriated or deported immigrant would often turn around a short time after arriving on Mexican soil and recross the border (as happens today). This practice persisted even in the face of repeated anti-Mexican attacks by racist mobs and vigilantes, aroused by the Ku Klux Klan and ever fresh tides of Anglo-American nativism. In 1922, for example, a liquored-up mob carrying burning torches stormed a jailhouse in Weslaco, Texas. Shouting racist epithets and howling raucously, they hauled out one of the bewildered Mexicans awaiting trial and strung him up to the nearest lamppost, where he was left to expire as jeering spectators and jail guards looked on.[17]

Despite this atmosphere of terror, the migratory flow continued at a feverish pace during the 1920s, its "revolving door" character well established. Employers anxious to hire Mexicans did not suffer from the racist hysteria or from Congress's "restrictionist" mood on immigration legislation in the 1920s for two reasons: first, the racist violence accompanying simultaneous deportations/importations through the "revolving door" kept Mexican migrant workers tractable; second, strict immigration quotas were established for southern Europeans but not for Mexicans, who were less likely to stay and unionize.

In 1924 employers received additional help from an immigration law that was, like the Simpson-Mazzoli bill sixty years later, ostensibly aimed at limiting Mexican immigration but in fact served to guarantee admission of and control over Mexican immigrant workers. The Immigration Act of 1924 created the US Border Patrol, the country's only national police force. This assured armed enforcement of the criteria differentiating between "legal" (eight-dollar head tax, ten-dollar visa fee, literacy test, no contract labor) and "illegal" immigrants. The 1924 law further provided for instant deportation of those who became public charges, violated US law, or engaged in anarchist or seditionist acts.

Ever since, US employers have had Mexican immigrant laborers at their mercy thanks to a specialized, federally funded police force that keeps the "revolving door" in motion. In the aftermath of the Palmer Raids, the deportation or threatened deportation of Mexican "illegals" by the US Border Patrol further constrained immigrant labor's organizing endeavors. The threat was backed up, and still is, by factory raids, harassment of Mexicans by INS agents, and surveillance and enforcement activities by the Border Patrol and local law authorities, acting with remarkable coordination and usually at the employers' behest, to get rid of labor agitators, to avoid paying the last week(s) of salaries, to drain off any excess that might accumulate in the surplus pool of unemployed workers, or simply to keep immigrant labor tractable.

Other laws of the 1920s excluded immigrants from receiving public medical assistance if they had lived in the United States for less than five years, further increasing Mexican migrants' vulnerability. In addition, a number of futile attempts were made in the late 1920s—the "Box laws," named after Congressman John O. Box—to restrict the number of Mexican immigrants. Box concurred with the sentiment expressed by Congressman Martin Madden of Chicago that Mexicans were "the worst element that comes into the United States . . . the most undesirable people who come under the flag."[18] Mexican government protests, employers' needs, and public objections by the *colonia Mexicana* frustrated the restrictionists. Also working against them was the fact that the federal government was pushing a cooperative spirit of "Pan-Americanism" with the Latin American republics as a means of protecting growing US corporate investments in the region. Many congressmen were unwilling to undermine this Pan-American policy by so overtly slamming the door on America's nearest Latin neighbors.

The well-attended US speaking tour of internationally renowned writer and Mexican presidential candidate José Vasconcelos in 1928 further put the restrictionists on the defensive. Vasconcelos galvanized stateside Mexican sentiment against the racist statements of American labor leaders like Samuel Gompers and the anti-Mexican activities of the Ku Klux Klan, with which he compared the "exclusionist" unions and the immigration restrictionists.

Acting either independently or with only token support from America's mainstream unions, a number of labor organizations continued to incorporate Mexican immigrant workers during the 1920s and 1930s. They sometimes obtained the backing of Mexico's labor unions and of local Mexican consulates. In May 1928, for example, the California-based Confederation of Mexican Workers Unions held a convention attended by twenty-one unions representing both agricultural and industrial workers. It drew support from the official labor confederation of Mexico, the Confederación Regional Obrera Mexicana (CROM). The Longshoremen's Union and the CIO-affiliated United Cannery, Agricultural, Packing and Allied Workers of America, whose locals were often led by American communists, were among the few (and the first) American unions to launch organizing drives among Mexican immigrant workers in the thirties.

The communists did not discriminate, unlike the AFL. As two Mexican immigrant workers informed Mexican anthropologist Manuel Gamio in 1930,

> "I don't belong to any union because they don't want to admit the Mexicans. Once the workers in asphalt, all Mexicans, organized a union but they wouldn't admit us into the Asphalters' Union of the AFL because they said that these same Mexicans were going to take their jobs away from them by accepting lower wages. So our union was broken up."

> "When a strike is near the American unions make it easy for all those who want to join. But when they are not on a strike they make all kinds of difficulties, especially for the Mexicans, so that they can't be members of those unions."[19]

Mexican workers, in spite of the fact that they made up only a small percentage of American union membership, were at the forefront of many of America's most militant and important strikes of the 1920s and 1930s. These included the famous Imperial Valley cantaloupe strike of 1928; the Imperial Valley lettuce strike of 1930; the Pittsburgh miners' strike of 1932; the El Monte strawberry strike in Los Angeles County in 1933; California's cotton strikes of 1933 and agricultural strikes of 1936; the canners', packers', and pecan shellers' strikes of 1938 in San Antonio, Texas; and, through the Spanish-speaking Section 96 of the

International Ladies Garment Workers Union, the ILGWU strikes of 1933–36 and 1939. The El Monte berry strike obtained the support of the Mexican consulate, unified Mexican and Japanese workers, and led directly to the growers' recognition of the union and the formation of California's 10,000-member Confederation of Mexican Peasants and Workers in 1934. All these strikes showed a remarkable degree of worker self-organization. They received the support of communists and other radicals, leading to constant Red-baiting and frequent attacks by goon squads in the pay of employers or local law authorities.[20]

The ultimate card to be played by employers in the face of such labor organizing was the "revolving door." Mexican labor organizers or union members could be swiftly and legally deported, since few of them had taken the literacy test or paid the immigration head tax or visa fee. Whipped-up anti-Mexican racism made the policy even more harsh. It was in an atmosphere of jingoistic hysteria that Mexicans were deported by the hundreds of thousands in the 1920s and 1930s (and into the present). This massive deportation was coupled with school segregation and other routine racist offenses against Mexicans, dating from the nineteenth century.

The employers' other major card in the face of labor unrest was state collusion in the subjugation of immigrant labor. A Mexican community newspaper in Chicago complained in 1926, "While the Department of State in Washington is demanding guarantees for its citizens in Mexico, we are being made the victims of the police in Chicago and other cities."[21] To put down the 1936 Orange County farmworkers' strike, growers called upon more than 400 sheriff's deputies and special guards. If on-site repression failed, the state turned a blind eye to violent evictions, as when Mexican strikers in Santa Paula, California, were replaced in 1941 by Oklahoma Dust Bowl refugees.

In his 1964 classic work *Merchants of Labor*, Ernesto Galarza commented on the complex network of state-employer collusion in violence, racist vigilantism, and the maintenance of multinational, multiracial migrant labor pools used by employers to get their way.

> Behind the [California growers'] Associated Farmers and the vigilante committees, there stood the less conspicuous commodity federations, whose leadership was in close touch through interlocking directorates that extended their lines of communication into every major power center in the state. . . . The labor force conceived as a pool, recruited

from the surplus stock of people in Asia, Mexico, and the backward counties of the United States, held together by mass coercion, was adequate.[22]

Racist practices, state-employer collusion, and massive deportations of Mexican workers have disguised the "revolving door." This reality was illustrated in the early 1930s, at the height of the Great Depression. By the end of 1932 in the United States, growers had suffered a 70 percent decline in their income, industrial production had plummeted 50 percent, and unemployment was affecting 25 percent of the labor force, or 12 million workers. The first workers to be laid off were women and racial minorities, including about 500,000 Mexicans. Meanwhile, unemployment in Mexico tripled, and US employers, especially hard-hit growers, welcomed the sight of an expanded and totally desperate labor pool so near at hand. They thought that hiring these workers at substandard wages would help boost profit rates and promote "economic recovery"—a common practice used during times of depression and recession to combat the "tendency of the rate of profit to fall."[23]

Most American laborers would not work for the low wages offered to Mexican immigrants. Only the most down-and-out, such as the Dust Bowl victims from Oklahoma and other states, would accept the miserable working and living conditions imposed on Mexicans. With American employers and workers alike seeking a scapegoat for their economic troubles (brought about by capital's overinvestment and overproduction in the late 1920s), there occurred a fresh outbreak of anti-Mexican hysteria.

The US government orchestrated a nationwide campaign to deport Mexicans. Local officials gladly cooperated in what became a veritable "Mexican scare." For example, C. P. Visel, the Los Angeles coordinator for unemployment relief, admitted that he intended at the time to frighten "illegals" and force them to leave the region. Social workers and relief agencies advised US-citizen Mexicans to take their families "back to Mexico." To send a trainload of Mexicans to the border cost Los Angeles County a mere $77,000, compared with $348,000 to keep them on relief—a savings of $271,000 a trainload. Authorities rounded up and deported at least 400,000 Mexicans. Some estimates go as high as a million or more, including tens of thousands of US-citizen Mexicans. The deportations added to Mexico's unemployment and made the Mexican "labor pool" even more vulnerable to superexploitation.

Yet in 1930 there were an estimated 640,000 Mexican-born Mexicans (and as the decade progressed, an estimated million) living alongside the 1.4 million American-born Mexicans in the United States. Of the Mexican immigrant workers, most of whom had no immigration documents, 70 percent were employed in agriculture, 15 percent in factories and workshops, 10 percent in mining, and 5 percent in comerce, business, and the professions. In other words, it can be estimated that during the early years of the Great Depression less than half of the Mexican "illegals" were actually deported, so necessary was their labor to US capital. And many of the deportees turned around and reentered not long afterwards.[24]

Even so, in the midst of the attacks on Mexicans, some employers began to worry that the massive deportations would make the "revolving door" stop. They clamored for some kind of government assurance of access to cheap Mexican immigrant labor. The head of the Department of Agriculture, among others, responded to their pleas by informing the American public, "We have depended upon these people; they are not a social burden but honest men and workers who have helped so much to develop this country. Certainly they merit consideration, if for no other reason than at a minimum they are necessary and because their absence will be sharply felt by all those persons who employ workers in large numbers."[25]

And so the border doors went on revolving inexorably, year after year. The heat of anti-Mexican racist hysteria rarely subsided, reaching new heights in 1943 with the so-called Zoot-Suit Riots of Los Angeles, San Diego, and Oakland, California (since made part of American cinema folklore by the first commercial Chicano movie, the musical *Zoot Suit*, released in 1981). US soldiers and sailors on furlough, supported by local police forces, stormed Mexican neighborhoods to "depants" Mexican or Chicano youth dressed in the flamboyant outfits known as zoot suits, and to "get the greasers."

The climax of several nights of very one-sided rioting came on June 7, 1943, when thousands of servicemen and civilians shouting, "Let's get 'em! Let's get the chili-eating bastards," swept through the East Los Angeles *barrio* and yanked Mexicans from bars, movie theaters, and cars, clubbing them mercilessly. Filipinos and blacks were also "fair game." One black, pulled from a streetcar, had his eyes gouged out with a knife. The irony is that according to widely reported statements by officers and enlisted men at the time, the US military encouraged and condoned these attacks even though US-born Mexicans were the most decorated ethnic group of World War II.

In the end, with the press portraying the sailors as heroes and the zoot-suiters as hoodlums, full-scale urban warfare threatened to erupt. When the police were clearly unable to reestablish order in Los Angeles, military shore police were called in to quell the disturbances. The overwhelming majority of those arrested, detained, or otherwise charged with criminal action were Mexicans, the victims of the attacks; no punishment was ever meted out to the servicemen or their commanding officers.

For its part, the Mexican government vigorously protested these acts of racist violence and in fact helped to bring an end to the Zoot-Suit Riots. But it was too economically strapped to provide more than token assistance in the repatriation of its citizens from the United States in the 1920s and 1930s—or since. In 1931 it created a National Committee of Repatriates, backed by public and private monies and organizations. And throughout the decade it provided occasional "agrarian colonies" on which less than 5 percent of the repatriated workers settled. More than 70 percent of the "repatriates" reemigrated to the United States.[26]

Article 123 of the Mexican constitution calls upon Mexican consuls abroad to make sure that any contract between a Mexican citizen and a foreign employer is "legalized by the competent municipal authority" and that the employer is responsible for the costs of the citizen's repatriation to Mexico. In practice, however, the Mexican state has largely limited its actions in *colonias mexicanas* to encouraging celebrations of significant national events such as the Grito de Dolores (September 16, Mexico's Independence Day) and to rhetorical or symbolic demands expressive of national dignity. In the face of cold reality, it has in fact been unable to do much more.

In a characteristically demagogic expression of this futility, President José López Portillo told the Mexican people after his September 1979 meeting with President Jimmy Carter, "I told the President of the United States that . . . we stand behind our Chicano brothers and we stand behind our undocumented citizens."[27] The facts are that López Portillo never made more than symbolic gestures on behalf of either his "Chicano brothers" or Mexican migrant workers—while the oil-rich Mexican government went bankrupt during his notoriously corrupt administration.

3

"Revolving Door" for "Outlaws": Braceros and "Illegals"

> *"Is this indentured alien—an almost perfect model of the economic man, an 'input factor' stripped of the political and social attributes that liberal democracy likes to ascribe to all human beings ideally—is this bracero the prototype of the production man of the future?"*
> —Ernesto Galarza, *Merchants of Labor*, 1964

> *"There comes a large cloud of dust*
> *with no consideration*
> *Women, children and old men*
> *are being driven to the Border*
> *Goodbye beloved countrymen*
> *we are being deported*
> *But we are not outlaws*
> *we come to work."*
> —"El Deportado," Mexican folk ballad

Many Americans have fallen for the scapegoat approach used throughout the history of Mexican and other immigration to the United States. The early targets of Anglo-American racism were Indians and African slaves. Later, it was the Germans and the Irish who drew Americans' xenophobic wrath, followed by the Chinese and Japanese. More recently, anti-immigrant sentiment has been expressed against Scandinavians, Jews, Greeks, Italians, Filipinos, Koreans, Vietnamese, Arabs, and others.

Unfortunately, many Americans from the racial and ethnic groups that were once so virulently attacked find it satisfying today to vent their own frustrations upon the largest available immigrant pool—Mexicans and other "Latinos" (as Latin Americans call themselves). Too few Americans recognize the Mexican immigrants for who they actually are: human beings suffering extreme forms of oppression and persecution while performing many of society's basic unskilled and semiskilled tasks. Too many Americans tend to see Mexicans as "aliens," that is, strange-looking or odd-sounding foreigners who have no right to live or work in the United States. Hence, the press frequently refers to them not as workers, immigrants, or people but as "aliens," "illegals," "undocumented workers," or simply "criminals." Incorrigible bigots, of course, cite "the brown peril."*

Yet if so many employers and all consumers depend so heavily on these people, then why is it that they are viewed as a "problem" or as "illegals"? Human beings can *do* illegal things, but can a human being actually *be* illegal? Moreover, since when under capitalism is it an illegal act to sell one's labor power for a low wage to an employer engaged in a socially approved business? Will halting all Mexican immigration (an impossible task short of a fascistic militarization of the border) solve the alleged problem of unfair competition with US workers? On the other hand, will "legalizing" immigration for some of the Mexicans in fact help the situation?

A number of prominent voices in American society seem to think so. They include agribusiness and industrial employers, newspapers like the *New York Times*, various powerful lobbyists and opinion makers, and even some AFL-CIO leaders. These authorities claim that proposed legislation such as the Simpson-Mazzoli bill, advocating selective legalized permanent and temporary immigration, is a long overdue "solution" that will overcome the "problem of illegals" and abolish the injustices of the past. They argue that legal channels for Mexican immi-

---

*Throughout this work, the terms "undocumented," "illegal alien," "wetback," and so on are put in quotation marks to highlight their obviously racist connotation. Of workers without proper immigration papers, those stopped or searched most frequently by authorities tend to be nonwhite; and, as we shall see, even US *citizens* of Latin American descent are harassed during periodic factory or neighborhood roundups conducted against "illegals."

gration will offer "guest workers" fair living and working conditions and eliminate once and for all the large-scale phenomenon of "illegals."

Yet history clearly invalidates the arguments of those who champion the Simpson-Mazzoli bill. The 1942–64 bracero program is a case in point. [Designed to allow Mexican workers legal entry into the United States, the bracero program set up recruiting centers in Mexico that provided specific contracts for work across the border.] Unfortunately, these recruitment centers could offer only a fraction of the jobs sought by the hundreds of thousands of applicants. Since most of the contract centers were near the border, it was a simple matter for a rejected applicant to sneak across and compete with the official braceros for jobs in agriculture, services, and the lower ranks of industry. Employers, in fact, encouraged this "illegal" migratory flow since they stood to benefit greatly from an expansion of the low-wage labor pool of job-hungry Mexicans. The US government colluded with the employers' active recruitment of "illegals" on a regular basis. Thus, the bracero project resulted in extreme abuse both of legally admitted workers and of vastly increased numbers of "illegals."

If the bracero experience is any indication, then another "guest worker" program will in no way reduce the influx of "illegal" Mexican immigrant workers. On the contrary, it will lend it considerable momentum, far beyond current levels. Yet the same arguments used three and four decades ago to introduce and administer the bracero program are now being advanced for similar "guest worker" programs.

A number of false propositions served then, as now, to legitimize the legalized importation of Mexicans and to disguise the consequences. These propositions are: there exists a chronic shortage of manpower in the United States; only recruitment of Mexican labor can alleviate this shortage; the Mexicans are recruited to do stooped labor; Mexicans are employed only during critical harvest peaks when there are not enough American workers; employment of Mexicans is necessary to prevent the loss of perishable crops; the main benefits go to small farms, strengthening "family farming"; the Mexican economy is aided rather than harmed, since the migrants remit large portions of their wages; the migrants benefit since they learn methods of modern agriculture and the values of democracy; and the migrants' rights are protected by the US Department of Labor and the Mexican consulates. As becomes clear in this and succeeding chapters, each one of these claims stands reality on its head.

The Bracero Program and PL 78

Manpower shortages caused by America's entry into World War II in December 1941 brought the prior decade's ongoing deportations of Mexicans to a screeching halt. During the next few years, the border doors did not merely revolve—they were suddenly thrown wide open. In 1941 the Southern Pacific Railroad petitioned the government for 6,000 laborers for maintenance-of-way operations. Cotton and beet growers in Arizona, New Mexico, and Texas clamored for fieldhands. Orange and lemon growers in California asked for 50,000 Mexicans.

In 1939 there were still 10 million Americans unemployed, but by 1942 some 14 million Americans were in the armed forces and another 10 million civilians had found employment in the booming war industries. Many low-paid farmhands joined the military or got better jobs in defense plants. In February 1942 some 100,000 Japanese and Japanese-Americans were thrown into concentration camps, further shrinking the nation's labor supply in agriculture, services, and nondefense industry. Agroindustry growers, concerned that farmworkers' organizing activities of the 1930s had begun to close the gap between farm and industrial wages, obtained wage stabilization policies from the government, freezing wartime wages close to or even below 1940 levels.

Pressed by employers for immediate action to bring in tens of thousands of Mexicans, especially to harvest the next season's crops and maintain the nation's railroads, the US government entered into negotiations with Mexico. Since 1938, the year it expropriated with compensation US and British oil properties, Mexico had been subjected to a worldwide petroleum boycott by the Allies and had turned to the Axis powers of Japan, Germany, and Italy for its oil trade. Now, as a result of urgent bilateral negotiations, Mexico agreed to enter World War II on the side of the Allies, to pay further indemnities to the oil companies in exchange for the end of the blockade, to increase silver and agricultural exports to the United States during the war, and to provide American growers and other employers the laborers they so desperately needed.

On August 14, 1942, Presidents Manuel Ávila Camacho and Franklin Delano Roosevelt signed a bilateral executive agreement known officially as the bracero program.[1] It called for the legal immigration of Mexican workers according to US agricultural employers' needs for the duration of the war. It provided for nondiscriminatory conditions in wages, work, health, sanitation, and lodging, equivalent to those offered American employees in the same areas of work. Since these protections for the braceros were rarely honored, and since enterprises besides agribusiness benefited, US employers in general were delighted with the program and pressed for its postwar continuation.

Thus, what started ostensibly as an emergency wartime measure to solve an American labor shortage was periodically reenacted. Effectively controlled by modern agribusiness and other employers or their agents inside and outside of government, the program resulted in widespread abuse of both braceros and "illegal" Mexican workers, who in some cases became virtual slaves. Their ill-treatment and low wages helped keep American workers' wages down. The bracero program served to perpetuate the misery of American farmworkers, already made notorious in works of literature, photography, and muckraking journalism of the 1930s. It held back the unionization drives of American farmworkers another two decades. Above all, it contributed to making American agribusiness a global giant with lucrative investments in almost every nation of the world.

A 1951 presidential commission found that bracero labor was used by only 2 percent of the nation's farms and that these farms had not been suffering a labor shortage prior to the bracero program. Rather, the commission reported, large employers had asked for braceros in order to drive down American workers' wages and to defeat union organizing efforts among domestic farmworkers.[2] A more recent study of the bracero program concluded that it contributed to a growing coordination of government and corporate actions to increase the profits of US corporations at home and abroad. This study showed that the bracero program undermined Americans' economic and political rights while fueling US-corporate economic expansion to the detriment of both immigrant workers and the American people.[3] Lee G. Williams, a US Labor Department executive who from 1959 to 1964 oversaw the day-to-day operation of the bracero program, has called it "legalized slavery, nothing but a way for big corporate farms to get a cheap labor supply from Mexico under government sponsorship. . . . The braceros were hauled around like cattle in Mexico and treated like prisoners in the United States."[4]

In Spanish, *bracero* (from *brazo*, "arm") means "working hand." Half of the 52,000 braceros recruited during the first year of the program (1942–43) were rushed into railway maintenance work from coast to coast. The rest harvested the nation's crops. Their numbers rose dramatically from that point on but were still dwarfed by the number of Mexican "illegals." For each bracero entering the country during the program's 22 years of existence there were an estimated four "illegals"—known in those days as *mojados*, or "wetbacks," because so many supposedly swam or waded across the Río Bravo to enter the country. US-citizen Mexicans objected to this derogatory label, which was sometimes applied to them as well, especially during periods of mass deportations. Besides, from a Mexican or Chicano nationalist point of view, it was the "anglos" who were "illegally" in the Southwest, not the Mexicans, who were the first to settle there after the Indians.

By July 1945 there were some 58,000 braceros employed in agriculture and 62,000 working on the railroads (these figures do not include an estimated 70,000 "illegals"). The number of deported "illegals" alone exceeded that of braceros from 1946 on. By 1950 some 430,000 braceros were passing through Mexico's three main recruitment centers, Hermosillo, Chihuahua, and Monterrey, while the number of deported "illegals" was surpassing half a million, reaching a peak of 1.1 million in 1954. While figures for the deportation of "illegals" provided by the Immigration and Naturalization Service may not be altogether reliable, they at least suggest just how quickly the border doors were revolving. From 1944 through 1953 the INS reported deportations doubling almost every other year, rising from 29,000 in 1944 to nearly 900,000 in 1953, or about 5 million for the 10-year period—a figure roughly equivalent to the number of braceros legally admitted during the entire 22-year period of the bracero program.

After taking control of the bracero program from the War Manpower Commission in 1948, the US secretary of labor regularly colluded with growers in the erosion of bracero wages and the large-scale importation of "illegals" at harvest time. Employers, organized into powerful interest groups like the Imperial Valley Farmers Association and the San Joaquin Farm Production Association, used the "illegals" to make sure the government would not think they depended only on braceros. In this way, they were able to persuade the government that enforcing fair labor conditions under the bracero program was not only impossible and costly but also unrealistic and unnecessary, since lower-paid "illegals" could always do the job. Deportations of "illegals" after harvest time, or whenever the surplus labor pool grew too large or cumbersome, served to maintain an aura of legality around the bracero program and to keep the revolving door rotating at a clip commensurate with employer needs.

The periodically renegotiated bilateral bracero agreement prohibited the use of Mexicans as strikebreakers and their employment where domestic workers were available or where it would adversely affect local wages or working conditions. But these terms were routinely violated. Consequently, energized by the labor of abysmally underpaid and extremely hardworking Mexican braceros and "illegals," who travailed on a roughly equal basis in large-scale commercial farming, America's world-famous agricultural productivity rose sharply. US farmhands ranked a poor third as a proportion of the labor force in the biggest firms producing the nation's leading crops, especially in California and Texas. Far from prospering, "family farms" went into severe decline during the period of the bracero program, their acreage halved. During the 1950s some 38,000 farms went out of business in California alone.

In the agriculture sector as a whole, including small farms, Mexican immigrants accounted for up to one-third of the seasonal labor force. Their presence all but extinguished that of the American migrant laborer. By 1960 Mexican immigrant workers represented more than a quarter of the Southwest's labor force. Nationally, they accounted for almost 19 percent of agriculture workers, seasonal or other. Nearly 5 million braceros and many more "illegals" had entered the country since the bracero program's inception. Farm labor conditions generally deteriorated for two decades, until the union organizing drives led by Cesar Chavez, Dolores Huerta, Antonio Orendain, and others in the 1960s and 1970s led to improvements for at least a small minority of workers (see Chapter 7).

After World War II, US employers and the Mexican government were so pleased with the bracero program that its continuation was never placed in serious doubt. Aside from the obvious economic advantages, employers were fearful that ex-farmhands returning to the fields from military service or employment in the war plants would renew their prewar union organizing activities. This in fact happened in both agriculture and industry when more than a million American workers went on strike in 1945–46, seeking compensation for their acceptance of wage freezes and no-strike pledges during the war, when big corporations had raked in superprofits.

Mexican braceros proved useful for "scabbing" many of these postwar strikes. The 1947 Taft-Hartley Act limiting labor's rights, and the Cold War offensive against labor militants, also helped big business. A veritable witch-hunt swept through labor's ranks, cleansing the unions of organizers and other alleged "communists." These steps consolidated the generally antiforeign, racist, anticommunist, and uncombative character of American labor unionism that has prevailed since.

The American Federation of Labor and the Congress of Industrial Organizations (merged in 1955 as the AFL-CIO, today's officially recognized labor union movement) did not at first seriously seek to organize or help farmworkers. Not until 1959 did it make a financial commitment to undertake a farm labor organizing campaign in California. In fact, the AFL-CIO colluded with agribusiness employers through its refusal to resist in any sustained way the actions of agribusiness sympathizers in top government positions—people like Don Larin, deputy director in charge of farm placement for the Department of Labor in the 1940s and 1950s. Among Larin's many notorious acts on behalf of agribusiness was the "Tobin-Larin rule" (issued by himself and Secretary of Labor Maurice Tobin in 1952) prohibiting US farmworkers from limiting their availability to a specific place of employment, and thereby forcing them to apply for jobs elsewhere if braceros were already employed. Larin also made sure that farmworker wage levels and the policing of the bracero program were left ultimately to the discretion of the growers. When Mr. Larin was named later in the 1950s to direct the farm placement division of California's Department of Employment, the AFL-CIO endorsed his appointment.[5]

In 1951 the Mexican government tried to introduce some order into the bracero program by insisting that the US government supervise contracting. As a result, the 1942 binational executive agreement on braceros was given formal approval by the US Congress in the form of Public Law 78 (PL 78). At Mexican insistence, PL 78 exempted braceros from contributing to the US Social Security system. This saved employers their part of Social Security payments, adding substantially to profit margins already swelled by the low wages paid braceros.

PL 78 gave the US secretary of labor the authority to recruit Mexican workers and "illegals" who had resided in the United States for at least five years and to set their wage levels. Ostensibly an amnesty provision, this was a kind of forerunner to current proposals for long-time resident "illegals." In practice, PL 78 continued to stimulate the "illegal" migratory flow and frequently resulted in the hiring of resident "illegals" who had been in the United States less than five years. It further assured a large labor pool from which employers could choose workers on their own terms. Once inside the United States, braceros not hired within five days were to be returned to Mexico, so most workers accepted whatever terms of employment were offered.

During the 1950s nearly 3.5 million braceros and far more "illegals" worked in the United States. By 1959 California and Texas accounted for about three-fourths of these laborers. Mexican braceros and "illegals" worked in 275 important crop areas throughout the nation, often in what became known as "mixed crews," despite PL 78's unenforced proviso that no braceros could be provided to employers hiring "illegal" Mexicans. In effect, low-paid Mexican labor toiling long hours under miserable conditions built American agribusiness into the world potentate it is today.

The bracero program was financed largely by the US government—that is, by American taxpayers. Former braceros interviewed by this writer in Michoacán understood better than most Americans do to this day how the program functioned. One of them summed it up this way:

> The US government was paying money for the braceros. They were rented the American government, which paid this government. Mexico owed money to the United States and was paying it off with the braceros. We braceros were the money all along the line—rented out by the Mexican government to the American farm associations which paid off the US government which checked all of it off to the Mexican debt.

The braceros thus subsidized both governments and private enterprise, especially agribusiness. Private enterprise was in effect doubly subsidized: by US taxpayers and by imported Mexican laborers who had paid for their own upbringing and sustenance. During the war years alone, the cost of the bracero program ran to an estimated $55 million. In subsequent decades, as the numbers of braceros and "illegals" rose and the "revolving door" shifted into high gear, the costs of administering Mexican immigration and deportation reached astronomical heights. After 1951 growers had to pay for the transportation and subsistence of the braceros—tasks accomplished in great part by a flourishing semicriminal underground network of hired hands, smugglers, and fast-buck hustlers on both sides of the border. Yet once again the buck was passed down the line to the braceros. The provision of food for the braceros, for instance, led to wage checkoffs of between 20 and 50 percent; insurance checkoffs approached 2.5 percent of a bracero's paycheck.

Mexican taxpayers also helped finance the program. The Mexican government was obligated to assemble prospective braceros at the different contract centers. The US Department of Labor then selected workers from these "worker pools established and maintained by the Mexican Government."[6]

A 1949 interim bilateral agreement legitimized the employment of "illegals." Known as the "drying out" (of "wetbacks") measure, it permitted "illegal" Mexicans in the United States to be employed and to have their immigration status adjusted accordingly—in effect, to become braceros. The US Employment Service of the Department of Labor was instructed to give preference to those Mexicans who had been properly "dried out." This in turn helped consolidate an underground system of recruiting "wetbacks" from inside Mexico. In 1950, when the Korean War was helping the United States recover from a serious recession, less than 20,000 new braceros were admitted but nearly 100,000 "wetbacks" were "dried out."

The McCarran-Walter Immigration Act of 1952 went even further. It made it a felony to import or harbor—but not to employ—a deportable alien. The green light for employing such people was a supposed concession to Texas congressmen and so became known as the Texas Proviso. It really allowed harboring as well, since many employers were involved in transporting, housing, and feeding the migrants they hired. In fact, the McCarran-Walter Act prohibited citizens' arrests of "wetbacks," a tactic used effectively the previous year in California's Imperial Valley by the small but struggling National Farm Labor Union, an underfinanced semiautonomous AFL affiliate. The Texas Proviso, unlike the bracero program, has never been removed from US immigration law. Given employers' preference for desperate "illegals," its existence has allowed them to carry on business more or less as usual regardless of the public debates raging around defunct bracero programs or new guest worker proposals.

The McCarran-Walter Act also restricted the admittance of suspected communists or other "subversives," thereby making it easier for the INS to stop known or suspected Mexican labor organizers at the border. It listed various grounds on which "aliens" could be deported or excluded, and it even provided criteria for "denaturalizing" naturalized American citizens.

These draconian measures, striking at America's traditional civil liberties, only added to those of the earlier McCarran-Walter Immigration Act of 1950, which provided for the construction of concentration camps, six of which were built in 1952. Many Mexicans, including US citizens, feared being placed in a camp, labeled subversive, or deported. In this way, the McCarran-Walter Acts achieved one of their central purposes: to discourage or intimidate would-be political or labor union activists. In fact, numerous US-born Mexicans *were* deported in the 1950s. As the Los Angeles Committee for the Protection of the Foreign Born protested in 1954, "The McCarren-Walter Law is aimed at the heart of American labor. . . . With this law, under the pretext of hunting 'illegals' and 'subversives,' immigration service officers serve as a terroristic police force in Mexican communities, as a strike-breaking, union-busting force in the fields, shops, and factories."[7]

The Taft-Hartley Act, McCarthyism, the 1950 Smith Act (making it a crime to "conspire to teach" the overthrow of the government), the McCarran-Walter Acts, the bracero program—all were interrelated parts of a frontal assault on labor activism and the free exercise of Americans' basic civil liberties. In the name of anticommunism and patriotism, they created an atmosphere of psychological terror throughout society. Countless people lost their jobs, served jail terms, were deported, or went into exile. American protest on any significant scale was effectively silenced for an entire decade, "the silent fifties."

In the case of Mexicans, the new laws, parts of which were later found unconstitutional, intimidated every Mexican civil rights organization founded before and after World War II. During the height of the Cold War, Mexican civic, student, and labor groups engaged in "purges" of suspected "subversives." The result was that America's Mexican communities were placed, if not in a defenseless position like the braceros and "wetbacks," in a highly defensive one. A massive and militant offensive against racism and economic oppression was thereby postponed until the 1960s. Even so, Mexicans made remarkably persistent endeavors to obtain justice.

Typical was the making of the film *Salt of the Earth* and the real-life events it recorded in the early 1950s. In June 1951 miners of the International Union of Mine, Mill and Smelter Workers, Local 890, met in Hanover, New Mexico, to discuss their limping eight-month-long strike. Most of the men were Mexican, some of them "illegals." The employer, Empire Zinc, had obtained an injunction against the men's picketing. In a scene that became a classic in cinema history, the wives of the picketers said, "We'll walk the line for you and keep the scabs out." Many of the "macho" men snickered at this proposal but after heated debate accepted it. The women picketers were in turn arrested but proved difficult to subjugate in the town's overcrowded jailhouse. Gradually, more women and children took over the picket lines, and in early 1952 Empire Zinc finally agreed to a new contract.

Salt of the Earth records this microcosm of labor, ethnic, and women's history in faithful detail. The strikers themselves composed most of the film's cast, including the male lead. The female lead, a Mexican film star, was refused a visa to enter the United States. Many blacklisted filmmakers and actors driven from Hollywood by the witch-hunt and the "Hollywood Ten" hearings brought their talents and cameras to record the evolution of the strike. Like the strikers, the filmmaking personnel were repeatedly harassed, beaten up, shot at, and so on. Armed vigilantes met at the local American Legion Hall and proclaimed the slogan "Get out of Grant County or go out in black boxes."

Considered too subversive to be seen by the American public, *Salt of the Earth* was banned but has become since the sixties a cult film among progressives and cinema buffs. The entire experience of the artists, workers, and migrants involved with the film and the strike reflected the difficult situation of the Mexican community at the height of the bracero program and PL 78.[8]

Open Border, "Operation Wetback," and the "Revolving Door"

In 1951 a presidential commission on migratory labor stated, "In effect the negotiation of the Mexican International Agreement is collective bargaining in which the Mexican Government is the representative of the workers and the Department of State is the representative of our farm employers." It pointed out that the bracero program was having adverse effects on American workers, a conclusion reaffirmed by a panel of experts appointed by the secretary of labor in 1959. These effects included depression of wages, displacement from jobs, deterioration of living conditions, weakening of labor organization, and the use of braceros as strikebreakers.[9]

By 1953 the manipulation and abuses of Mexican immigrant workers had become so obvious that the Mexican government and press began referring to "Eisenhower's open border" and the need to enforce the wage and work standards of the bracero program, notoriously honored in the breach. That fall, bilateral negotiations broke down on the issues of wages.

Federal minimum wage legislation had never embraced farmworkers. The use of the (employer-defined) "prevailing wage" for a particular locale at a given time continued to characterize American agriculture. Federal "certification" of bracero wages, also defined in practice by employers, was often used by the same employers as a guideline for the wages of other workers. The bracero "benchmark" wage thus served as a drag on wages in general.

Mexicans were understandably appalled by the government's certification methods for bracero wages. The innocent- and fair-sounding proviso of the prevailing wage in actual practice permitted employers and labor recruiters to drive wages down, in part because of the bracero-generated increased labor pool. Federal certification only served to consolidate the wage-depressant impact of the importation of Mexican laborers. In fact top bureaucrats in charge of overseeing the bracero program brazenly served the interests of agribusiness.

It was well known that the chief of the Labor Department's Farm Placement Service, Edward F. Hayes, was a stockholder in the Di Giorgio Fruit Corporation. Hayes later testified that both growers' needs for braceros and the prevailing wage were ascertained through "our constant contacts. . . . The grower sends the order to us."[10] As Glenn E. Brockway, director of the Mexican program on the West Coast, put it, "It should not be left to the discretion of the workers to decide by which method they will be paid."[11]

Washington's powerful and insulting response to Mexico's justified concern was to open the border to any Mexicans who wished to cross, starting in January 1954. This assured an even larger labor pool and lower prevailing wage. The result was tumultuous as thousands of workers broke through Mexican police and army lines to rush into the United States. Mexican soldiers opened fire on migrants climbing the border fence near Mexicali. Some INS officials and labor recruiters engaged in "body-snatching," helping to pull Mexican workers over the border.

At this time, the US Department of Labor openly engaged in unilateral recruiting of Mexican workers—an illegal but highly successful act. PL 78 was promptly amended by Congress to authorize Labor Department recruiting of Mexicans. This left the Mexican government with little alternative but to accept the usual false promises on fair wages and other outstanding points of contention concerning braceros, since now by law, as well as by January's proven practice, the United States could open the border at will (a border impossible to close, in any case).

In March 1954 a joint declaration was issued whereby Article 15 of PL 78 read, "The determination of the prevailing wage shall be made by the [US] Secretary of Labor." US employers audibly sighed with relief. They had long since established a network of organizations and reporting devices necessary for successful collusion with the secretary of labor in determining the prevailing wage. As Assistant Secretary of Labor Rocco Siciliano acknowledged on March 2, 1954, "Neither the State Department of Employment nor the US Department of Labor can set or fix farm wages or wage rates under the Mexican Nationals program. They are authorized only to discover what employers themselves are in fact paying."[12] Mexico "saved face" by including in the joint declaration some antidiscrimination rhetoric and the establishment of a bilateral commission to look into problems associated with legal and illegal migration.

In spite of January's "open border" practices, US authorities were by July deporting Mexicans in greater numbers than ever before in history. AFL-CIO officials joined a national outcry against "too many Mexicans taking jobs from Americans" as "Operation Wetback" was proclaimed in Washington. INS officials, the Border Patrol, the FBI, other federal agents, the army, the navy, and local sheriffs and police swung into action in a veritable militarized dragnet operation that sent 1 million to 2 million Mexicans to the nearest jailhouse, detention center, or border crossing. An atmosphere of nativist hysteria and anti-Mexican terror swept the land. Local officials were more busy and brutal in making the roundups than even the well-armed Border Patrol.

No one of Mexican appearance, whether a US citizen or not, was immune from the dragnet. Once again in the long dark history of American nativism and anti-Latino hysteria, it was "open season" on the Spanish-speaking. House-to-house raids in Mexican neighborhoods scooped up numerous US citizens. Their civil rights were violated not only by the absence of search warrants but also by their detention in jails and/or deportation to Mexico, a foreign land in which many found themselves disoriented and "without a country."

"Operation Wetback" left permanent scars in every Mexican community. Similar deportation operations in later years served to keep most Mexicans, US citizens or not, in a state of perpetual tension.

The timing of "Operation Wetback" presented a clear anomaly: how could the contradiction between an "open border" involving "body-snatching" and a "closed border" involving "body-deporting" possibly be explained?

Employers had been shaken by the "wetback strikes" organized by the National Farm Labor Union back in 1951–52. Serious social problems had surfaced in areas where Mexicans had become numerous and housing and health facilities had become a dangerous disgrace. The Korean War had ended. High unemployment brought about by the 1953 business recession was now compounded by returning soldiers out of work. A scapegoat was needed.

Moreover, managing the size, discipline, and wage level of the labor pool had long been the biggest headache for administrators of the bracero program. The use of "illegals" or "wetbacks" had proven essential, as had its sister operation, "drying out." Yet sometimes there were not enough of these surplus workers available; at other times there were more than the normal surplus requirements, and the dangers of mass rioting or starvation became immediate. Hence the "revolving door": expelling Mexican immigrants with one hand while blaming them for all kinds of economic and social problems, yet pulling them back into the country with the other. The Mexican worker was both highly sought and highly persecuted, a dialectic historically institutionalized by the "revolving door," and one that well suited employers.

And so the border door spun around and around—before, during, and after "Operation Wetback." The INS apprehended 875,000 Mexicans in the recession year of 1953, and only 160,000 more than that during the "Operation Wetback" year of 1954. In 1955, with deportations running at 242,000, the number of braceros under the bilateral agreement was actually increased. In other words, the US was sending a double message: Mexicans get out; Mexicans come in. The door revolved, Mexicans were harassed, wages held steady or dropped, and labor stability was assured for at least another decade.

The results from the viewpoint of employers could not have been more satisfactory. For example, the prevailing wage in the Imperial Valley, California, remained at seventy cents an hour from 1951 to 1959. Throughout the 1950s the average wage of all hired workers in agriculture, including braceros, dropped about fourteen dollars per year. Omitting braceros, it rose a few dollars a year—remaining well below the level of World War II's frozen wages. When the wage rose, it was by fits and starts, accompanying or following union organizing or labor protest activity of one kind or another.

The National Farm Labor Union (NFLU) sought to reverse the adverse effects of the bracero program. In California it called a strike against the Di Giorgio Fruit Corporation in October 1947. An overwhelming majority of Di Giorgio farmworkers (860) honored the strike, in spite of Red-baiting, police harassment, lack of funds, and the use of braceros as scabs. A March 9, 1949, report signed by three US congressmen, one of whom was Richard M. Nixon, condemned the NFLU and whitewashed Di Giorgio.[13] In 1950 the NFLU struck tomato growers in San Joaquin County, where it restored wage rates in spite of police protection for Mexican scabs.

Since the right of braceros to join US unions had been granted by the original wartime bracero agreement, the NFLU recruited Mexicans into its ranks. As a result, a watered-down provision for bracero self-organization was written into the 1951 bilateral agreement, limiting bracero rights to "maintaining the work contract." In the spring of 1951 NFLU members struck cantaloupe producers in the Imperial Valley. At the time, some 4,000 braceros were employed in the area; they continued to work under police guard. More braceros were brought in to break the prolonged strike. Union appeals to both governments were ignored.

The NFLU's courageous but unsuccessful efforts were demoralizing to farmworkers and union organizers alike. NFLU leader Ernesto Galarza later summed up the long-run effects as follows: "Domestic laborers were forced to yield on wages, compelled to abandon the fields as [Mexican immigrant] domination advanced and left to reckon alone with agricultural corporations on whose behalf their government negotiated agreements for terms and conditions that no employer ever tendered an American citizen."[14]

For their part, braceros knew that implementing their right to "self-organization" could lead to their being labeled "subversive" and to their instant deportation. Rather than unionize, militants instead engaged in periodic work stoppages or spontaneous protests. They had few supporters in the rest of society and no major defenders of the rights they were granted by international agreement. The US Labor Department was either too understaffed or too much in collusion with employers to lend a hand. As West Coast program director Glenn E. Brockway observed in 1955, "It is somewhat incompatible to be working with those who hire the workers and attempt to merchandise the available labor supply and have their co-operation and perhaps next week take an enforcement action against them."[15] The Labor Department cooperated fully in strangling the braceros' right to "self-organization." It went along with employers' disclaimers about abuses and approved of just about anything employers did to prevent braceros from organizing themselves. In 1957 it went a step further and agreed to an INS request to help finger labor agitators in the braceros' ranks.[16]

In the absence of serious Labor Department oversight of bracero contracts and rights, an ironic and unprecedented trend developed: some of the growers' associations began to assume responsibility for protecting the braceros. They did this for a number of reasons. First, they preferred self-policing to outside interference in their internal affairs. Second, there existed cases of blatantly bloodthirsty and cruel growers who needed a bit of wrist-slapping from their business peers. Third, the occasional defense of braceros gave the public a better image of the employers and the bracero program, as well as covering up a multitude of sins.

Routine violations of braceros' rights became legendary in the fifties, but they have been forgotten by today's legislators who vote for new "guest worker" programs. These violations guaranteed the intended impact of the bracero program on the American economy: lower overall wages, higher productivity, heightened antiforeign sentiment and anti-Latino racism, and strengthened labor discipline. Among the better-known employer violations were collecting passports or other documents as a means of discouraging labor resistance, firing braceros in order to avoid payment of the final weeks' wages and to discourage labor protest by others (a practice still common today), and falsifying payroll records (also a current practice).

Employers were expected to provide braceros with work for only three-fourths of the contracted time. Once contracted, a bracero found himself used for all kinds of additional work he had not bargained for. The minimum guarantee of four months' work was reduced, by 1960, to four weeks, with a maximum of six months. Employers preferred to use "wetbacks" for periods of work longer than the minimum.

Abuse of braceros, who at least had legal though unenforced rights, was made easier by widespread trampling on the human and labor rights of "illegal" Mexican immigrant workers (the so-called wetbacks). The entire system thrived and in fact depended upon graft. At every step of his journey, a Mexican worker, legal or "illegal," had to pay someone off: for selection in his municipality or village; for preference at a contract center or from labor smugglers and traffickers; for clearance from one or another authority; for recommendations; for employment itself, whether contracted or not. Even back home at the end of the round trip, the graft was not over. In the words of one Michoacán oldtimer,

> Here in Mexico they formed a bank that we had to deposit a
> certain percentage of our dollars in, and that bank grew rich
> off us braceros. In the end the bank disappeared and all the
> bracero savings were lost. That was from 1942 to somewhere
> around 1948.

Loansharks moved freely through ramshackle, unsanitary encamp-
ments of Mexican immigrant workers, profiting from their misery and,
not incidentally, making them more tractable as laborers. A worker's
willingness to do the bosses' bidding grew in rough proportion to his
accumulation of debts. For those who survived the difficulties of border
passage described by Isauro Reyes in Chapter 1, transportation accidents became common as legal standards went unsupervised and un-
met. On-the-job accidents further crippled Mexican immigrants
(although immigrants were not specifically identified in the statistics).
California agriculture's toll in 1957 reflected the pattern: 79 deaths and
16,595 lost-time injuries. Industrial poisons and insecticides led to
longer-term disabilities or deaths.

It is often alleged that Mexican immigrant workers were the real
beneficiaries of the bracero program, for otherwise why would they
have continued to come for so many years? It is true that immigrants
derived at least a few minor material benefits, but these were usually
outweighed by the abuses and risks. Those who died or were disabled
or humiliated obviously did not benefit. Hardly any learned English or
even a new trade, a trend that has continued to the present. Only 8
percent of the Michoacán migrants surveyed in 1980–81 said they had
learned any skill at all.

Although subjected to long workdays at miserable wages, frequent
racist and nativist harassment, and various other hardships, ex-braceros
and present-day migrants comment remarkably little on their personal
sufferings. Yet, as revealed in Chapter 1, there is an obvious concern
about death. One Michoacán woman commented that in 1979 four
cadavers were returned to her village from Texas—yet no one seems to
know how these men died.

The migrants direct most of their resentment at immediate superiors at the workplace, who are usually members of other minority
groups, such as Latinos, Filipinos, and blacks. They rarely speak out
against their employers. "Wherever I've worked, the employers have
been good. They took care of us. They provided us a radio during the
strawberry harvest and always warned us when the *migra* [INS agents]

were around." They attribute this attentiveness to the fact that they are such highly valued workers.

> They like the Mexican a lot because he's the hardest-working person the United States has. Mexicans work more than any other race. Just give him a little water, a hit of home brew, a few beers, and the Mexican will work. . . . No people work as hard as the Mexicans. You should see it. And the Mexican receives a lower wage, the blacks over there work less and earn more.

Even the *migra* is rarely badmouthed by the migrants—although a few told this writer of being beaten up and chained by Border Patrol agents. The first criminal indictment ever filed against INS agents was handed down by a federal grand jury on September 26, 1979, accusing four agents of thirty-eight overt acts of brutalization of Mexicans and a subsequent coverup. Six weeks earlier the Border Patrol announced a policy of diverting "illegal aliens" from Mexico into the deserts and mountains east of San Diego, even though, as one patrol agent told reporters, "we realize it could mean death for many from exposure or thirst." The general migrant attitude seems to be that the INS may be vicious and racist but it is filled with incompetents whom the migrants can "outwit." Former INS commissioner Leonel Castillo, who resigned in late 1979, spoke as harshly of the *migra* as any Mexican migrant interviewed by this author. Castillo told reporters in August 1979 that INS policy was a "disgraceful black mark" and compared the migrants to "indentured workers." Mexican migrant workers do, however, speak quite negatively about the Mexican authorities.

> At times, it's not so much the *migra* who bother us in getting over there as it is the Mexicans in the border areas who watch us, rob us, and so on. . . . The very Mexican police, the police agents, take our money, beat on us and all that.

Besides the Mexican police shakedowns, the migrants are also robbed by *baja pollos* (colloquially, "those who take money from chickens") when trying to cross the border.

To sustain the momentary and small-scale economic gain that comes from migration Mexican workers must make repeated trips to the United States. This cycle causes a serious erosion of family life, since wives and children are repeatedly left behind to fend for themselves. Some of the migrants become, as Isauro Reyes pointed out, "irresponsible" in family matters. Many wives and even children have to take over responsibility for planting, weeding, and harvesting the crops at home when their men are away. A migrant's dollar remittances normally go directly to the father-in-law, as patriarchal control of the Mexican family persists even during the husband's absence. As one Michoacán mother commented, "At times, the north is a curse for a woman."

Upon return, the migrant husband seems as determined as ever to keep "his woman" under his total control. In much of Mexico—especially rural areas, where 40 percent of the population still resides—wife-beating is an accepted practice. Most Mexican migrants have not been favorably impressed by how Americans conduct their family affairs. Male Michoacán peasant migrants commented almost in unison to this writer,

> Over there a woman can leave her husband because she can get welfare. Here a woman alone is in a most difficult situation. . . . There the family is topsy-turvy, libertine. Here sons twenty-five and thirty years old have a right to order their mothers about, but there, there's no respect. Anyone from the family can go to the bars, the dancehalls, with a divorced man. . . . Here one's family obeys, but there one must obey the woman; she writes the check, she gives the little bit for soda, cigarettes. She manages what you earn. Whereas in Mexico, no, in Mexico one makes his money and doles it out to his woman for household expenses. . . . But over there the woman is law, she orders the man about.

When there is no other recourse, a woman emigrates. Interviews with Michoacán women, however, revealed that for those who stay in the United States any length of time the material gains are offset by personal hardships. One mother, for example, age thirty-five and still living in Denver, works ten-hour days at a factory as a seamstress and is going blind. She has raised many children, one of whom is an INS agent.

A bracero's dollar remittance to his family reportedly averaged about $500 a year, or about a third of his total earnings. In actuality, for a few the remittances were this much or more, while for most they were far lower. The braceros' average weekly wages ranged from $9.43

to \$51.55. Since most stayed only forty-five days per visit, it was almost impossible to save money. As one Michoacán peasant put it, "In forty-five days you couldn't do anything. With very good luck you might bring out a hundred dollars, but if your luck was bad you didn't make enough even to cover your expenses—it was too little time." Nowadays migrants earn more, of course, but since most stay only a short time—between two and six months—their dollar remittances do not add up to much until they have made many trips. Of those Michoacán villagers surveyed by this writer and others in 1980–81, only a fifth sent more than a hundred dollars a month home, while almost half sent nothing at all or simply could not remember sending any. Yet many worked up to sixteen hours a day, and few had not suffered either a physical injury or physical exhaustion from the amount and intensity of work they performed.

The actual impact of migration to the United States varies greatly according to whether the sending community lands "good" jobs or not. That is why in Michoacán and other parts of Mexico today one can see two neighboring villages whose living standards are as different as those of Harlem and Westchester. The village whose emigrants earned more and remitted higher amounts may have new stone or brick houses, paved streets, and even a new church constructed in an American-style modern design modeled after what the emigrants saw in the United States. The neighboring town whose emigrants earned little and remitted less may remain unchanged, its roads unpaved, its homes made of adobe or thatch, unimproved except for—in the rare case—a new gas stove or electrical appliance purchased with US-earned dollars.

The workers' dollar remittances, though paltry by US standards, favorably affect Mexico's balance of payments. Estimates of the money sent or brought back range as high as a billion dollars a year, making migrants' remittances third after oil and tourism as a source of Mexico's foreign exchange. At the same time, these remittances are made possible only by depriving Mexico of quantities of hardworking laborers needed for sustained economic growth. In addition, the "revolving door" deportations create unemployment problems for the Mexican government, especially in the congested northern border states. Since the migrants never obtain permanent jobs, Mexico's unemployment problem is not alleviated in the least; only its short-run impact is. Meanwhile, the likelihood of Mexico's workers organizing in Mexico or rebelling against the "revolutionary" government that has ruled them since 1917 is reduced to the degree that workers feel they might improve their lot by migrating to the United States.

To this day the migrants are open to the idea of another bracero or guest worker program. Their need for wages better than those available in Mexico has not diminished. But interviews suggest that the migrants do not wish a repeat of the 1942–64 experience; they want the guarantees of such a program, without the abuses. They don't mind accepting a lower wage than American workers, but they want it to be a decent one by their standards. "Of course," one Michoacán villager told me, "they have to give preference to the Americans—it's their country after all. I would say they could give, for example, if three dollars for the American then two-fifty for the Mexican." More ideal from the migrants' point of view would be the introduction of factories and good-paying jobs in the Mexican villages and small cities where so many of them live. "I imagine," said one, "that Mexico's problems come from people with money stashing it in foreign banks and that is why we are so poor here in Mexico. That money could be setting up factories and industries here."

By attracting Mexican peasants, the bracero program assured a deepening of Mexico's bifurcated agriculture: rich landholders and foreign agribusinesses on the one hand, impoverished *ejidatarios* and smallholders on the other, their emigration often resulting in the need to rent or even in the loss of the little land they possessed. Proletarianization of Mexico's peasantry sped up during the bracero period and its immediate aftermath, accelerated by mechanization of agricultural production inside Mexico. The 1970 census showed that 51 percent of all *predios* (farms) were under 5 hectares (half of these less than 1 hectare) and occupied, all told, 0.6 percent of the land (1 hectare is approximately 2.2 acres). In other words, about half of Mexico's "farmers" clung to subsistence parcels while gaining their income by hiring themselves out to others, usually through internal and external migration.

In addition, deteriorating work conditions for rural laborers inside Mexico added to the internal and external migratory flow. The average number of workdays for rural wage earners fell from 190 a year in 1950 to 90 in 1970 and 65 in 1980. By the mid-1960s the average annual wage of day laborers in Mexico was in decline, yet it was still more than a small farmer could make from his meager crop production. Out of economic desperation, some 3 million rural inhabitants started migrating to the cities or to the north. By the early 1970s Mexico's farming population had decreased in absolute numbers. Those who found steady, even if seasonal, jobs by migrating often abandoned their small rural parcels. Those who were less successful returned to the countryside to engage in subsistence farming in little-noticed spurts of "reverse migration."[17]

Thus, more and more of Mexico's rural population were driven into the lowest ranks of the wage labor force, vulnerable to exploitation on either side of the border, in town or city, in agriculture, services, or industry. The result of enforcing the "legality" of the US-Mexico border by means of the bracero program was not merely an increase in the number of Mexican immigrant workers legally and illegally crossing into the United States each year—it was, in effect, the creation of an internationally mobile pool of inexpensive surplus Mexican labor power sufficient not only for US agribusiness's survival and expansion but also for a sudden increase in the tempo of Mexico's industrialization, unprecedented since the turn of the century. This in turn made possible what has become known as the "silent integration" of the Mexican and US economies, examined in the next chapter. The porous common border became a convenient "legal fiction."

But this fiction has real consequences. The border today, as during the bracero program and earlier, is a boundary often used to harass Mexican immigrants, to discipline American labor, to permit a free flow of capital and commerce, and to deceive the people of both nations. As the next chapter explains, both governments, their rhetoric to the contrary, make use of the border for the mutual advantage of a wealthy minority of Americans and Mexicans who dominate the two increasingly integrated economies.

The End of the Bracero Program and the Changing Character of the Migratory Flow

Sufficiently frightened by the labor union organizing activities and bracero work protests of the early 1950s, employers had by the 1960s set in motion a series of steps that reduced their dependence on large numbers of Mexican immigrant workers, at least in agriculture. These steps included the consolidation of an atmosphere of fear and terror as represented by "Operation Wetback" and the "revolving door," increased mechanization of agricultural production, and creation of subpools of other foreign workers. As a result, the number of braceros contracted each year peaked at about 440,000 in 1959 and had sunk to 177,000 by 1964.

The use of subpools of workers of different nationalities to help America grow has a long history. In 1950 growers in Salinas, California, recruited some 300 unemployed Filipino workers from Honolulu. They proved, however, too familiar with modern industrial relations, declaring a militant work stoppage shortly after their arrival. They were sent packing. In 1956 California farmers reached an agreement with the Japanese government to import more than 1,000 Japanese contract workers. The INS and Department of Labor approved, finding legal authority in Public Law 414 regulating immigration. The same law was used in August 1956 to establish a quota of 1,000 farm laborers from the Philippines.

Thus, in an ironic twist of history, employers turned to Asians to reduce their dependence upon increasingly demanding Mexican laborers, just as they had turned to Mexicans to replace Asians at the turn of the century and during World War II. The entry of Asians into the United States was now considered easier to regulate and control. By the mid-1970s the recruitment of Asians was in full swing and opened doors to Filipinos, Koreans, Vietnamese, Cambodians, and others, paralleling immigration trends of a century ago. This increased recourse to inexpensive Asian labor came at the very moment Mexican immigrant workers were achieving new forms and new heights of organizational coordination and protest activity. Many of the Asians, especially the Vietnamese, Cambodians, Laotians, and Koreans, were viewed not only as another subpool of cheap labor but also as ideologically supportive of the American system.

In addition, in the 1950s, as today, employers made effective use of another subpool of laborers known as "green-carders." These were Mexican immigrants admitted under the regular visa program for "resident aliens." Between 1956 and 1960 nearly 200,000 Mexican citizens were granted US visas in this way, most of them to work in agriculture. Day permits for crossing the border were also issued in large numbers to residents of northern Mexico. These Mexicans were frequently used by agribusinesses located within about 25 miles of the border, such as those in California's Imperial or San Diego counties or Texas's Lower Rio Grande Valley. Both the green-carders and the holders of day permits were routinely rushed into strike situations in the 1960s and afterwards to serve as scabs.

East Coast growers, of course, drew Mexicans into their subpools of labor to supplement or replace Puerto Ricans, Jamaicans, and other Caribbean peoples. In the veritable mosaic of pools and subpools of foreign immigrant labor in the nation, Mexicans composed, as they do today, the largest and most productive number.

Eventually, however, the AFL-CIO could no longer turn a blind eye to the consequences of this form of economic management. As NFLU organizer Ernesto Galarza pointed out, "Commercial agriculture, bidding in a world stirred by agrarian revolt, invited inspection. What it had to show, behind its dazzling efficiency, was the managed, not the autonomous, man . . . the man of the barracks, the man in a camp who spent all of his time under supervision. . . . Some of these total communities were surrounded by barbed wire."[18] From 1959 to 1963 growing numbers of AFL-CIO leaders and members protested the negative impact of the bracero program on American labor. They lobbied for its termination.

In addition, Cesar Chavez and other US citizens of Mexican descent began a militant union organizing campaign among Mexican and Filipino farmworkers in California. Eventually this activity spread to other states and commanded AFL-CIO support and consumer backing through nationwide lettuce, melon, and grape boycotts (see Chapter 7). Together with employers' reduced needs for Mexicans, signs of this new labor activism led to the termination of the bracero program in 1964. On May 29, 1963, the House of Representatives voted to terminate PL 78.

The end of this kind of contract labor coincided with a new trend toward exporting factories, agroindustries, and jobs to cheap labor areas in Latin America and Asia. As part of American capital's continued expansion on a global scale, US-based "transnational corporations" (TNCs),[19] including a number of agribusiness firms, began to operate overseas. Mexico's low wage structure, a factor behind Mexican emigration northward, was also a factor attracting US-based TNCs to that country in quest of higher profit rates. Wage differentials between California and Mexican farmworkers, for example, were at least eight to one. Agronomist Ernest Feder calculated a $95 million annual difference in strawberry agribusiness profits based only on these wage differentials.[20] It is not surprising that United Brands (formerly United Fruit Company, well known for its interventionist role in Central American countries in prior decades) dominates much of Mexico's strawberry industry today.

Similar calculations could be made for other cash crops. From the end of the bracero program to 1975, about 10 percent of US manufacturing investment in Mexico went into the food industry, doubling its profits in a decade. US-based TNCs appropriated between 25 and 35 percent of the Mexican food industry's total gross product and profits. By 1975 US agribusinesses were employing almost three-fourths of Mexican agrarian labor, even though they absorbed less labor per unit of production every year because of mechanization. By the late 1970s fruits and vegetables accounted for half of Mexico's agricultural exports (for the US winter and spring markets). To escape California's militant unionizing labor force, Del Monte moved its entire white asparagus production to Mexico and in 1975 made over $8 million through worldwide exports. During this period Ralston Purina and International Multifoods joined Mexican investors to control the poultry industry; Coca-Cola accounted for nearly half of Mexican soft drink sales; and Anderson-Clayton ran the Mexican cotton industry, once the pride of private Mexican capital, like a fiefdom—before the Mexican government took over cotton financing.

Like Heinz, John Deere, Ralston Purina, and other US giants investing in Mexico, Anderson-Clayton diversified its investments into additional areas—cattle feed, chocolate, planting seeds, edible oils, chickens, and insecticides. TNCs also moved heavily into the livestock raising and animal feed industries, Mexico's most profitable rural enterprises during the late 1960s and early 1970s. From the production and sale of machinery and fertilizers to the processing and merchandising of agricultural goods, most of Mexican agriculture came to be dominated by US agribusiness.

However, these shifting investment patterns did not end Mexican emigration to the United States. Nor did they reduce Mexican unemployment. On the contrary, the migratory flow increased, now under radically altered circumstances. This happened in part *because* of the rapid increase in US corporate investment in Mexico. American agribusiness was interested in profiting from Mexico's trade at both ends, by dominating Mexico's agricultural exports and imports alike. While the average Mexican's caloric intake declined 10 percent from 1967 to 1976, Mexico was forced to import more and more of its food from the United States—25 percent by 1980. Animals and foreign consumers were eating more basic foodstuffs produced in Mexico than the Mexicans themselves. In 1981 Mexico's agricultural imports—$3 billion worth of corn, grains, *frijoles* (beans), sugar, and edible fats and oils—were greater than its agricultural exports.[21]

US-based TNCs concentrated themselves in the fastest-growing and most dynamic sectors of Mexican industrial and agricultural production. Their capital resources gave them an initial strong advantage over Mexican investors. The sheer size and scale of the TNCs' Mexican investment, plant, and technology increased the corresponding amount of capital required for any future creation of jobs inside Mexico, further favoring the TNCs over their less wealthy competitors. New US direct investments quadrupled during the 1970s, while Mexico's outflow of dividends, interest, and other payments to foreign investors doubled the sum of new foreign investments. This "suction-pump" effect of foreign investors receiving more from Mexico than they put into its economy—together with Mexico's increased borrowing from foreign lenders, declining terms of trade, and periodic flights of domestic capital—generated a process of relative decapitalization, rapidly growing indebtedness, and inadequate opportunities for employment expansion. By 1982 Mexico had amassed the largest debt to US banks of any country in the world.

Since 1978 US business investments have been doubling almost every year in Mexico. These mostly capital-intensive investments have aggravated Mexico's unemployment problem by reducing the number of labor hours required for maintaining production and by further elevating the amount of capital needed for the creation of new jobs. It is no coincidence that in every Mexican state visited by this author during the 1980s, the communities sending the most migrants to the United States were not those with the most impoverished agrarian base. On the contrary, they were those that had experienced at least middle levels of agricultural technification—hybrid seeds, fertilizers, tractors, etc. Moreover, there were indications that as the costs of "modern" agriculture increased a struggling farm family's needs, family members resorted more to emigration than ever before.

Thus, US private interests in Mexico helped create a situation conducive to the further temporary emigration of workers to the United States. US government promotion of TNC activities in Mexico—which contribute to Mexico's unemployment and underemployment problems in ways already suggested here and further elaborated in the next chapter—is ignored when the US blames Mexico for exporting large numbers of migrant workers.

Meanwhile, US capital's needs for low-wage immigrant labor rose sharply after the 1973–75 recession as US corporations struggled to remain competitive on a world scale. When American workers protested against "runaway shops," they were told by some employers that more Mexican immigrant workers were required to allow profit margins sufficient to keep their firms operative in the United States. Agribusinesses and ever more varied sectors of American industrial and services production sought to combat recessions and "stagflation" (stagnation with inflation), including in many instances falling rates of profit, by saving even more on wages. This entailed unionized workers' "givebacks," governmental bailouts of failing firms, and, of course, bringing in more Mexican workers. The demand for more Mexicans was accompanied by the usual scapegoating of Mexican "illegals" and cries for regaining control of American borders, a blending of contradictions long since institutionalized in the practice of the "revolving door" so profitable for employers.

US labor unions and jobless Americans complain about "millions" of Mexicans crossing into their territory. Yet, the American government and US employers allow the "illegals" to go on cleaning toilets in Houston, packing meat in Chicago, picking crops in the Imperial Valley, and assembling parts in Los Angeles. These migrants, whose numbers are actually lower than the press makes out, find temporary work and carry home to Mexico what is left of their wages after they pay their living expenses and pay off the traffickers and loansharks who "help" in their migration. The Mexican migratory flow provides cheap nonunion labor to American agribusinesses, hotels, restaurants, automotive plants, electronics factories, and garment producers who depend on such labor at set periods of time. The flow also helps the government and businesses in Mexico to raise generations of workers at minimal cost.

Contrary to most news reports surrounding new immigration legislation, the migration of Mexican workers represents an unequal exchange in which Mexico—through the export of human capital—subsidizes the US economy. Data obtained from interviews by Mexican researchers on hundreds of thousands of migrants in the late 1970s show that they are not the poorest, the most likely to be unemployed, or the least educated workers in Mexico. In other words, however miserable their condition, they are not at the bottom of the social pyramid. [22]From this it may be inferred that the migration out of Mexico represents the transfer to the United States of a significant investment by Mexico (mainly by Mexican workers in feeding and reproducing themselves) in the form of human capital.

The same studies by Mexican researchers permit us to provide a fairly accurate social profile of the "illegal" Mexican labor force working in the United States today. Nine out of 10 of these estimated 2.9 million workers[23] are male, although in recent years more women and children are migrating than ever before. Most of the migrants are between 18 and 25 years of age. More than 50 percent are bachelors, of whom over 80 percent come from 10 states in central and southern Mexico: Chiapas, Chihuahua, Guanajuato, Hidalgo, Jalisco, México, Michoacán, Oaxaca, Sinaloa, and Tlaxcala. Most of the other migrants come from Durango, Veracruz, and Zacatecas in central Mexico. The migrants usually go to California or Texas, most for only a few months; 85 percent of all "illegal" Mexican entrants to the United States depart within one year. They are temporary immigrants; their permanent homes are in Mexico. More and more migrants arrive from Mexico's cities, fewer and fewer from the countryside.

The demand for their labor has grown in different areas, with an accelerated expansion in services and industry more than compensating for a tapering off in agriculture. Even migrants from rural areas who traditionally harvested US crops are turning up increasingly in low-wage sectors of American industry. For example, of more than 200 migrants surveyed in Isauro Reyes's village, 25 percent said their last job in the United States was in industry, 5 percent said they last worked there in construction, and 5 percent said they worked in services.

This growing, ever more diversified demand for a steady, predictable flow of Mexican labor is the main factor to be considered in the present situation of renewed talk about a "guest worker" or bracero program (whose roots and character are discussed in Chapter 5). That the demand is real was illustrated throughout the 1970s and early 1980s by a number of attempts to enact legislation on Mexican immigration (see Chapter 8).

Not even the "revolving door" can be kept swinging fast enough to accommodate the present needs of US business. Moreover, as more and more of the migrants hear about union efforts to combat their exploitation, the necessity for new legislation to control the migratory flow grows acute from the point of view of employers (these organizational developments—10 percent of the migrants are now unionized—are examined in Chapter 7). But to understand all this, we must first turn to the interrelationships of the two nations' economies and to the character of the post–1973 economic crisis.

4

Silent Integration, or, The Border as Legal Fiction

"If they throw one out through Laredo,
ten will come in through Mexicali.
If another is kicked out through Tijuana,
six will come in through Nogales."
—"El Corrido de los Mojados," migrant
workers' folksong

"Closing the crossing [to all traffic, legal
or otherwise] is a bit like raising the
Berlin Wall."
—*New York Times*, March 9, 1985

The previous chapters examined the history of Mexican immigration into the United States and its impact on US economic growth. One of history's largest movements of a people to a new land, Mexican migration in the period 1890 to 1930, greatly affected Mexicans' lives in both countries. The 1942–64 bracero program further linked Mexicans across the border. The border's "revolving doors" served then, as now, not only to keep employers satisfied but also to create a continuous linkage between permanent and temporary Mexican communities in the United States.

The out- and influx of Mexico's growing labor pool benefits employers *inside* Mexico, domestic and foreign. Since the 1940s, when the "Green Revolution" technified agriculture and Mexico's so-called "economic miracle" industrialized the country, Mexico has generated an increasing pool of surplus labor. This modern epoch of industrialization, guided by a strong authoritarian-technocratic state, has been accompanied by the "silent integration" of Mexico's economy with that of the United States. A key element in this integration, the border, guaranteed the two-way flow of capital and goods, helping to "modernize" and consolidate the Mexican surplus labor pool and to internationalize the industrial "reserve army" of labor. The recent penetration of capital-intensive transnational corporations (TNCs) into the commanding heights of Mexican industry and agriculture has only intensified this process.

This chapter examines the "silent integration," concluding with a look at its impact in the border areas. It is precisely there, where the official border line runs and the fences are built, that the border's fictitious quality and use by international capital becomes most evident—and most directly and dramatically affects the future of millions of Americans and Mexicans.

Integration of the Mexican and US Economies

The integration of the Mexican and US economies observed today is not a new phenomenon, but its form is. Prior to Mexico's 1938 oil nationalization and post–World War II industrial transformation, the integration was characterized by Mexico's producing and exporting mineral and agricultural goods and importing manufactured products and raw materials for production, which often occurred in foreign-controlled "enclaves" (mines, oilfields, sugar refineries, etc.).

Today, the Mexican state owns or controls the oilfields and most of the mines and refineries. US investors, instead of exporting manufactured goods to Mexico, save on taxes, tariffs, wages, and transportation and marketing costs by producing manufactured goods directly inside Mexico itself. Their major exports to Mexico are capital goods and new technologies, including "know-how agreements" that facilitate their profit-making inside Mexico and their influence over the Mexican state.[1]

The 1890–1930 period of large-scale Mexican migration to the United States coincided with the clearest expression of the earlier "enclave" form of economic integration. Then, as today, the border was a porous imaginary line across which capital and labor flowed with remarkable proportional correspondence. In years when US capital flooded Mexico, Mexican migrant workers flooded the new job sites in Mexico and the areas of economic boom north of the border. When US capital slowed its movement into Mexico, as during the 1907 economic recession, Mexican workers slowed their movement into the United States and Mexico's new job sites.

The reasons underlying this synchronized movement of capital and labor across the border were identical: capital's expansion, successes, and failures, or, in a word, the business cycle. When economies grew, so did the labor force needed to make them grow. In other words, when both countries' economies boomed, Mexican labor mobility was heightened. Roads and railroads linked points of production and trade from the canefields of Morelos or the oilfields of Veracruz to the clothing factories of Los Angeles or the stockyards of Chicago, and many Mexican workers rode the rails to *el norte* in quest of higher wages. But when hard times set in, Mexicans retreated to their villages and small plots of land to survive as best they could.

By 1897 US investors had more money in Mexico than in any other part of the world, including Canada, Europe, Asia, or the rest of Latin America. Their investments in Mexico had increased fivefold by 1911, exceeding those of the Mexican bourgeoisie and about double those of all other foreign investors. On the eve of the Mexican Revolution of 1910–20, foreigners owned nearly 20 percent of Mexico's land surface, most of the 80 largest commercial and industrial establishments, and 90 percent of all investments in mining (of which 80 percent were American). The United States was receiving 74 percent of Mexico's exports. Many Mexican mines, factories, and landed estates were policed by what were known as "white guards," or private armies in the pay of American millionaires and other foreign investors.

Corresponding with this impressive, if colonized, economic growth, Mexico's population expanded to 15 million by 1911, nearly double what it had been in 1875. Millions of low-paid new workhands, whose real wages were equivalent to those of their fathers and grandfathers, contributed mightily to the riches extracted from Mexico by foreign investors. By some estimates, Mexico's industrial proletariat by 1911 constituted as much as 15 percent of the adult labor force—or about 110,000 mine and 625,000 manufacturing workers.[2]

Today's double use of cheap Mexican labor—for the benefit of employers on *both* sides of the border—dates from this earlier period of integration of the two nations' economies. A similar expansion of Mexico's population and of the industrial proletariat accompanied the next period of sustained Mexican economic growth, 1940–65, the "economic miracle" years of Mexico's industrial transformation. These were also the economically expansive years of the United States' misnamed and historically short-lived "affluent society." In both countries, expanding economies meant more jobs, and because of the far greater scale of US production and growth, the demand for abundant cheap immigrant labor became particularly intense there, even as it had done at the turn of the century.

From 1940 to 1965, Mexico's population grew from 19.6 million to 42 million, and its industrial proletariat expanded to nearly 25 percent of the economically active population. Industrial production jumped 120 percent, agricultural output 100 percent. Modern, usually imported technologies were introduced—tractors, reapers, fertilizers, hybrid seeds, and a myriad of industrial techniques and parts necessary for the assembly-line production of automobiles and other consumer goods.

Once again, rapid economic transformation of Mexico was accompanied by a radical increase in the flow of US investments into Mexico and of migrant workers into Mexican job sites and into the United States. But now the form of integration of the two economies altered, even as did the form of Mexican migration (from "illegal" to "legal"— the 1942–64 bracero program). US investments centered more on heavy industry and modern agriculture and less on mining and rails. They were more capital-intensive and less labor-intensive, although they continued to depend on inexpensive Mexican labor. "Joint ventures" of American investors with the Mexican "revolutionary" state and private Mexican investors became commonplace.

Now Mexico's production and trade, though as dependent on the United States as before, were no longer "enclaves." The state owned the oil and minerals and helped oversee the economic transformation of Mexico into a semi-industrialized "giant" by Latin American standards. The strong Mexican state, which dated from the days of Porfirio Díaz, now altered its official rhetoric from "Order and Progress" to "Revolution and Progress"—with the understanding that order would be maintained since "we've already had a revolution here." The Mexican state did not take the place of private capital but rather assisted it, stimulated it, and complemented it. As economist Alonso Aguilar felicitously described it, paraphrasing a Mexican banker, "It is the duty of the state humbly to set the table, and the job of private enterprise to eat what it finds there." Agustín F. Legoretta, director of the private Banco Nacional de México, was more blunt: "The state and private enterprise are, at bottom, the same thing."[3]

Expenditures by Mexico's capitalist state soared from only 8 percent of the gross domestic product (GDP) in the 1930s to 25 percent in the 1960s, 45 percent in the 1970s, and, with the expansion in oil production, over 50 percent today. The state contributed 40 percent or more of total investment in every decade since the 1930s (except the 1950s, peak years of post–World War II and pre–Vietnam War foreign investment). Most state investment went into economic infrastructure: electrification, highway and airport construction, irrigation, public education, and so on. From 1953 to 1972 the state subsidized private industry to the tune of $3 billion by selling energy and fuel at a discount from the Federal Electricity Commission (CFE) and Petróleos Mexicanos (PEMEX). It also assisted private capital by exercising control over worker and peasant organizations.[4]

Each successive Mexican government sought to aid private capital in reducing operating costs and increasing sales. Each held real wages constant (as during the Porfiriato) and maintained "labor peace" by military force—most notably during the 1959 railroad, telephone, and industrial strikes. Moreover, Mexico has maintained one of the lowest corporate tax rates in Latin America: of all the region's countries with a population above 7 million, Mexico still has the lowest tax revenue as a percentage of GDP. Mexico also actively procured international loans, which further tied the nation's solvency to foreign, primarily American capital. It offered credits and tax incentives to private industry while allowing foreign investors like General Motors, Anderson-Clayton, General Foods, and Coca-Cola relatively free remittance of profits abroad. These policies, amounting to state giveaways to private interests, helped convert Mexico into the world's largest debtor to US banks.

Thus, Mexico's supposedly "mixed" economy, far from pitting public against private capital, in fact allied the two in a process of capitalist monopolization fully supported and guided by an authoritarian-technocratic state. The state, claiming to act on behalf of "national" capital, subsidized private monopoly capital, both domestic and foreign. Leading Mexican businessmen moved in and out of government ministries with ease while hobnobbing with top Mexican politicians and prominent American investors at exclusive country clubs and resorts in both countries. One American academician approvingly described the silent integration of the two nations' economies as an "alliance for profits."[5]

The billions of dollars' worth of foreign investments that poured into Mexico after World War II, including joint ventures with Mexican private and state enterprises, forged structural connections that allied foreign capital with Mexican monopoly capital and the state bureaucracy. Corrupt trade union leaders eagerly joined the consequent dance of dollars. Typically, in exchange for a TNC's hiring union labor, Mexican union leaders guaranteed protection for the employer's interests in case of labor conflict outside the factory gates or on the shop floor.[6]

The state encouraged Mexico's initial steps toward modern industrialization through its policy of protective tariffs and "import substitution," introduced during World War II when the United States was unable to export its usual quantity of manufactured goods. Mexican industrial production increased 35 percent during the war years, and Mexico's exports doubled. The United States purchased from Mexico minerals and varied foodstuffs, as well as silver to help finance its war production, and advanced large credits for Mexico's industrialization program. A number of private investors, fleeing US wartime price regulations and high taxes, also invested in Mexico. Immediately after the war, US corporations increased their investments and began purchasing many of Mexico's new industries, a trend that has deepened to the present day.

By the early 1970s three-fourths of all new foreign investments in Mexico were acquisitions of existing companies. US-based TNCs had penetrated the commanding heights of Mexico's economy, achieving the following percentages of control: automotive, 57 percent; rubber, 76 percent; mining, 54 percent; tobacco, 100 percent; industrial chemicals, 50 percent; food and beverages, 47 percent; chemicals and pharmaceuticals, 86.4 percent; machinery, 51 percent; computers and office equipment, 88 percent; commerce, 53 percent; and so on. As if to symbolize the silent integration of the two economies, 71 of the top 100 US manufacturing concerns (ranked by sales) had investments in Mexico by 1977. From American capital's point of view, to paraphrase a famous saying, "What's good for General Motors is good for both countries."[7]

Moreover, as Table 2 reveals, foreign investors earned up to double and sometimes triple their total investment, sending most of their profits back home. So-called technology transfers, by which foreign investors bring into Mexico machines and parts at inflated prices and send money home supposedly to buy more technology, served to hide additional profits not reported in statistics like those in Table 2. As the manager of one US affiliate in Mexico said in 1975, "The use of payments for technology is the easiest legal way to transfer profits out of the country."[8] Foreign pharmaceutical firms, for instance, were report-

TABLE 2
Foreign Investment and Income in Mexico, 1960–1980
(million US dollars)

Year	New direct foreign investments	Total net foreign income on investments*	Reinvested profits
1960	62.5	141.5	10.5
1961	81.8	148.1	25.2
1962	74.9	159.3	36.2
1963	76.1	182.9	34.4
1964	83.1	242.2	56.3
1965	110.1	234.9	73.5
1966	111.1	277.4	73.7
1967	105.4	321.4	105.3
1968	111.1	367.7	112.2
1969	166.3	435.5	139.6
1970	183.9	473.6	154.2
1971	168.0	339.6*	nd†
1972	189.8	403.8	nd
1973	287.3	485.6	nd
1974	362.2	556.9	nd
1975	295.0	686.0	nd
1976	299.1	816.9	nd
1977	327.1	633.2	nd
1978	383.3	707.4	nd
1979	810.0	1,073.4	nd
1980	1,622.6	1,580.3	nd

*For 1960–1970, profits remitted abroad and profits reinvested, interest royalties, and other payments; for 1971–1980, same *minus* profits reinvested (for which there are no data).
†nd = no data.

Source: Nacional Financiera, *La economía mexicana en cifras* (1970); Banco de México, *Estadísticas básicas de la inversión extranjera en México* (nd), Cuadro 5; and Sepafin (1981).

edly making up to $400 million a year on "transfer pricing"—the over-pricing of technology imports and underpricing of exports.

By transfer pricing, disguising profits as costs for technology imports, and underpricing exports, TNCs are able to increase their capital accumulation manyfold. These practices reduce the profits they declare and have to pay taxes on. Transfer pricing thus has the effect of partially decapitalizing Mexico in the name of capitalizing it. By 1970 so-called technology transfers were remitting to the United States from Mexico almost twice as much money as officially declared profits.[9]

Integration's Costs: Dependence, Monopoly, and Unemployment

The major consequences of Mexico's industrialization and economic integration with the United States have been deepening dependence, concentration of wealth, and unemployment. These trends can be observed in both countries, but clearly Mexicans have suffered them to a much greater degree than have Americans. In Mexico the triple alliance forged by the state with the Mexican bourgeoisie, TNCs, and global lending agencies generated three problems that stood out in bold relief by the early 1980s: a $96 billion foreign debt (1984), the annual interest payments on which could not be met; insufficient employment for at least 52.5 percent of the work force, by official figures; and inadequate food production to meet the minimal nutritional needs of the populace.

Much talk is heard of the two nations' "mutual dependence," but Mexico's dependence has far more devastating consequences than does that of the United States. In spite of its growing dependence on foreign oil and laborers, particularly those of Mexico, the United States has a much more productive economy. Mexico's far less productive system has, through the process of silent integration, dug itself deeper into debt and dependence upon foreign loans, capital, and technology.

Mexico is the United States' third-largest trading partner, after Canada and Japan. It imports, mainly from the United States, 82 percent of the machines, tools, materials, and parts needed by industry. Much of its heavy industry is located in the north, from the "Pittsburgh" of Monterrey to the "Detroit" of Saltillo. Expensive imports for industry underlie Mexico's perennial trade deficit, which by 1980 was four times what it had been a decade earlier. Tourism receipts cover less than a third of the deficit; moreover, oil revenues cannot match the more than $10 billion nonoil deficit in trade. At least a third of the negative trade balance derives from TNCs' purchases of materials needed by their Mexican affiliates (for every product a TNC exports from Mexico, it imports eight for its installations).

And the more the TNCs invest in Mexico, the more the country is sacked. In 1980 new direct US investments surpassed the $1 billion mark; in the first three months of 1982 alone, some $1.5 billion in foreign profits were remitted abroad. Declared foreign profits and interest receipts for a single year, 1977, exceeded those for the entire decade of the 1960s. Seventy percent of foreign investment is American; 78 percent of foreign investment is in manufacturing industry.

Increased foreign investments and profit remittances, technology purchases, foreign debts, and trade imbalances have created a "suction-pump" effect that drains Mexico of much of its wealth and greatly benefits US industrialists, trading firms, and bankers. Although heavily weighted to the advantage of US corporate interests, the flow of capital is not just one-way. By 1980 Mexican companies had established affiliated enterprises in Europe, Japan, Latin America—and the United States. The state's central bank, Banco de México, reported $6.45 billion leaving Mexico between 1976 and 1979 in such private ventures, an amount equivalent to new loans taken out by the public sector in 1978–79. And although it periodically gripes about "capital flight," the Mexican government encourages silent integration by selling "petro-bonds" and stock shares in Mexican industry in US money markets, by selling most of its petroleum to the United States at prices well below those of OPEC, by opening up state bank branches in New York (e.g., Somex, a bank with majority state shares), and by tolerating the emigration of workers and peasants to the United States.

From such economic integration comes the common saying "When the United States sneezes, Mexico catches cold." This was illustrated when the effects of the US recession hit Mexico in the mid-1970s. By late 1975 more than 32,000 workers had been laid off in border assembly plants, crippling many local economies. The impact in central Mexico was similar. For example, in the Federal District (Greater Mexico City) half a million workers were dismissed and 3,000 small companies went bankrupt in just one year, 1976. Capital flight, dollarization of the economy, and pressures imposed by the International Monetary Fund (IMF) forced a nearly 100 percent devaluation of the peso in late 1976, almost doubling Mexico's real foreign debt (to almost $50 billion), as well as the real costs of imported capital goods.

These developments worked to the further advantage of the TNCs while hurting Mexico's nonmonopoly firms, which were unable to compete. In fact, the 1970s set the stage for the far larger economic crisis Mexico would suffer with the next downturn in the American economy—the debt and bank crisis of 1982 (examined in the next chapter).

As already observed, Mexican governments have guided this process with a certain amount of foreknowledge in order to industrialize the country. However, Mexico's industrial transformation has always been partial and lopsided because it relied too heavily on the traditional superexploitation of cheap labor, failed to adequately develop the capital goods sector (the machines that make the machines), and delivered control over most of the economy to foreign investors or lending agencies and their allies among Mexican businessmen.

Mexico's industrial output increased fivefold between 1940 and 1965, but imports of foreign (mainly US) industrial or capital goods and replacement parts increased 12.5 times. After 1965 industrial growth slowed and technology imports skyrocketed. As during the 1940–65 period, US corporations tied their sales of technology to further sales and investment possibilities, using a panoply of means, including patents, licenses, and know-how agreements. In analyzing Mexico's dependence on this technology, economists Fernando Fajnzylber and Trinidad Martínez Tarrago have pointed out its inappropriateness both in terms of cost and labor utilization. They conclude that "fewer and fewer productive jobs have been created per unit of capital invested. . . . Capital has been increasingly remunerated at the expense of workers' incomes."[10]

The same results have been observed in the much-heralded "Green Revolution" in world agriculture. Introduced in Mexico in 1943 by the Rockefeller Foundation and Mexico's Ministry of Agriculture, the Green Revolution was intended to foster use of pesticides, fertilizers, and modern equipment and methods in order to increase yields per acre and replace many acres of traditional foodstuffs with specialized crops for export, animal feed, and food processing. UN researcher Cynthia Hewitt de Alcántara concludes her widely acclaimed study of Mexican agriculture by calling the Green Revolution

> waste: waste of natural resources; . . . of manufactured agricultural inputs (and the foreign exchange needed to acquire many of them); . . . waste of profits generated by rapid tech

nological change, that went into conspicuous consumption or speculative investment; . . . above all, waste of human skills possessed by the landless workers, *ejidatarios*, and *colonos* [private possessors of state lands in agrarian colonies], whose control over their own land was taken away in the course of agrarian technification.[11]

The Green Revolution set Mexico on the road to becoming an importer of its traditional subsistence crop, corn. An agrarian nation, Mexico now gets one-fifth of its corn from the United States. From 1967 to 1976 the average caloric intake per Mexican declined 10 percent. Animals and foreign consumers eat more basic foodstuffs produced in Mexico than do Mexicans themselves. The world's ninth-largest food producer, Mexico ranks sixtieth in life expectancy and food consumption per person.

Large-scale commercial farmers and foreign agribusinesses, aided by the Mexican government, which continues to favor them with the best hydraulic and irrigation resources and 85 percent of state credits, have taken over most of Mexico's countryside, dispossessing millions of peasants in the process. By 1965, in a typical region developed by the Green Revolution's new technology, like the Yaqui Valley of Sonora, 80 percent of the peasants who received lands under agrarian reform had been dispossessed. Many peasants farming small and medium-sized parcels got the new technological inputs on credit and often had to sell or rent their land outright after defaulting.

"Rent parcels?" groaned one Sonora peasant to this writer in 1963. "Why, here entire *ejidos* are rented out." By 1970 some 70 percent of Sonora's *ejidos*, presumably unrentable under the agrarian reform law, were rented. In other areas of high-profit capitalist agriculture, like the Zamora Valley of Michoacán, famed for its US-controlled strawberry industry and for the provision of cheap migrant labor to California, the figure for rented *ejidos* ranged as high as 80 percent.

In central Mexico's Bajío, the nation's traditional foodbasket, one-fourth of sorghum production is absorbed by Ralston Purina—which, together with Anderson-Clayton, annually removes 3 million tons of corn and 6 million tons of sorghum from human consumption for the animal feed industry. Fruit and vegetable exporters dominated by TNCs account for almost 30 percent of the value of the main agricultural products in the Bajío's Guanajuato State, ironically the "cradle of national independence" more than a century and a half ago.

Mexico's National Center of Agrarian Research recognizes the enrichment of TNCs, the dispossession of peasants, and the increase in hunger, but the government, complicitous in these trends, looks the other way. In fact, it habitually sends its forces of repression to subdue peasant or worker protest. The pages of recent Mexican history are bloodied by army massacres of peasants, workers, and students. The most notorious act of official violence occurred in the Tlatelolco housing project of downtown Mexico City on the eve of the Olympic Games, October 2, 1968, when some 500 demonstrators were killed, 2,550 wounded, and 1,500 arrested.

In controlling dissident movements, Mexico's government routinely welcomes the assistance of US government agencies. For example, post-Watergate revelations show that the FBI cooperated with the Mexican state in harassing the sizable Independent Peasant Confederation (CCI) in the 1960s.[12] When not resorting to repression, the Mexican government attempts to coopt dissident movements by offering their leaders economic subsidies or other forms of government legitimation, as it did with CCI leader Alfonso Garzón. Today, under Garzón's coopted leadership, the CCI supports the state as vigorously as it once challenged it.

State tutelage of organized peasants and workers and repression or cooptation of independent groups helped assure the "success" of the Green Revolution, which in turn helped generate the economic and food crisis Mexico faces today. Food imports account for up to one-fifth of Mexico's balance-of-trade deficit and, together with shortages in locally produced food staples, fuel Mexico's rising rate of inflation (about 100 percent a year in 1983–84). Dispossessed and hungry peasants stalk the land, crowd the cities, and, in some cases, eventually decide to migrate: "*Vámonos al norte, pues!*"

The most immiserated are reduced to Stone Age conditions. In some areas, for example, women and children hunt small animals or collect wild fruits and herbs on mountain slopes. Others, having migrated to cities, seek food in garbage dumps where entire communities have built shacks, mingling with the scavenging dogs and rats.

Moreover, even though it employs most of Mexico's rural workforce, highly mechanized modern agribusiness absorbs less labor every year. Female labor, more easily exploited, has largely replaced male labor in the food processing industry. Fewer workdays for rural laborers assure the growth of the Mexican surplus labor pool.

This situation suits business interests in the United States and Mexico. The technification of agriculture and the industrialization of Mexico that it helped make possible were welcomed by the more privileged groups. Increased agricultural yields provided two decades of relatively low-cost food for the urban population, and held down the costs of labor and the level of industrial wages. Agricultural modernization also supplied inexpensive raw materials (such as cotton, tobacco, hemp) for industry. Increased agrarian exports became a principal source of Mexico's foreign exchange, useful for the importation of capital goods and luxury items.

Because of the state's role in Mexico's modern industrial and agricultural transformation, and because of increased domination by domestic and foreign monopolies, Mexico's economic system can be characterized as dependent state-guided monopoly capitalism. US capital does not control Mexico's economy in its entirety, but it wields sufficient influence to make a critical difference—and therein lies Mexico's structural economic dependence. Were the United States to impose an economic boycott of the kind directed at China for twenty years and now maintained against Cuba and Nicaragua, Mexico might well lose its economic viability overnight.

By late 1984 the state's share of Mexico's $96 billion foreign debt was about $66 billion, almost one-fourth of the nation's GNP (gross national product), or 15 times what it had owed in 1970. That amounts to around $1,200 for every adult Mexican—more than most Mexicans make in a year. The United States has an even larger debt, but Americans owe it to themselves, while Mexicans owe it to foreigners. What if foreigners tighten the credit screws, as they did briefly in 1976 in response to nationalist rumblings from the Mexican president's office—or as they did earlier against the democratically elected government of Salvador Allende in Chile?

As Chapters 5 and 6 illustrate, economic dependence causes Mexico to give in to most of foreign capital's demands on such occasions. Mexico's only bargaining chips are a relatively independent foreign policy, abundant oil reserves, and the threat to cut off emigration of its workers to the United States. Yet because of economic dependence and rising rates of unemployment and underemployment (more than 50 percent in recent years), the Mexican government's use of migrants as a bargaining chip has lost much of its force.

The Border as an Instrument of Integration, Not Separation

The United States and Mexico have a common border that is nearly two thousand miles in length, one of the world's longest and least "controllable." A historical product of conquest and settlement, that border is rich in symbolic and mythological import. But it is an impossible task to seal off the entire border.

During "Operation Intercept" in 1969, President Richard Nixon prescribed something like this in calling for a "shock treatment" to persuade Mexico to collaborate in a crackdown on drug smuggling: the border was virtually closed to northbound traffic. Since such an operation cannot be sustained for more than a brief period of time, the action was largely symbolic.

In March 1985 President Reagan ordered a partial shutdown of the border in the name of hunting down drug-related "terrorists" connected to the abduction and murder inside Mexico of a top American operative of the Drug Enforcement Administration (DEA). Reagan's action led to mass protests on both sides of the border by disgruntled merchants and laborers, most of them Mexican, who depend on the border area as a separate economy linked to both nations. Most observers felt that Reagan's intense pressure upon the Mexican government had a lot to do with his publicly stated desire to overthrow the Sandinista government in Nicaragua and his displeasure with Mexico's leading role in the Contadora Group of nations calling for demilitarization of Central America, an end to US interventionism, and peace.

Periodic drug crackdowns are more symbolic than real, since many high officials on both sides of the border are involved in the notoriously profitable drug trade. It is common knowledge that in Mexico the army engages in harvesting marijuana and that high police officials are involved in drug trafficking—so much so that in response to the assassination of the DEA official, the Mexican government levied charges against a select number of police officers.

From 1973 to 1977 the Mexican police received $47 million from the DEA, presumably to combat the harvesting and trafficking of drugs. The police spent much of the money on hardware for use against political dissidents. In the Sierra Madre of the northern states of Sinaloa and Durango, 7,000 Mexican soldiers aided by 226 DEA advisers fought a "special war" against Indians and peasant land occupiers under the pretext of searching for marijuana fields. Herbicides of a type used in the Vietnam War were sprayed on food plants, causing starvation among the Indian population.

Meanwhile, Mexico's share of the US heroin market reached nearly 90 percent in 1974, a time when "Mexican brown" became easily available and the number of American heroin addicts reached an all-time high of 600,000. Today, Mexico accounts for 36 percent of the heroin market, 30 percent of the cocaine supply, and 9 percent of the marijuana consumed in the United States. The figures for marijuana are suspect, however, because in November 1984 a Mexican government raid reportedly turned up 10,000 tons of marijuana on only a few plantations—almost as much as the estimated annual American consumption. Among those arrested in the raid were seven Mexican federal police officers.[13]

It is now known that Federal District police chief General Arturo Durazo Moreno built a fortune on the drug trade and other illicit activities. In 1985 he was in a Los Angeles jail awaiting possible extradition to Mexico on charges of corruption. Federal security director Miguel Nassar Haro was also detained in the United States, in early 1982, for alleged involvement in a $30 million car theft ring. He, however, was released on bail; the CIA requested that he not be prosecuted since he had been its most important source of information in Mexico and Central America.

In addition to drug and other smuggling activities, controversial issues involving the border include capital transfers; commerce in fruits, vegetables, machinery, and raw materials; shipment of assembled products from TNC plants; use and abuse of water resources; wind-blown or water-carried pollution; tourist traffic; and, of course, the flow of migrant workers. The bracero program and the corresponding concentration of immense pools of cheap labor in northern Mexico generated a veritable population explosion in many cities on both sides of the border, contributing to the region's economic dynamism. Tijuana's population rose from 16,846 in 1940 to 151,939 in 1960; that of Ciudad Juárez from 48,881 to 261,683; and Mexicali's from 18,775 to 171,648.

This expanded labor pool in turn spurred the economic transformation of industry and agriculture that made the US Southwest the region with the fastest-paced economic growth of the post-1960 period. According to Census Bureau data, manufacturing employment increased by 67.3 percent in the Southwest between 1960 and 1975, compared with a 3.2 percent increase in the Great Lakes region and losses of 13.7

percent in the Midwest and 9 percent in New England. Census figures for 1972 showed why: the average value added per wage dollar for the Southwest was $3.48, compared with $3.30 for the Northeast and $3.35 nationally. In other words, the labor force in the Southwest was less organized than in other parts of the country and therefore could be more highly exploited.[14]

The Mexican north was also dynamized. Mexico's northwest adopted the agribusiness model of production, financing, and marketing that already prevailed in California, Arizona, and Texas. US-based TNCs increasingly directed the flow of capital and labor across the border as Mexico's industry, agriculture, commerce, and banking, particularly in the north, became more and more integrated with the economy of the United States.

This cross-border economic integration has made the area's residents very dependent on one another. During the Mexican economic crises of 1976–77 and 1982–83, for instance, retail sales in US border towns reportedly fell off by 50 to 75 percent. Not surprisingly, California's San Diego and Imperial counties recently requested a federal grant to develop not only the two counties but also Mexicali and Tijuana, construing both sides of the border as one development region.

The border is equally artificial in relation to water resources. In 1962 this writer was the first American to report in the United States the widespread damage done to soils and crops in Baja California's Mexicali Valley by Colorado River water flowing into Mexico after passing over heavily fertilized agribusiness fields in Arizona and leaching them of their salts. Salinity-caused damage practically ruined the lives of tens of thousands of Mexican peasants. The border proved to be, in this case, literally porous.[15]

In the case of capital flows and trade, the situation is practically identical. American investors pour funds and plants into Mexico and transfer back to the United States twice as much in profits and other remittances (Table 2). Meanwhile, Mexican investors, especially in recent years, put their savings into US real estate ventures and bank accounts.

Yet here again, as with other commodities, the border's fictitious character has its legal side, making it theoretically possible for each nation to enforce protective tariffs demanded by select producers in various sectors. In practice, Mexico suffers in this regard, annually complaining about US tariffs on its manufactures (such as shoes) and agricultural goods (such as tomatoes).

The Role of the Maquiladoras

The fictitious character of the border and its consequences for both labor and capital are nowhere more vividly illustrated than in the startling economic and cultural transformation along both sides of the border during the post-bracero period, 1965 to the present. America's Southwest became the economic heartland of the nation's future, showing faster rates of economic growth, less unemployment, higher productivity rates, faster-growing commerce, and greater agricultural and high-tech industrial output than any other region in the United States. And the story is similar in Mexico, where the six border states experienced a faster rate of economic growth than any other region. With only 15 percent of the population, Mexico's border states account for 22 to 25 percent of the value added in the nation's main nonoil sectors of economic production and distribution (manufacturing industry, agriculture, and commerce).

This modern-day transformation, rooted in the history of silent integration, received its main impetus in 1964–65 when the United States terminated the bracero program. Mexico, in part to absorb the shock of increased unemployment caused by the return of the braceros and "dried-out wetbacks," many of whom crowded the border area, introduced its Border Industrialization Program of labor-intensive assembly plants (*maquiladoras*). The Mexican government allowed the US-owned *maquiladoras* to import parts duty-free, while the US government allowed the return of assembled products in like manner (US tariff items 806.30 and 807.00).

These developments sped up the tempo of the traditional migratory flow northward from central and southern Mexico, and by 1974 one-third of the border population consisted of migrants (only 3 percent of whom were employed in the *maquiladoras*).[16] The Border Industrialization Program, then, vastly augmented the populations of Mexico's major border cities and ultimately added to the numbers of people and commodities passing north and south through the revolving border doors.

During the decade after 1965, there occurred for many major US-based TNCs a monumental historical shift in the international flow of the labor-intensive phases of modern production. By 1972 nearly a third of the value of *all* US components sent abroad anywhere in the world for assembly went to Mexico. *Maquiladora* firms showed an annual income growth rate of 30 percent from 1971 to 1977 (years that included both prosperity and recession phases of the business cycle). By 1977 more than a billion dollars' worth of *maquiladora*-assembled products per year was being returned from Mexico to the United States.

"Runaway shops" became part of the daily lexicon of American labor. Mexican workers received wages that ranged from one-fifth to one-seventh of those paid US workers in like industries (today, after recent devaluations of the peso, the figures are one-twelfth to one-fifteenth). Moreover, Mexicans worked longer days and produced more per hour at greater risk to their health. For example, Mexican women performing electronic assembly operations with the naked eye produced 25 percent more than their US counterparts using microscopes.[17]

Mexican secretary of industry and commerce Octaviano Campos Salas stated in 1965 that the goal was "to offer an alternative to Hong Kong, Japan, and Puerto Rico for free enterprise."[18] Besides traditional US manufacturers like General Motors, Dupont, and Dow Chemical, such diversified giants as Transitron Electronic Corporation, Litton Industries, Fairchild Camera, Hughes Aircraft Company, and Lockheed Aircraft, many of them among the top twenty subsidized clients of the Pentagon, moved into Mexico. The electrical and electronics industries accounted for more than a third of the *maquiladoras*, textiles and footwear for more than a fourth, and transportation equipment and machinery, furniture, processed foods, and others for the remainder. Subsequently, Mexico permitted the establishment of foreign *maquiladoras* in the interior of the country as well. By 1983 US companies owned some 650 of these *maquiladoras*, most of them near the border.

It was in the border area that the *maquiladora* program proved particularly profitable for US corporate interests. A TNC paid wages according to Mexican norms but sold the finished products across the border according to much higher US price norms. The legal fiction of the border, in other words, permitted a vast increase in the profits of US-owned private corporations setting up assembly plants in northern Mexico. The proximity of the two markets—one for the labor supply and the other for the sale of finished products—and the waiving of duties reduced the costs of production, transportation, and marketing to a pittance at every stage. Moreover, sizable portions of the wages earned by *maquiladora* employees were spent on the US side of the border, adding to the economic boom of America's Southwest.

Wall Street Journal reporter Peter F. Drucker, among others, has described this "production sharing" as neither an exporting nor an importing activity for Mexico, even though standard trade statistics show it as such. According to these trade figures, border transactions, led by *maquiladora* activity, have become Mexico's second most important source of foreign exchange. They amount to about 18 percent of Mexico's income on current account (compared to only 0.5 percent of US income from export of goods and services). In 1979 nearly a third of Mexico's foreign exchange earned from manufacturing exports derived from *maquiladora* transactions that in fact represented in great part US company profits.[19]

In actuality, then, the *maquiladoras* represent a deepening of Mexico's economic integration into the United States through the linkage of different stages of the production process, as well as what many authors have described as "a new international division of labor." As US manufacturing firms have become more finely tuned to the sophistication of modern technology and the cheapness of modern transportation, they have moved entire segments of their production overseas. Modern production is marked by an increasing complexity of design of finished products yet a growing simplicity of the individual operations necessary for their manufacture. As a result, TNCs export tedious manual operations to peripheral areas, seeking an expanding pool of newly defined "unskilled" and "semiskilled" laborers (many of whom are women). This is what is meant by a "new international division of labor."[20]

Economist Calvin P. Blair has characterized the US-Mexico economic integration as "border symbiosis." "The Mexican city," Blair observes, "typically furnishes some workers to the agriculture and service trades of the US side. It also acts as an entrepot for goods moving into the Mexican interior, serves as an assembly point for location of one of the 'twin plants' which produces for US markets. . . . The sister city on the US side provides similar entrepot and expenditure stimuli to its Mexican counterpart, and it often contains the other half of the 'twin plants'."[21]

Once again, the integration of the two nations' economies has produced more benefits for the United States than for Mexico. Unemployment has gradually increased in Mexico's border states and decreased in those of the United States. Whenever labor unrest, the formation of labor unions, or a recession has occurred in northern Mexico, the *maquiladoras* have routinely dismissed personnel, closed down, or moved to another part of Mexico. Each new locale of such plants has experienced a brief economic boom until the next economic downturn or threat from employees organizing.

Consequently, far from dropping, unemployment rates in those border cities penetrated by the *maquiladoras* (notably Tijuana, Mexicali, and Ciudad Juárez) have risen, boosted by the arrival of thousands of persons from other parts of Mexico in quest of work. Through 1983, fewer than 225,000 jobs had been provided by the *maquiladoras*.

Of those Mexicans employed by the 500 border area plants established between 1965 and 1975, most (85 percent) were poorly paid single women between sixteen and twenty-five years of age. Three-quarters of them had a background of migration, usually from smaller cities north of the nation's capital. They had an average educational level superior to the national norm—sixth grade instead of third grade. Mexican sociologist María Patricia Fernández has documented in heartrending detail the multiple abuses these superexploited women experience at the hands of their male superiors both at work and at home. By age thirty, many are too ill from unhealthy work conditions and physical abuse to continue.

Fernández goes on to point out the lack of long-term secure employment for women and their "downward mobility" to less skilled jobs as they grow older. Older women still able to work have begun migrating to the United States. Most teenage women employed in *maquiladoras* become the economic mainstay of their extended families. Many are abused sexually by plant managers and bosses, and a number are rotated out of the *maquiladora* workforce by their mid-twenties and driven to prostitution in order to continue supporting their families.

Because of growing rates of male unemployment and relatively low wages for women, Mexican family income in the border areas ultimately declines and the labor force is made yet more exploitable. In the absence of equal pay for equal work, "feminization" of the workforce has devastating consequences for every member of the international working class. Concludes Fernández, "The recent incorporation of large female contingents into the new international proletariat expands the number of workers of both sexes; it broadens the labor supply, with the probable long-run consequence of not only driving wages down but also of debilitating all workers' organizations."[22]

Some Mexican authorities view these trends with equanimity, since economic hard times for labor in Mexico usually translate into the arrival of more, not fewer, *maquiladoras*. For example, in the fall of 1982, when more than a million regularly employed Mexican workers were being laid off, Aureliano González Baz, a Ciudad Juárez lawyer who promotes the *maquiladora* road to industrialization, stated that Mexico's fourfold devaluation of the peso over the previous nine months and resultant lowering of salaries meant that Mexico would now be able to compete on a world scale with Hong Kong, Taiwan, and Haiti as a source of labor.[23] In the words of a manager of a Fisher-Price Toys plant in Tijuana, "Essentially, we are buying labor, and the [peso] devaluation is going to make it less expensive to purchase that labor."[24]

Maquiladora-style industrialization compounds silent integration and the suction-pump effect of foreign capital taking out of Mexico more than it puts in. Eighty-five percent of the products of these assembly plants are exported to the United States. Profits are not reinvested in Mexico; less than 2 percent of declared earnings remain in the country. Mexico does not benefit technologically, since the plants are labor-intensive and 98.3 percent of the machinery and materials for production are imported. In other words, there is practically no "economic multiplier" effect generated by the *maquiladoras*.[25]

The main "multiplier" turns out to be the impact of economic fluctuations in the United States on Mexican border cities and towns, where more than 60 percent of business transactions are conducted in dollars and the prices of basic necessities approach or surpass those in the United States. Mexican shoppers usually prefer, whenever possible, to buy on the US side of the border. A handful of wealthy Mexican merchants, bankers, and speculators have fattened from the border area's high prices and many dollar transactions, which have produced a small but powerful local commercial bourgeoisie.

For Mexico as a whole, however, the *maquiladoras* have made economic development more lopsided, enriching the northern bourgeoisie, impoverishing the working class and peasantry, and leaving the nation relatively decapitalized. National investors are less and less able to raise the capital necessary to create new jobs on a par with the pace set by foreign corporations using expensive modern machinery.

Border economic development has stimulated the growth of America's Southwest, which in turn gives its economic and political leaders a more influential voice in US affairs. The 1980 census showed that a majority of Americans now live in the Sun Belt and the West, whose states account for a majority of seats in the House of Representatives and Senate, as well as in the Electoral College.

Economic development of the Mexican border states has likewise given their leaders increased leverage in determining the future of Mexico. Today, the distribution of economic activity in Mexico testifies to an important new development: the actual production of commodities of whatever kind is far more intense in the border region than elsewhere.

It is important to keep in mind that in the absence of production, neither trade nor economic growth can occur. In the border states, manufacturing industry accounts for about 50 percent of the value added in all economic activity, as compared with only 25 percent for Mexico as a whole; in agricultural production, the corresponding figures are 19 percent and 12 percent. Border states produce 21 percent of the value of Mexico's basic agricultural products; Sonora dominates agricultural production, with Tamaulipas a distant second. Nuevo León, Coahuila, Chihuahua, and Baja California lead the way in the border area's *maquiladora*-dominated manufacturing industry.[26]

Most of the gross production in Mexico's north is foreign-dominated. The rest is largely in the hands of a powerful bourgeoisie known as "the Monterrey Group," a junior partner of foreign capital, historically renowned for its ultrareactionary political character but far more complex and sophisticated today in its handling of political affairs. The local commercial bourgeoisie and the Monterrey Group in Mexico's north are the main economic powers behind that region's growing political movement for a "two-party democracy" to break the near-monolithic grip of the official political party of Mexico, the Institutional Revolutionary Party (PRI). The second party they back, the Party of National Action (PAN), has long been a conservative force in Mexican politics. The two-party system they advocate is modeled, not surprisingly, after that of the United States.

Thus, in politics as well as economics, Mexico is moving closer to the United States. It is not a colony, like Puerto Rico is or Alaska and Hawaii once were. But in the long run, irresponsible talk of Mexican statehood is not as farfetched as first it might appear. Powerful economic forces in both nations' ruling groups would like to see the border not merely continue to be a legal fiction but disappear altogether.

That day is far off, however, given the history of Mexican nationalism and the usefulness of the border for extricating the monopolies from the periodic economic crises they themselves bring about through overinvestment, overproduction, and mismanagement. The value of the border and of Mexican immigrant workers during such crises, then, is the subject of the next chapter.

5

The Use of
Immigrant Workers
in the Economic Crisis

"I believe leaders of the business community, with few exceptions, have chosen to wage a one-sided class war in this country—a war against working people, the unemployed, the poor, the minorities, the very young and the very old, and even many in the middle class of our society."
—United Automobile Workers union president Douglas Fraser, letter of resignation from the Labor-Management Advisory Committee, July 19, 1978, circulated by UAW

Since the late 1960s the integrated economies of the United States and Mexico have been in some form of crisis. By the early 1980s the economic crisis had become global and prolonged in scope.

An exploration of the economic crisis in the two countries reveals how underpaid migrant workers have become an important resource for employers to combat economic woes, particularly falling profit rates. Present and future population and job market trends demonstrate how the prolonged economic crisis and employers' increased resort to inexpensive migrant labor are leading to the emergence of a two-tiered society, not just in Mexico but also in the United States—a social pyramid marked by the shrinking of the so-called middle class into a shell of its former self. Finally, the crisis-reinforced generation of yet more migrant labor has prompted many US employers to demand a tough immigration policy to stabilize matters at the border and assure a predictable supply of inexpensive Mexican laborers.

The Character of the Crisis in the United States

However varied their explanations for the US economic crisis, few economists disagree about its broad contours. It started in the late 1960s, deepened in the 1970s, and became global by the 1980s. It has included three recession periods—in 1969, 1973–75, and 1979–83— each deeper than the preceding one. The persistence of high unemployment rates, low productivity, and rising consumer prices and interest rates amounts to what is called "stagflation," or stagnation combined with inflation, meaning insufficient production of goods and jobs, with rising prices. Stagflation in turn contributes to high interest rates and federal budget deficits (including the tripling of the deficit under President Ronald Reagan by late 1984), which threaten to make matters worse. The ripple effects of the crisis in less industrialized countries had become, by the 1980s, a tidal wave portending massive defaults on national debts to US banks and a consequent international financial crash reminiscent of 1929.

War as a possible way out of the new economic crisis no longer appeared easy or quick, as it had in 1937 after the collapse of the previous year's economic "recovery." For the United States, the Vietnam War had been both a socially and politically destabilizing experience. Furthermore, the growing threat of local conflagrations becoming continentwide wars or even triggering a nuclear holocaust made them far less viable as government policy.

Throughout the crisis, the upswings following downturns in the US business cycle were ever less vigorous, ever less self-sustaining, ever less capable of reducing unemployment to the 4 or 5 percent rates of the 1950s and 1960s. Unemployment rates rose from an average of 4.8 percent of the labor force in the 1960s to 6.2 percent in the 1970s and 8.2 percent for the 1980s (through mid-1985). Unofficial estimates of unemployment were almost double the official figures, since the Bureau of Labor Statistics (BLS) routinely excludes those no longer looking for work while counting as "employed" anyone who works as little as one hour per week or is in the armed forces. Throughout these crisis years, industrial production ranged from only 77 to 86 percent of capacity.

At every turn, the federal government lavished favors upon big corporations to encourage them to invest more and spark a lasting economic recovery. Indeed, the effective tax rate on large firms dropped severely throughout the 1970s and 1980s. The progressive federal income tax declined, while regressive Social Security payroll taxes more than tripled. Even in 1980, *prior to* the Reagan administration's generous tax cuts for employers, such corporate giants as Chase Manhattan, Squibb, and Monsanto paid no federal income taxes, while Exxon, Bank of America, and the nation's ten largest banks paid from 1.3 percent to 3.1 percent of their income. That same year the tax rate for a working family of four with an income of $20,000 was 10 percent.

Meanwhile, federal bailouts of failing industries and banks became commonplace: the Penn Central Railroad, Lockheed Aircraft, Franklin National Bank, Chrysler, the Hunt Brothers, the First Pennsylvania Bank and 25 other savings and loan associations, the Continental Illinois National Bank and Trust Company, and more. From 1969 to 1985 most big corporations, including those saved by federal bailouts, continued to make copious profits—even ones socially embarrassing in the harsh light of an overall stickiness or decline in real wages.[1]

Yet the corporations' expected *rates* of profit were not sufficient to cause them to plow these returns back into production or R & D (research and development) for improved techniques of production. Instead, they played the international money markets, speculated in real estate or other areas, invested in the national debts of countries around the world, shifted more funds into gold-plated military and other nonproductive activities, and bought government bonds and one another's stock. As early as September 1981 President Reagan's treasury secretary exclaimed, "Where are the expansion plans? It's like dropping a coin down a well—all I'm hearing is a hollow clink."

Corporate mergers and buyouts became an everyday occurrence. Yet only the largest monopolies and conglomerates, instead of the economy as a whole, received a shot in the arm from these many-faceted wheelings and dealings. By 1979 *Fortune* magazine's top 500 industrial firms accounted for 80 percent of all manufacturing sales and more than 75 percent of all profits and persons employed. This monopolization trend escalated in 1981, the first year of the Reagan tax cuts, when US corporations bought up other companies at the rate of $82.6 billion a year, or four times their expenditures on R & D. That same year in Europe some $1.5 trillion was floating around the "Eurodollar" markets in quest of bargains. Chase Manhattan Bank alone had over $10 billion outstanding in credits to the Mexican government or private Mexican borrowers. The three largest US banks—Chase, Citibank, and Bank of America—reportedly had an estimated 40 percent of their capital tied up in Mexico, whose debt represented 17.1 percent of all US bank loans to third world countries and the Eastern bloc.

In other words, in the eyes of most big-time investors, speculative financial activities yielded higher short-term returns than productive long-term investments and were thus preferable. The gigantic transfer of funds from consumers to oil companies facilitated by the pro-oil policies of the Carter and Reagan administrations, for instance, did not result in significant new oil drilling but rather in the companies' "purchase of circuses, retail chains, and real estate."[2]

The upsurge in speculation was illustrated during the 1976–83 period by a fourfold increase in the trading of futures contracts (buying and selling of contracts involving bets on the course of future prices), from 36.9 million to 140 million contracts traded. In the words of *Business Week*, investors were "rushing into futures because of the small margin required and because of the variety of contracts being traded." In so doing, they were "shifting their dollars away from the traditional capital-formation mainstream—out of investment and into something close to out-and-out gambling."[3] Accordingly, *Business Week* entitled the cover story of its September 16, 1985 issue "The Casino Society."

Among industrialized countries—with the exception of France— the United States by 1984 had the most unequal distribution of income. In 1980 it had already slipped to the rank of eleventh in per capita GDP (gross domestic product—total output of goods and services before expense deductions and tax payments). And although the United States was unable to compete with the other industrial powers as successfully as it had done in the 1950s and 1960s, as evidenced by its skyrocketing trade deficit, the European powers were scarcely better off. In West Germany in 1983 unemployment averaged 9.1 percent; in Britain, 11.5 percent; in France, 8.3 percent; and among 15 members of the Organization for Economic Cooperation and Development, 8.3 percent. Estimates of unemployment rates for the European nations in 1984–85 were even higher. In other words, the economic crisis had gone global.[4]

In the so-called recovery year of 1983, net private nonresidential fixed investment (the common measure of productive investment) fell to 1.5 percent of the US net national product (total output of goods and services after taxes and expenses)—the lowest figure in nearly forty years, in spite of the Reagan administration's slashing of social programs, raising of depreciation and other allowances for industry, and near doubling of the defense budget. Preston Martin, a Reagan appointee to the Federal Reserve Board, referred to this as "growth recession"—a slow recovery in production growth accompanied by rising unemployment.

Roger Brinner, an economist at Data Resources, Inc., a private forecasting firm, predicted that the "growth recession" would last until at least mid–1986. He used as evidence the fact that during the first quarter of 1985 (when 130,000 more factory jobs were lost), economic growth slowed from 1984's "recovery" pace of 6.8 percent to a meager 0.7 percent annual rate. In light of subsequent declines in industrial output, Charles B. Reeder, chief economist at E. I. du Pont de Nemours and Company, stated that "the industrial component of the economy is in a recession."[5] The year 1985 showed only a 2.3 percent GNP growth rate, the slowest growth in the US economy since the recession year of 1982. Once again, a much-heralded "recovery" seemed to be undermined by the deep structural characteristics of the prolonged economic crisis.

With hindsight it is possible to locate the roots of US economic problems in the Vietnam War, the inflated rates of waste in war and/or nonproductive "defense" industry, the postponement of recessions, federal and corporate mismanagement, overproduction in the face of inadequate markets at home and abroad, loss of US domination over select foreign markets, declining real wages and a resulting shrinkage of future markets for expansion, and slackened productivity. President Lyndon B. Johnson once told GIs stationed in South Korea that had it not been for the Vietnam War, the United States would have suffered unemployment rates on a par with those of the Great Depression. Some of that "delayed" unemployment remained in the mid-1980s. As *New York Times* economic commentator Leonard Silk pointed out in 1982,

> Call it a repression—a chronic state of underemployment and industrial slack that has dogged the economy for the greater part of the past decade, a condition brought on by repressive actions by governments in the industrial world. . . . When did this Great Repression begin? Since history is a seamless web it is hard to date it precisely. But the escalation of the Vietnam War in 1965 and 1966 seems the logical point.[6]

If one assumes, as the federal government and most economists do, that a sustained high *rate* of profit for corporate investors is critical for economic growth, then one has to trace the economic crisis to the tailing off of the rate of profit after 1965. There are two common measures of corporate profitability: the after-tax rate of profit on domestic nonfinancial corporate business operations, for which figures are readily available; and "Tobin's Q" measurement of profit *expectations*, named after 1981 Nobel Prize winner James Tobin.[7] By either measure, the rate of profit, with only occasional short-lived upturns, has shown an overall, dominant downward trend from the mid-1960s through the early 1980s.

Declining profit rates and profit expectations not only led to a shift of investments into short-term speculative activities such as futures contracts but also intensified capital's long-term quest for low-wage labor. In this context, rising rates of labor immigration and the setting up of "runaway shops" in the 1970s and early 1980s were US capital's response to what Karl Marx once theorized as "the tendency for the rate of profit to fall."[8] The loss of jobs for US workers caused by overseas runaway shops (rising from an estimated 1 million jobs lost by 1965 to 2.5 million by 1980) helped hold back labor union demands for wage hikes.

From January 1979 to January 1984, according to a BLS survey released December 1, 1984, some 5.1 million workers with at least three years' tenure lost their jobs because of plant shutdowns or staff cuts. A subsequent congressional study found that only 60 percent of these displaced workers were able to find new jobs, and only 42 percent of displaced blacks who had held their previous jobs at least three years found new employment. The same study found that 94 percent of the 23.3 million people added to nonagricultural payrolls from 1970 to 1984 were in the service-producing sectors, where the 1984 average hourly wage for production and nonsupervisory workers was $7.52.

In theory, more unemployment and reduced wage levels contribute to higher rates of profit. However, driving real wages down in this case compounded the problem of shrinking domestic markets for goods by reducing the amount of money America's wage-earning consumers had to spend. Reduced consumption, or buying, resulted in reduced production by US business. This, in part, is why Silk (and others) characterize the crisis as one of "chronic unemployment and industrial slack."

Nonetheless, most US employers have still preferred attacks on wages and the power of labor unions, aided by increased labor immigration, to any alternative strategy for combating their economic woes. And as the international economic crisis has deepened, the supply of inexpensive, easily disciplined immigrant workers has grown by leaps and bounds south of the border.

The Character of the Crisis in Mexico

If Mexico caught cold when the United States sneezed during the 1973–75 recession (see Chapter 4), then we can say that it experienced acute pneumonia during the more severe recession years of 1981–83. In late 1981, in spite of the government's long record of imposing wage ceilings, or limits on wage increases, Mexican bankers and industrialists began withdrawing their money from Mexico—up to $100 million a day by mid-1982. Hoping to increase sales, the government slashed oil export prices and broke earlier nationalistic promises by announcing that the state-owned oil company, PEMEX, had signed a five-year contract to sell crude oil directly to the United States for its Strategic Petroleum Reserve (SPR)—the first such direct purchase from a foreign government agency by the US Energy Department. In February 1982 the government devalued the peso by 65 percent, claiming this would stave off fresh demands by the International Monetary Fund (IMF) for yet another austerity program. But these and other measures were all in vain.

In August 1982 a full-scale financial panic erupted. The Mexican government announced it could not pay its debt for the next ninety days. The peso was devalued twice more, completing a tenfold decline in its value vis-à-vis the dollar since 1976. Countless small businesses and farms closed down. More than a million workers were laid off. Hunger stalked the land. Money speculation along the US-Mexico border grew to alarming proportions. Tens of thousands of workers at the border's *maquiladoras* were laid off. Many of them, together with huge numbers of Mexican laborers arriving from the interior of the country, began slipping across the border in quest of work.

The historic causes and effects of Mexico's crisis have been sketched in Chapter 4. The "silent integration" of Mexico's economy with that of the United States did not lead to a complete industrial transformation of Mexico or to a self-sustaining pattern of economic growth. On the contrary, it drained Mexico of much of its economic surplus, "dollar-ized" its economy, and added to its unemployment problems. While the Mexican government continued digging itself into debt with foreign creditors, Mexican employers relied upon an abundant supply of cheap labor to obtain their profits rather than invest in the nation's industrial transformation and develop a robust internal market of adequately paid consumer-workers. Aware of these problems, the government of President Luis Echeverría (1970–76) sought to lay the foundation for complete industrialization by pumping money into the economy's capital goods sector—the manufacturing of the means of production (heavy equipment, machine tools, etc.).

Echeverría's technology development plans happened to coincide with those of US-based TNCs, recently buffeted by setbacks suffered in Vietnam and the US dollar's loss of hegemony on the international money market. The United States' terms of trade had deteriorated because of the activities of OPEC and similar cartels. The rising number of revolutionary governments and liberation movements throughout the world had intensified rivalries among the developed capitalist nations for shrinking markets. Moreover, during the Vietnam War years of "guns and butter," when the government had assured Americans they could have both high war expenditures and abundant consumer goods and social programs (President Johnson's "War on Poverty"), US corporations had overproduced. The eventual result was a crisis of overproduction and rising production costs leading to frequent worker layoffs—a combination of stagflation with recession.

All these problems left US-based TNCs short on markets, sources of cheap labor, and liquid capital (cash). As part of their response, the TNCs' boards of directors opted for a strategy of intensified capital goods exports and the selling of more industrial installations abroad, particularly to such low-wage, semi-industrialized areas as Mexico. Stepped-up technology sales meant quick access to cash, since purchasing nations often paid immediately through credits obtained from bankers and international credit institutions. In fact, during the 1970s, technology sales and capital goods exports became the fastest-growing source of liquid capital for US-based TNCs, crucial for their survival and growth at a time when they were being put on the defensive.

Thus, Mexico became one of the first test cases for US corporate capital's strategy of displacing part of its own crisis onto the third world. President Echeverría's advisers argued that the 1972 Law on Registration of Technology Transfers, which required registration of TNC's technology purchases from abroad, would provide enough government oversight to forestall any "sacking" of Mexico. Yet they conceded that even with the registration of technology purchases there was no adequate way to prevent the TNCs from overpricing technology imports and underpricing exports of subsequently produced goods.

Three years later, the National Council on Science and Technology publicly acknowledged the failure of the 1972 law—and the previous thirty years' development strategy in general. Technology purchases had been registered irregularly, usually after contracts had been negotiated and payments made. Although Mexico's capacity to produce the means of production had advanced somewhat, its capital goods sector remained largely foreign-owned and dependent upon foreign "know-how." Technological growth, based largely on purchases from the United States, had turned out to be very expensive and had added to the state's need to borrow, thereby plunging the nation further into debt and dependence upon foreign banks and corporations.

Despite this admission of its mistakes, the Mexican government stuck to its technology development strategy, and from 1976 to 1980 the importation of production goods tripled, much of it for the oil industry. Of all capital goods developed in the 1970s, more than 80 percent were imported. It was estimated that for every $1.00 of new foreign investment entering Mexico, $2.50 to $3.00 left the country in the form of profits, royalties, and other payments, and through tricks of transfer pricing on technology imports.

The Echeverría government's development strategy reinforced the structural basis of the economy's "dollarization" and relative decapitalization. The ninefold rise in Mexico's production goods imports in the 1970s, for example, contributed heavily to the more than sixfold increase in the public sector foreign debt during the same period. Interest payments and amortization on the foreign debt typically absorbed half or more of Mexico's export earnings, further decapitalizing the nation.

President José López Portillo (1976–82) sought to stem the financial hemorrhaging by turning Mexico into a one-product economy—oil would solve the problem. But rapid development of the oil industry only increased the need for production goods imports. PEMEX soon accounted for a third of the foreign debt. The economy "overheated," and the petro-bubble burst in 1982. Mexico turned out to be a textbook case of how a country's efforts to increase productive capacity without emphasizing its own resources, research skills, and technology leads to increased wealth for its more industrially advanced "partner" and increased indebtedness for its own economy.[9]

Mexico's 1982 economic collapse provided both domestic and US employers with a tool for at least partial economic "recovery"—an expanded "reserve army of unemployed," from whose desperate ranks employers could obtain new cheap labor to exploit for a time before discarding again. This was the strategy adopted by many corporations everywhere to combat a recession that had become worldwide. An expansion of the international reserve army of labor through massive layoffs, an increased resort to highly exploited temporary workers, and the lowering of real wages—all have continued to be basic components of big business's policy of using immiseration to stem declining profit rates and bring itself out of crisis.[10]

Meanwhile, panic and unrest swept through Mexico's cities and villages. In a desperate and politically shrewd move, President López Portillo announced on September 1, 1982, that he was expropriating Mexican private banks, with compensation. This move "in the national self-interest" stabilized the situation politically for a few months, allowing the bankrupt government to appear in control while it turned to foreign creditors for its economic salvation. Later, particularly during the early years of the new government of President Miguel de la Madrid Hurtado (1982–88), shares in the expanded state banking sector were sold to "the public," with preference given to the formerly "private" bankers.

As early as September 1979, President López Portillo had anticipated Mexico's economic crisis by noting the heavy costs of the IMF austerity program imposed at the height of Mexico's 1974–76 recession: "When stabilization programs, justified by transitory conditions, are perpetuated," he told the nation's congress, "greater injustices result than those supposedly being corrected. Fatally, salaried workers' wages are restricted; capital centralizes; and the state's room for maneuver is reduced. The state's capacity to resolve conflicts is annulled, its possibility of governing cancelled." In 1982 López Portillo was attempting to reclaim the state's ability to maneuver, blaming greedy Mexican bankers and high US interest rates for a crisis that went far deeper.

The international banking community, afraid that a Mexican default might ignite a run on the banks and bring about global financial collapse, quickly bailed Mexico out of its immediate debt crisis. The US government arranged a cash-in-advance billion-dollar oil purchase for its SPR at a per-barrel figure too low to be announced. The US "bailout" included another $1 billion from the Commodity Credit Corporation to cover grain imports, and $925 million toward a $1.85 billion "bridge" credit from the Bank of International Settlements. As part of an additional $4.5 billion standby IMF credit, Mexico agreed to accept an austerity "stabilization" program similar to the 1976 arrangement, which, in hindsight, had only deepened the nation's crisis. Mexico also stood by its 1981 agreement to double its natural gas exports to the United States to about 600 million cubic feet a day.

All told, the international bailout of Mexico in August 1982 totalled $10 billion and mortgaged the nation to foreign interests for the foreseeable future. The Mexican government practically guaranteed US receipt of the bulk of Mexican oil and gas sales at less than market value, thereby converting Mexico into the United States' principal oil supplier and the world's third largest exporter of oil to the noncommunist world (after the Soviet Union and UK). On September 6, 1982, Finance Minister Jesús Silva Herzog, Jr., announced that in 1983 Mexico would pay only the interest on its debt.

The truth is that then, as today, Mexico could not pay even the interest unless it doubled its oil production to 5 million barrels a day (it had almost that capacity in 1985). Such an increase in the tempo of petrolization of the economy spells more foreign borrowing to finance PEMEX expansion, sudden injections of capital into an overheated economy already plagued by runaway inflation of nearly 100 percent a year, and a deepening of the very crisis that triggered the initial August 1982 panic. While PEMEX subsidizes Mexican industry by selling it hydrocarbon products at one-third the world market value, Mexico's people experience repeated price hikes in the same products for their vehicles and homes. As a Michoacán peasant who still makes frequent trips to the United States complained to this writer, "What do we gain from that fabulous wealth if the poor are crying from hunger?"

But financially strapped Mexico has plunged headlong into the stratospheres of oil and credit "development." By early 1983 the IMF and foreign commercial banks and creditors had patched together another $10 billion bailout of Mexico. Similar emergency steps were implemented over the next two years. Thus, the bursting of Mexico's petro-bubble in August 1982 threatened to be but a prelude to a much larger economic debacle some time later in the 1980s or 1990s.

Some observers thought the September 1985 earthquakes that took 25,000 lives and left hundreds of thousands homeless might trigger another economic collapse. The CIA reportedly estimated a 20 percent likelihood of the Mexican political system's breakdown. Once again the IMF and international banking community were scrambling to guarantee future Mexican payments on the debt. The subsequent decline in oil export prices to less than $20 a barrel further weakened Mexico's hand.

Compounding the Mexican government's problems has been the growing social discontent caused by its earlier repression of popular protests, its implementation of the IMF austerity measures, and the economic crisis. Workers and peasants have started to take to the streets in protest against their being made the victims of corporate and state mismanagement. On October 18, 1983, on May Day 1984, and on June 5, 1984, Mexican workers brought the wheels of production and distribution to a partial halt through two general strikes and one massive public demonstration. They did this in spite of the government's stepped-up repression of their decade-long movement for labor union democracy, including arrests, beatings, torture, murders, and "disappearances" (about 500 people still unaccounted for as this book went to press). Militant sections of their annual May Day demonstration in 1985 were dispersed by police gunfire and tear gas.

In the course of these labor and popular struggles, huge numbers of Mexicans have gained experience in attempting to democratize the nation's labor unions (the so-called Democratic Tendency labor movement, largely crushed in the late 1970s) or to organize independent trade unions free from the influence of the *charros*, as corrupt and violence-prone labor and peasant union bosses are pejoratively labeled. A popular cartoon of the 1980s portrays a worker addressing a comrade clothed in prisoner's garb: "Trade union democracy? Where?"—to which the prisoner replies, "Well, in Mexico, in Poland . . ."

Since 1980 various national marches on Mexico City have numbered well over 100,000 people. These demonstrations have included participation by the urban poor's independent National Council of Popular Urban Movements (CONAMUP), the independent peasants' National Plan of Ayala Network (CNPA), the rank-and-file workers' network coordinator COSINA (National Trade Union Council), the national teachers' strike movement, and many similar groups. After the 1985 earthquakes, many grassroots organizations joined a single coordinating committee for earthquake victims (known as the CUD), which in turn launched angry street demonstrations and sit-ins demanding popular control of reconstruction efforts. Although splits in the popular movement have never been overcome, the natural question arises: is Mexico on its way to a Poland-type or Iran-type eruption?[11]

One way to prevent such an eruption, as employers on both sides of the border have long realized, is to keep border doors revolving—to allow more and more "illegal" Mexicans to migrate across the border as a means of funneling off discontent. US employers need the inexpensive labor, and the Mexican government needs the corresponding "escape valve" for the pressures generated by crisis-induced budgetary cutbacks and mass layoffs.

As we have seen, Mexico is not just a market for commodities produced by the US and other industrial nations—it is also a supplier of a commodity of a very different and fundamental kind: labor power. Historically US employers have turned to immigrant labor power as a basic means of generating economic growth. During the prolonged economic crisis from the late 1960s to the present, resort to a particular kind of labor power has become more and more necessary for employers to recover their expected rates of profit: economically desperate, low-paid workers, whether immigrants or others.

It is in this context that international finance capital's involvement with issues of "the poor" can best be understood. As early as the 1960s, the US Agency for International Development (AID) and the World Bank, leader of a medley of international development enterprises sponsored largely by the United States, began advocating "investment in the poor" as a solution to the agrarian problems that they had helped to generate through proagribusiness projects like the Green Revolution in Mexico (see Chapter 4). With other lending agencies, they helped finance the delivery of more technical inputs to subsistence farmers. Instead of dispossessing peasants and incorporating them as free labor into the overflowing ranks of the rural and urban proletariat, these agencies now aimed to keep farmers producing on small parcels. In the words of World Bank director of agriculture and rural development Montague Yudelman, "The traditional, small-farm sector will have to become the producer of an agricultural surplus rather than the provider of surplus labor, as it has been in the past."[12]

On September 26, 1977, World Bank president Robert McNamara (former Ford Motor Company executive and US secretary of defense during the Vietnam War) outlined the urban component of this "investment in the poor" strategy. He said that the bank planned to create and aid independent producers in the development of artisan enterprises, domestic workshops, small grocery stores, and the like.[13] The strategy extended to women as well, especially once issues of "women's rights" had become fashionable. As an unclassified AID document put it,

> [Women's] contribution to production must be enhanced. . . .
> The US recognizes that women in developing countries already have the skills in agricultural production, processing, and marketing which provide a broad and relevant foundation on which to build. . . . The US [favors]: fostering labor-intensive economic activities to provide more income-earning

opportunities; increasing productivity through the introduction of appropriate technology, credit and other inputs; . . .
giving people control over their own reproduction.[14]

In all these ways the international development agencies have been
tying the urban poor to international credit systems in the same way
they earlier tied subsistence farmers to foreign loans and new foreign
farm technology.

The TNCs and other large companies involved in the implementation of these development plans accumulated new profit dividends
through sales of technology and products to the newly developed farms
and urban enterprises. During the late 1970s and early 1980s, this
strategy worked fairly well. It involved many poor people in new day-
to-day projects, thus forestalling social unrest while preventing the surplus labor pool from growing too large or unmanageable.

Nonetheless, oil-fueled inflation undercut the limited gains of this
attempt to deal with poverty. Mexico's legal minimum wage today
suffices to purchase less than half of what a family of five needs to
maintain itself, and only 40 percent of the economically active population receives even that. In other words, whether unionized or not,
the vast bulk of Mexico's rural and urban workers are superexploited—they earn wages insufficient for their own sustenance and
reproduction on a daily basis. As a result, most Mexicans adopt a
multiple wage-earning family strategy, with every able-bodied person
working at least part-time.

In the course of prolonged economic crisis, as total wages become
less able to meet even the bare requirements of living and as employers
and the state refuse to assume these costs, the burdens fall upon the
shoulders of the wage and nonwage working classes. Workers are thus
expected to assume the costs of economic crisis even as they pay the
price through "overemployment" of the entire family in the face of
rising rates of unemployment.

Official income statistics on Mexico's class structure tend to underestimate the ever sharper polarization separating the rich from the
poor. Strictly on the basis of comparative income, at least 65 percent of
the Mexican population qualifies as lower class, 10 percent as upper
class, and the rest falls somewhere in the middle. But in reality, the
intermediate classes consist of a shrinking minority of well-paid professionals and state bureaucrats and an immense majority of underpaid

schoolteachers, professionals and paraprofessionals, and others increasingly unable to make a living.

Statistics cannot measure the harshness of daily economic reality. Mexican census categories obscure class lines, conceal unemployment, and fail to capture the complexity of economic survival strategies undertaken by "middle-class" and working-class families, village communities, or rural *ejidos*. The truth is that almost every Mexican who can works. For most Mexicans, their survival is at stake. Even when an entire family works, it often cannot make ends meet.

Prior to the massive layoffs of 1982, the Ministry of Labor estimated that there were 8.5 million subemployed persons in Mexico. Fidel Velázquez, the octogenarian boss of the official Confederation of Mexican Workers (CTM), claimed there were more than 2 million unemployed according to the government's own testimony. In other words, some 10.5 million Mexicans, or 52.5 percent of the workforce, were without sufficient employment. It would take 800,000 new jobs a year just to keep unemployment from rising. Mexico was nowhere near achieving that. According to the 1980 census, 42.6 percent of the population was under fifteen years of age. Tens of millions of these youngsters began entering the job market in the 1980s.[15]

And then came the August 1982 economic collapse and the subsequent plummeting of Mexican real wages. Many of those millions of underpaid young Mexican workers are now knocking on the border door. And in contrast to any other time of economic crisis in history, they may be welcomed not merely with racism, abuse, and repeated deportations but—by employers at least—with open arms.

The Use of Immigrant Workers to Combat the Crisis

Unlike earlier historical periods, when economic crisis in the United States led to relative dropoffs in Mexican immigration, the period 1968–83—during which US unemployment rose dramatically—witnessed a sharp *increase* in the number of Mexican immigrant workers allowed to slip across the border into the United States. This does not mean that large-scale apprehensions and deportations did not accompany the ongoing demand for immigrant labor during the 1970s and 1980s, just as during the 1953–55 "Operation Wetback" period (see Chapter 3). For example, there were reportedly a million apprehensions in 1983, compared to only about 100,000 twenty years earlier. The border's "revolving door" has never stopped its efficient operation on behalf of employers.

But the level of immigration is now higher than it was a generation ago, and considerably higher than during the last period of prolonged economic crisis, the 1930s. Increased immigration during economic hard times is on the whole a new phenomenon for the United States—and one demanding an explanation.

Paradoxically, the crisis itself is the main explanation. In many small farms or branches of agribusiness, in garments and textiles, and in various other areas of industrial manufacture, services, and trade, immigrant labor has become crucial. As the *Wall Street Journal* said in 1976, "Legal or not, the present wave of Western Hemisphere immigrants is already enriching and contributing to North American society. . . . Illegals may well be providing the margin of survival for entire sectors of the economy."[16]

Less than half the Mexican migrants to the United States still go into agriculture. The others are now employed in the services sector, industry, and construction. A rapidly growing portion are entering either industry proper or subcontracted workshops for garments, automotive parts, or electronics. A detailed *Wall Street Journal* report, May 7, 1985, summed up the current situation in its headline: "Illegal Immigrants Are Backbone of Economy in States of Southwest—They Make Computer Parts, Package Arthritis Pills, Cook, Clean and Baby-Sit—Prisoners in the Bunkhouse."

Industrial employment of migrants is on the rise because corporations, in order to combat the crisis, are attempting to deunionize and rotate the labor force in a concerted effort to improve profitability. In the course of rotating the workforce, they are increasing mechanization and cutting costs by permanent layoffs and recourse to more easily disciplined low-wage immigrant workers, many of whom earn less than the minimum wage. Laid-off workers, ever more desperate for jobs and partly persuaded that the Mexicans may indeed be "taking our jobs," become more amenable to nonunion employment and less interested in the apparently unfulfillable promises of the occasional union organizer.

Discussions of Mexican immigrants that focus solely on the unskilled worker ignore the small but significant number of migrants who are trained professionals (an estimated 20,000 in 1981). In fact, the drain of income and skills caused by this out-migration further hinders Mexico's economic development and helps sustain an international reserve army of labor from which US employers can draw both skilled and unskilled laborers at a low price.

Mexico suffers extreme shortages in all areas of skilled labor, from engineers to auto mechanics. The composite educational level of Mexican workers migrating to the United States is above the third-grade average of the Mexican population as a whole—an often overlooked but not insignificant part of the "brain drain." About 14.4 percent of the migrants have seven or more years of education, and almost all of them have been employed prior to migration. This export of Mexican human capital, consisting of laborers whose education and training have been paid for in Mexico, subsidizes the US economy. Little wonder that even in times of economic crisis their presence is sought.[17]

And so the Mexicans (and other Latin Americans) have come, in a new and intensified wave. By 1984 low estimates placed the number of "illegal" immigrant workers in the United States at about 4 million, while high estimates approached 10 million. A fourteen-member panel on immigration statistics of the National Academy of Sciences issued a report, "Immigration Statistics: A Story of Neglect," in June 1985, noting that all figures were "woefully inadequate" and favoring the low estimate of 2 million to 4 million "illegals" actually residing in the United States. Another 5 to 7 million *legal* immigrants were expected to enter the country during the 1980s. During the 1970s California alone admitted an estimated 782,000 legal immigrants and 1,086,000 "undocumented" immigrants, according to Dr. Thomas Muller's recent study, *The Fourth Wave: California's Newest Immigrants.*[18]

Many people sought to blame this "fourth wave" of new immigrants for the economic crisis and high unemployment. Dr. Muller's study, however, like others before it, did not substantiate the charge. It found no decline in job availability for nonimmigrants in southern California, where nearly 70 percent of the new immigrants located. Of these, 75 percent were Mexican, and the study found "no statistical relationship between the size of the Hispanic population and black unemployment."

Yet neither did the Muller study contradict the fact that unemployment continues to affect many US citizens, especially blacks, in the Southwest and other locales of heavy Latino immigration such as Miami. The simple truth is that black Americans are tired of taking the worst jobs and unwilling to do the odious tasks immigrant workers are often asked to perform. Unlike the immigrants, black Americans are eligible for welfare. Moreover, they are familiar with the American system and have learned how to work within its interstices to make more money than employers offer immigrants.

Because employers recognize that immigrant workers are more docile and inexpensive than blacks, and because of the deeply ingrown antiblack racism of most employers, it is highly unlikely that a black would ever be chosen for a job over an immigrant. This would be the case even if unemployed blacks were willing and anxious to accept the low wages and miserable work conditions most Mexican immigrants accept. The same antiblack racism has without fail prevailed among employers during other waves of foreign immigration, such as the early 1900s. If history is any guide, the bitter wisdom of an antiracist American folksong applies here: "If you're white, you're right; if you're brown, stick aroun'; but if you're black, get back!"

Employers correctly perceive that it is easier to tame a Mexican immigrant worker than an unemployed black one. Of obvious advantage to employers is the fact that the immigrants are unable to speak English and are unfamiliar with the local culture. The greatest advantage for employers, of course, is the fact that the immigrant workers are "illegal," a status that makes them subject to instant deportation should they fail to obey orders, or find themselves no longer needed.

Dr. Muller's study, like so many others, confirms the picture given by earlier Labor Department statistics. These showed that in the eight Southwest and Midwest labor market areas experiencing the greatest increase in Mexican "illegal" immigration from 1968 to 1977, the unemployment rate was *lower* than the national average. Dr. Muller claims that from 1975 to 1981 some 325,000 new Spanish-speaking residents in Los Angeles County accepted wages that averaged only half those paid other workers, thereby helping to preserve the area's competitive advantage in manufacturing. For a number of decades, the large-scale presence of inexpensive Mexican, Asian, and Arab immigrant labor helped lower the general wage level in the Southwest. This in turn contributed to the Sun Belt industrial boom that, for a while at least, provided the contrast of factories and workshops opening up from Texas west but closing down in the Northeast and Midwest. Recently, of course, massive worker layoffs, plant shutdowns, and "runaway shops" have hit the Sun Belt hard as well.

Dr. Muller's study suggests that money spent in the local economy by newly arriving immigrants contributes to job creation for both black and white English-speaking citizens in the areas of education, health, and other social services. Notwithstanding, it is consistent with the racism and self-interest of most employers to perpetuate widespread black unemployment (or to tolerate growing white unemployment where necessary) and then put the blame on the shoulders of the very Mexican immigrants they recruit for low-paying jobs most Americans will not touch.[19]

A belt-tightening economic policy to combat the crisis would no doubt have been implemented with or without increased Mexican immigration. But the numerical upsurge in the reserve army of labor due to the "fourth immigration wave" and the 1982 massive layoffs of workers in Mexico has made it easier for the corporations to exact from the unions "wage givebacks" and other concessions in both the United States and Mexico. The role of millions of unemployed or poorly paid Mexican workers, immigrant or otherwise, as the backbone of an international reserve army of labor historically has been—and today remains—precisely that of disciplining all labor in both countries. As a reserve army of labor, migrants are essential to the corporations' attempts at combating the tendency of the rate of profit to fall.

Increased emigration of Mexican workers to the United States has proved fundamental to corporate interests in another way. The augmented migratory flow has been fueled by a rapidly deepening poverty in Mexico, particularly since 1981, when threats to economic survival began spreading to even the best-paid workers' families and some of the better-off ranks of Mexico's intermediate classes. Thus, a rise in the number of Mexican migrants not only helps US employers but also provides, now more than ever, an escape valve for the economic pressures building up inside Mexico.

In this sense too, migration serves as a weapon to combat the economic crisis and its effects on both sides of the border. In Mexico it cools off political pressures by sending workers to *el norte*. In the United States it displaces worker discontent onto the backs of Mexican immigrants who are blamed for "taking our jobs." Thus, Mexican emigration significantly reduces the potential for political protest that might further disrupt the two nations' economies.

The Mexican government's periodic verbal defense of migrant workers against abuses they experience in the United States obscures its role in supporting the economic system that drives Mexicans to emigrate. In actual practice, the Mexican government rarely lifts a finger to defend the migrants. This is no accident, since it knows that nearly seventy years after the end of the Mexican Revolution it has not been able to resolve the problems at home that obligate so many Mexicans to seek their survival abroad. From the government's viewpoint, it is better that these adventuresome, courageous, and economically desperate job-seekers leave the country rather than stay in Mexico to undertake the fight for lands, jobs, and decent wages—in sum, a more dignified life.

Affected both by a deeply ingrained history of racism and by a growing mass media bombardment of stories critical of Mexican immigrant workers in the late 1970s and early 1980s,[20] most Americans have little reason to question the common allegation that Mexican immigrant workers are draining taxpayers' contributions to social welfare programs such as food stamps, unemployment insurance, hospital service, or Social Security. In reality, however, the allegation is a false one that serves to conceal the very substantial contributions made by Mexican immigrant workers to the American economy.

A typical Mexican temporary migrant worker earns under $5,000, and deductions are automatically taken from these wages; some $50 million in taxes is annually collected from migrant workers. As the *New York Times* noted, "A 1978 report by a House committee showed that the typical illegal alien worker in San Diego County paid 17 percent of his wages in taxes, a much larger share than was paid by citizens earning the minimum wage."[21] But while paying so much into the tax system, the same worker receives next to nothing in the social benefits his or her contributions finance.

Bold and foolhardy indeed would be the "illegal" worker who appeared before the network of authorities overseeing government social programs like unemployment, food stamps, and welfare. In order to receive social services he or she would most likely have to prove citizenship; failure to do so could lead to swift deportation. Indeed, it is a well-established historical tradition for the INS to collaborate closely with the social welfare bureaucracy in those states receiving the most "illegal" immigrant workers.

A 1979 Labor Department study found over 75 percent of "undocumented" workers paying Social Security and income taxes, but only 0.5 percent receiving welfare benefits, and 1 percent using food stamps—quite a subsidy to the US economy. An anonymous questionnaire administered to more than 300 Michoacán migrant workers in the early 1980s revealed similar patterns and confirmed that the migrants rarely receive unemployment or health care benefits.[22]

Indeed, one hidden reason the US government has allowed an increased "illegal" migratory flow during the recent economic crisis is that the Social Security payments contributed by migrant workers account for a significant chunk of that system's trust fund—up to $80 billion a year by some estimates. In the words of a recent Ford Foundation report, "As more whites reach Social Security age, their support will depend on Social Security taxes paid by an increasingly Hispanic and black workforce."[23] In the absence of immigrant workers' contributions, the fund would be depleted even more rapidly than the current financing schedule suggests. According to US Census Bureau projections, Social Security arrangements will be almost impossible to sustain by early in the next century, when people over age sixty-five will make up one-fifth of the population. That is because active workers pay for most of the retirement benefits and by 2030 the ratio of active workers for every Social Security beneficiary will have dropped from the 1984 level of 5.3 to 2.7.

Union dues present a similar disadvantage to immigrant workers. Some 10 percent of all Mexican immigrant workers have joined unions in the United States, and the number may be rising as some mainline unions hard hit by falling membership and declining dues rush to sign up the unorganized (see Chapter 7). But while the union leaders take the dues to fill their emptying coffers, the economic crisis and unaggressive union leadership have combined to produce little or no improvement in the living or work conditions of most union members. The short-term, come-and-go Mexican migrants who pay union dues usually do not receive the long-term services those dues provide, such as pensions, hospitalization, retirement or strike benefits, and the like. Meanwhile, those immigrants who do not join unions benefit employers because they work for lower wages than do their unionized counterparts.

When all these considerations are added to the fact that migrants spend an average of 60 percent or more of their wages in the United States, their contribution to the American economy becomes obvious. *In general, US citizens benefit disproportionately from not just the migrants' labor and consumption but all the tax and benefit program checkoffs paid by immigrant workers—the very opposite of what Americans have been told and still generally believe.*

Technology, Immigrants, and Labor: "High-Tech but Low-Pay"

The widespread assumption of the 1970s that the technological revolution brought about by computers, telecommunications, cyber-

136 · Outlaws in the Promised Land

netics, and robotics would spur economic growth and fuller employment has exploded into dust in the 1980s. So has the view that the tailing off of the birth rate in the more industrialized countries and the consequent shortage of labor would further contribute to fuller employment, or low unemployment, in America and Europe.

Although high-tech industries have more than doubled the number of their employees in the past fifteen years, they have not constituted the sector creating the most new jobs in the United States. By far, the greatest job growth has occurred in low-skilled, low-paid service, maintenance, and white-collar occupations, particularly restaurant, health, sanitation, retail trade, and personal services. Many of these areas of expanding employment opportunity offer such rock-bottom wages that only temporary or newly arrived immigrants will sign on. Most citizens and long-term residents can do better economically by resorting to established street hustles in familiar territory or combining "underground economy" work and welfare.

From 1960 to 1982 the number of waiters, valets, maids, cooks, security guards, and others employed in services nearly doubled to become 13.8 percent of America's workforce. During the same period the white-collar share of the labor force rose from 43.4 percent to 53.8 percent, while that of blue-collar factory workers fell from 18.1 percent to 12.7 percent. The fastest-growing segments of the white-collar job market were the lowest-paid ones. For example, clerical employees accounted for 18.5 percent of white-collar jobs in 1982 compared with 14.8 percent in 1960.[24]

The growth in low-paid white-collar and services work has been closely related to the growth of the public sector: from 1960 to 1975, one out of every three new jobs was in the public sector, mostly in state and local government. Although the character of white-collar work varies according to profession, type of job, and other factors, it is widely recognized that, in the words of a 1972 federal study, "The office today, where work is segmented and authoritarian, is often a factory. For a growing number of jobs, there is little to distinguish them but the color of the worker's collar."[25] The same pattern is apparent among professionals and managers, who find themselves more and more in the role of employees.

The overall trend is one of "de-skilling" jobs so that anyone can do them. This is true in both highly mechanized and labor-intensive areas of work. Making laborers easily replaceable discourages demands for improved wages and benefits. It also serves to divide workers from one another and to increase the sense of alienation and helplessness many feel. Rotating workers, laying some off here, hiring others there, adds a fluid quality to the reserve army of unemployed and irregularly employed labor, expanding the number of people passing through its ranks. Together with increased immigration, the de-skilling, segmentation, and rotation of jobs is a general job market trend.

New technologies tend to segment and control labor, and not merely to increase production. Indeed, as labor sociologist Martin Oppenheimer has pointed out, "Technological advances segment work and thereby control workers, but conversely the control of workers creates imperatives for the development of new technology that will aid in such control."[26] The word processing "pool," the computer operator "pool," the computerization of work supervision, standards, and paychecks—all typify this new "high-tech" reality of controlling the ever more segmented and alienated workforce. Not surprisingly, as BLS and other statistics summarized by Oppenheimer show, labor productivity continues to go down in the face of this process, even though total production may rise.

Through the use of new technology we are being promised a new golden age of abundance and freedom. Best-selling authors John Naisbitt in *Megatrends* (1982) and Naisbitt and Patricia Aburdene in *Reinventing the Corporation* (1985) argue that America is becoming a "new information society" in which computers and satellite communications will usher in an age of "self-management" and a "democracy" of numerous self-sufficient enterprises based on small business values and "something for everyone."[27] These predictions are made in the face of a growing income gap between rich and poor and despite the increasing exclusivity of the technological dreamland, open only to the most highly trained and specialized workers.

Naisbitt and Aburdene are correct in foreseeing the emergence of a large segment of the workforce that is "permanent part-time." But these permanent part-timers are not the "intrapreneurs" Naisbitt and Aburdene envision as working "for fun" while creating new blueprints for the future while clipping stock coupons in their new homes. Rather, the permanent part-timers are the millions of less fortunate members of society, many of whom are immigrant workers who have managed to eke out a living—in spite of unprecedented levels of unemployment—by accepting low-paid part-time work. By the deepest point of the economic crisis in 1982, when 12 million American workers were unemployed (more than 11 percent of the workforce, including almost half of the nation's mainline factory workers), the technological revolution of the "new information society" had done little to create jobs for the millions of smokestack industry workers laid off from outdated plants unable to compete on the world market.

The introduction of more refined technologies has been accompanied by the transfer of many jobs to areas of low labor cost—including third world countries, where much of the publishing industry, for one, farms out its typesetting work. Even when large numbers of low-wage Chicanos and Mexican immigrants are hired by a high-tech firm, as in the case of the 1,700 recently unionized employees of Atari in Los Angeles, there is no guarantee that the company will not shut down and "run away." Atari did this in 1982, moving its manufacturing plants to Hong Kong and Taiwan. It claimed the move was necessitated by declining profits, even though its profits had risen from $80 million in 1980 to $287 million in 1981 and $324 million in 1982. Atari's real concerns were labor unionism, wages, and the *rate* of profit.[28] Thus, the economic crisis results in layoffs among high-tech workers as well as blue-collar factory workers, among immigrant workers as well as citizen workers.

The radical slowdown in the so-called economic recovery during the first half of 1985 was spurred by five consecutive months of reduced demand for business equipment like computers and a generalized weakness in the capital goods sector.[29] Indeed, as early as January 1985 the evening newscasts on American television were referring to "the new unemployment"—workers affected by 1984's wave of high-tech employee layoffs. On June 14, 1985, the nation's second-largest manufacturer of personal computers, Apple Computer Inc., announced it was laying off 1,200 employees—more than a fifth of its workforce.

"Silicon Valley" employers in northern California were laying off workers by the tens of thousands in 1985, causing economists to take note of the "depression" affecting the country's showcase high-tech region. Apparently, computer and other business machine manufacturers had overproduced, and many enterprises were discovering that computers did not save as much as expected on labor costs. San Francisco mayor Dianne Feinstein noted on a CBS national newscast in June 1985 that even though her city had spent large sums of money on computerizing its administration, its labor payroll had remained just as large.

The overall result has been unstable levels of employment and a distinct trend toward impoverished "permanent part-time work" that has affected not only mainline production workers but many middle-management "yuppies" as well. As Naisbitt concedes, whenever technology is introduced, both production and service jobs tend to become "de-skilled," while engineering and supervisory jobs become both fewer in number and more demanding. This reality is a long way from Naisbitt and Aburdene's utopian view of highly paid part-time work as "fun."[30]

No matter how high-tech jobs are defined, at most they account for only 3 percent of the US economy's employed workforce. Many of them are in low-skilled, poorly paid assembly work. Ironically, high-tech is the one area of production that, in its middle and lower echelons, most lends itself to the use of cheap immigrant labor. A 1984 *New York Times* "National Employment Report" acknowledged that "high technology has not saved the American economy" and accounts "for only a tiny fraction of the nation's total employment." Even the most optimistic projections show that by 1995 only one new job in twenty-five will be "technology-oriented." The *Times* special report quotes Massachusetts Institute of Technology professor David L. Birch as saying that 12 million to 14 million jobs must be created in the 1980s but only "4 or 5 percent of those will come in the areas that most people define as 'high technology.' "

Companies that produce the high-tech goods used in industry are themselves highly automated. Robots do the welding at Cincinnati Milacron, a maker of robotics equipment. Computer science college graduates no longer have much chance to start their careers as computer programmers; most, in fact, now start as computer operators, a task requiring little professional training. The *Times* special report concludes, "In fact, high technology's biggest contribution to the job market may prove to be indirect, in the service sector," citing American Express and Federal Express as "highly computerized and rapidly expanding businesses that are also major employers."[31] What the *Times* neglects to mention, however, is that the new jobs are usually the low-paid, easily rotatable ones that benefit employers but make life for working people more insecure and precarious.

It is becoming common knowledge that the introduction of high technology profits the corporations while generally hurting labor. For instance, of the estimated 20 million office workers in the United States, 80 percent of them women, less than 10 percent are union-organized. Approximately 7 million of them now work at video display terminals, and by 1990 the number is expected to pass 40 million. It is difficult for workers to organize or strike in such conditions, when a flick of a switch can shift the work from one city to another.

In addition, the new technologies make it possible to farm jobs out to individuals working at home. They accept lower wages and usually are not unionized. Such "clerical homework," consisting of rote tasks anyone can learn quickly, has become more and more common. Blue Cross/Blue Shield, J. C. Penney Company, and American Express have all begun shipping out work in this fashion. The same is happening in light assembly work. Apple Computer, for example, "jobs out" to a subcontractor who in turn distributes the work to a largely female home workforce.[32]

Wherever required skill levels are low or quickly learned, employers in almost all sectors of the economy have become increasingly interested in hiring immigrant workers. Thus we find immigrants performing a great variety of tasks throughout the nation. While in Los Angeles the majority of Mexican immigrants who find work are employed in manufacturing and services, in New York City immigrant labor is spread through a more diverse mix of activities. There the immigrant may establish a family business, usually a tiny vegetable stand or grocery store; drive a taxi; or work in apparel and other manufacturing sweatshops (the number of which almost tripled in the 1970s and early 1980s) or in the fast-growing "services and miscellaneous" sector (which expanded by 148,500 jobs from 1977 to 1983).

In California, on the other hand, many Mexican immigrants have been finding work in newly technified and modernized production systems. In Silicon Valley, for example, prior to its 1985 depression, the semiconductor industry was employing some 200,000 workers, 85 percent of them women. About 40 percent of the assembly workers were Mexican, other Latinos, or Asian. The wage hovered around $3.50 an hour, and only 5 percent of the workforce was organized. In Los Angeles, some 200 so-called undocumented, unskilled Mexicans run the machinery and sweep the floors for Electrosound Company, which produces 25 percent of the phonograph records US consumers enjoy in their homes; and 25 Mexican "illegals" at Tigart Industries in Alhambra operate its new sophisticated machinery. In both cases, the immigrants are almost the entire labor force.[33]

Population and Job Market Changes

As the June 23, 1980, *Business Week* observed, "The US will need immigrants to buttress the labor supply if the economy is to grow." Unlike Mexico, the United States by all estimates faces a labor shortage for generations to come. According to the US Census Bureau, declining numbers of US workers will be entering the labor force—some 7.1 million fewer people between the ages of 15 and 24 in 1990 than in 1980—and the decline will continue into the next century. The Census Bureau's projections, based on a "middle" series of assumptions about birth rates, death rates, immigration, and other factors, show the percentage of people under 18 years of age residing in the United States steadily dropping, from 26.7 percent of the population in 1983 to 22.9 percent in 2010. During the same time span, the median age of US residents will rise from 30.9 to 38.4 years. Meanwhile, Mexico's population, facing massive unemployment and underemployment at miserable wages, is expected to double in size by the year 2010.

Diminishing US labor force additions in the face of an increasing need for job stimulation and economic growth do not spell upward pressures on wages and benefits (as Naisbitt and Aburdene mistakenly assume). Recent experience indicates just the opposite. Average private sector nonfarm wages and salaries dropped by more than 6 percent in the 1980–84 period as nonunion wages edged ahead of union wages by more than a percentage point in early 1985.

According to the Bureau of Labor Statistics (BLS), between March 1979 and March 1984 jobs shrank by 2.4 million in the relatively well-paying areas of manufacturing, construction, and mining, but they increased by more than 4 million in the generally lower-wage service areas, including wholesale and retail trade and personal, business, and financial services. Real wages in all service areas declined about 11 percent between 1970 and 1980 (a time when blue-collar manufacturing wages rose 2 percent), dropping many employed people into the official "poverty" category.[34] Thus, for growing numbers of Americans, Naisbitt's futuristic dream society of plenty of jobs and money for everyone was more like a present-day nightmare of less and less to go around.

This trend accelerated throughout the first half of the 1980s. And for the rest of the century, the BLS projects most new job openings in such low-wage occupations as clerk, secretary, security guard, custodian, fast food worker, nurses' aide, and so on. The expansion of low-wage jobs coincides with the rise in numbers of newly arriving immigrant workers.

Projections are only estimates, and there can be a significant margin of error. Census Bureau projections show that after the year 2000 one-quarter of all Americans will be nonwhite, compared with 14.5 percent in 1982. Yet with the recent rise in the number of Latinos entering the country, most of whom are considered nonwhite, the 1982 figure seems far too low. In other words, the importation of foreign, nonwhite labor has already moved into high gear and is unlikely to be reversed in the near future.

It is almost certain that the second-largest minority in the United States is now or will soon be Latinos, not blacks. Many Latin American workers, fearful of the INS and other authorities, go uncounted by census takers. Justifiable concern about racism and "legal" status keeps many Latinos invisible. The Catholic Church's Ad Hoc Committee for Hispanic Affairs chose not to cooperate with the US Census Bureau in the taking of the 1980 census on the grounds that the confidentiality of the information could not be guaranteed.

Thus, the 1980 census data are definitely incomplete when it comes to the number of so-called Hispanics. That census tabulated 6.4 percent of the population "Hispanic" and 11.7 percent black, with the former group growing four times as fast as the latter between 1970 and 1980.

Subsequent Census Bureau estimates showed around 17 million Latinos in 1984, not counting more than 3 million Puerto Ricans living in Puerto Rico. Of the 17 million, about 60 percent were Mexican (double the number of Mexicans in 1970), and about 14.6 million were US citizens, leaving a Census Bureau figure of 2.4 million "illegals"— probably a severe underestimate, since the median of the most common unofficial estimates of "illegals" is 7 million. Adding this figure to the number of "legal" Latinos gives 21.6 million. Subtracting a small percentage of "illegals" who are not Latino still yields a number very close to the estimated number of black Americans in 1984.

This dramatic new demographic reality, itself a significant part of the "fourth wave" of Mexican immigrant workers and Latin American political refugees in the 1970s and 1980s, is a very serious matter in the minds of the nation's most prominent racists. As already noted, former CIA director William Colby stated in 1978 that Mexican immigration would in future years represent a greater threat to the United States than would the Soviet Union. Conservative politicians like Senator

Alan Simpson (R-Wyo.), sponsor of the Simpson-Mazzoli immigration reform bill (see Chapter 8), have repeatedly claimed that Mexican immigration threatens a territorial and cultural "Quebec-ization" of the United States.

Anti-Mexican sentiment reminiscent of the days of lynching or beating up on "the greasers" was—perhaps unwittingly—inflamed by the nation's two leading presidential candidates during their second presidential debate, October 21, 1984. Both Walter Mondale and Ronald Reagan accepted the basic premise of the question asked about the Simpson-Mazzoli bill, namely, whether "massive illegal immigration from economically collapsing countries . . . is the only real territorial threat to the American nation-state." Mondale's first words in response were "Ah, this is a very serious problem in our country and it has to be dealt with." To which Reagan added, "It is true our borders are out of control."

The very next question took this exaggerated form of anti-Mexican sentiment to its logical conclusion.

> Mr. President, the experts also say that the situation today is terribly different—quantitatively, qualitatively different— from what it has been in the past because of the gigantic population growth. For instance, Mexico's population will go from about 60 million today to 120 million at the turn of the century. Many of these people will be coming into the United States not as citizens but as illegal workers. You have repeatedly said recently that you believe that Armageddon, the destruction of the world, may be imminent in our times. Do you ever feel that we are in for an Armageddon or a situation, a time of anarchy, regarding the population explosion in the world?

In his reply, Reagan dodged the Armageddon issue and expressed what appeared to be genuine concern for a fair and just solution to the immigration issue.

> The problem of population growth is one here with regard to our immigration. And we have been the safety valve, whether we wanted to or not, with the illegal entry here; in Mexico, where their population is increasing and they don't have an economy that can absorb them and provide the jobs. And this

is what we're trying to work out, not only to protect our own borders but to have some kind of fairness and recognition of that problem.

This manner of addressing the question is typical among politicians who discuss immigration. Reagan's shrugging off of government responsibility with the phrase "we have been the safety valve, whether we wanted to or not" reinforces the message that there are no Americans involved in bringing Mexican workers into the country but rather that some out-of-control force is at work—yellow peril? brown hordes? Yet all researchers agree that US employers historically have very much, in the president's words, "wanted to" allow the illegal entry of Mexican workers and indeed have solicited it.

Because of the economic crisis, the dual role of such workers expresses itself with greater sharpness than otherwise. The immigrants are blamed for hard times ("our borders are out of control"), and yet they are urged to keep entering in order to maintain failing enterprises or to staff new ones.

As we have seen, both as a result of the crisis and as a major part of employers' strategy to solve it, America's job market has in recent years been transformed from one of relative job permanence and steady pay raises to one of job rotation, moonlighting or extra hours of work on the side, part-time work at low wages, subminimum wages for youth, and dual-"career" families or multiple wage earners per family. Accompanying these trends has been a steady restraint in wage increments, which have failed to keep up with the cost of living.

Few observers would quibble with Harvard Business School professor D. Quinn Mills's description of labor union restraint on wage demands during the modest economic "recovery" of 1983–84 as "amazing." A BLS wage report issued October 26, 1984, showed an average wage hike of 2.5 percent in labor contracts negotiated for 1.4 million unionized workers in the first nine months of 1984, compared with a 4.2 annual rate of inflation as measured by the Consumer Price Index. These figures did not include the much lower 1.25 percent wage hike negotiated by the United Auto Workers for 350,000 members with the General Motors Corporation. Mills claimed that the antiunion mood of government had led union leaders to moderate wage demands in hopes of saving jobs.[35]

Yet the practices of mainline union leaders in the 1970s and early 1980s—wage givebacks, no-strike pledges, and similar concessions to employers—have not stemmed the tide of union decline. A BLS survey released on February 7, 1986, found that union membership among young workers had dropped dramatically in 1985.

It is the complex web of labor, technology, and immigration trends affecting the character and availability of work in America during a period of prolonged economic crisis that is rapidly producing the outlines of a future two-tiered society separating rich from poor. The logic and politics of the situation are inexorably making immigrant labor an ever more central concern.

Toward a Two-Tiered Society

The 1960s trend of growing income inequality among wage and salary earners grew in the 1970s and 1980s, giving rise to the recognizable contours of a future two-tiered American society dividing a small number of well-off people from the rest of the population. A two-tiered society dominated by a handful of corporate magnates who command the loyalties of large numbers of affluent managers and highly qualified professionals is already forming. If present trends continue, this corporate/professional minority will eventually control a vast majority of poorly paid blue- and white-collar employees moving in and out of, or on the margins of, an ever larger and more international pool of available labor augmented by Mexican and other immigrants. Racial and gender discrimination components of this two-tier trend are already placing more and more blacks, Latinos, and women into the lower tier.

In income terms, many "middle-class" people are also being driven into the lower tier. According to a Federal Reserve Board study released in 1984, the bottom 70 percent of all families received 43 percent of total family income in 1969 but only 38 percent in 1982. Almost all their losses were gains for the most affluent 10 percent of American families, whose income share rose from 29 percent to 33 percent.

Income disparity is most striking at the bottom of the social pyramid. The poorest fifth of America's income recipients actually obtain a lesser share of total national income than the poorest fifths of such "backward" countries as India, Sri Lanka, and South Korea. Of course, the total income pie is larger in the United States than in the Asian countries, and the depths of American poverty are not as appalling. This, however, is small consolation to the 25 million Americans who have no health insurance or the parents of the 40 percent of the nation's infants and toddlers not yet fully vaccinated. Just since 1979 the number of Americans living below the federal poverty line has jumped by 20 percent.[36]

The much-heralded "rainbow coalition" promoted by the Reverend Jesse Jackson and others may not yet be a powerful political force, but it is already shaping up as a powerless tier. In 1982, one in seven adults and one in five children were living below the *official* poverty line. By 1984, the number of people in this category had risen to 35.3 million. Many poverty watchers, recognizing that the government's poverty criteria border on starvation, have put the number of poor at 50 million.

According to a congressional study released in May 1985, an extra 8 children per 100 were added to the poverty population from 1973 to 1983, lifting the child poverty rate to 22.2 per 100, the highest since the mid-1960s. Other than children, the largest group among the poor were female workers who provided the sole support of their families. Several commentators have referred to this trend as "feminization of poverty." Even studies claiming to show an improvement in women's wages in the twentieth century, such as a Rand Corporation study publicized in late 1984, have pointed out that the poverty-induced influx of more women into the job market has dropped the average 1983 woman's wage to 53 cents to the male dollar.[37]

Unemployment rates among black and Latino youth are so high, and have risen so steadily over such a long period of time, that a sizable portion of one generation has stopped looking for regular employment altogether. By 1984 some 78 percent of black youth in New York City were not finishing high school. An official 35.7 percent of the nation's black population was living below the poverty line—including 50 percent of all black children.

For the nation's Latinos, the situation is little different. In New York City their poverty rate is 10.1 points higher than that for blacks, while nationally it is only 5.7 points lower. In terms of median household per capita income, the Spanish-speaking family earns less than two-thirds what a white family earns and only a few percentage points more than what a black family earns. But official census figures, as already noted, omit large numbers of the Spanish-speaking, both US citizens and "illegal" immigrants. Many of the "omitted" are especially impoverished. Moreover, even by official figures, the family income of Latinos has been dropping more rapidly since 1972 than that of either whites or blacks. One recent census estimate shows the high school dropout rate among Latinos to be *twice* that of blacks.[38]

The nation's lowest-paying jobs, more and more filled by immigrants willing and anxious to accept half the normal wage for unskilled labor, hold no economic attraction for black or Latino youth—whom most employers, out of deep-set racism, refuse to hire in any case. Meanwhile, newly laid-off workers continue to have difficulty finding any employment other than in services, retail trade, and high-tech—at half their former wages.

The plummeting of more and more whites into the ranks of the nonwhite underclasses has not produced rainbow unity so much as racial friction. A 1980 *New York Times* survey indicated a growing negative attitude against nonwhites among those whites who most feared unemployment.[39]

The two-tier trend predates the Reagan presidency. The increase of 11 million jobs between 1973 and 1979 was largely in services and retail trade. The middle-income midriff of the population ("Middle America") was shrinking—not from dieting, but from economic hard times and basic structural faults in the American economy. Markets that had earlier boomed for this midriff section also began to contract, and so workers producing for "middle-class" consumers began losing their jobs as well.

The downward spiral from the "affluent fifties" became a plummeting fall in the seventies and eighties, with weaker and weaker updrafts of economic "recovery." BLS income figures for 1978–83 showed nearly 10 percent of the nation's working population falling from "intermediate" to "low" income; the proportion receiving "intermediate" income dropped from 55 to 42 percent. Michael Harrington's recent book, *The New American Poverty* (1984), calls these people the "reserve army of the future poor"—those with "good" jobs in the 1960s and 1970s, but now the group most vulnerable to the economy's underlying structural faults.[40]

As economists Gar Alperovitz and Jeff Faux point out about middle-income workers whom they refer to as "the middle class,"

> There is growing evidence that the combined effect of slow growth, automation, and the shift to services is depleting the middle class itself. Between 1965 and 1975 the number of people earning incomes in the middle range—roughly 20 percent below average to 20 percent above—shrank by 23 percent. . . . The accelerated loss of manufacturing jobs since 1975 has aggravated the situation.[41]

Labor analyst Jeremy Brecher, among others, concurs about the overall trend in the job market.

> The majority of workers will work in high-turnover occupations with no security, in which they are easily replaceable, frequently unemployed, or only employed part time. Middle-income workers will become increasingly [scarce] as more and more workers come to receive a "common labor" wage rate at or slightly above the minimum wage. Despite mass unemployment, the labor force will continue to grow due to continuing population growth, immigration, and a rising rate of labor force participation due to the poverty-induced need of women and children to go to work.[42]

From would-be social planners like Felix Rohatyn to free-enterprise monetarists like Federal Reserve head Paul Volcker, the nation's major economic gurus agree that the "shrinking middle" is a prevalent trend—and usually commend it as the only way to stimulate a sustained economic recovery. Ever since he oversaw the financial bailout of New York City, financier Rohatyn has advocated measures that add up to cutting the standard of living of the intermediate classes in order to obtain more capital for subsidizing big business and the economic infrastructure. These measures include new gasoline taxes, cuts in farm price supports, paring back Social Security, and so on. Banker Volcker frankly stated the approach of the new two-tiered era in 1979: "The standard of living of the average American has to decline. I don't think you can escape that."[43] The Reagan presidency has based its probusiness measures on this premise, aggravating the economic evaporation of the middle-income group in America.

Even such probusiness organs of the mass media as *Business Week* suspected prior to Reagan's presidency that state giveaways to big business and a crackdown on labor unionism (union deauthorization cases filed before the National Labor Relations Board tripled between 1966 and 1979) might not be enough to generate sustained economic recovery. In a special 1980 issue entitled "The Reindustrialization of America," *Business Week* acknowledged that the decline in real wages made labor so much cheaper than capital that the incentive for investment in more productive plant and equipment was undercut. As President Reagan's budget director, David Stockman, confessed in the *Atlantic Monthly*, he had abandoned the supply-side theory of economics even before submitting the first Reagan budget, knowing that it was no more than a giveaway to big business.[44]

"Inflation is still very high, growth is low, and the generation of employment is insufficient. . . . The government is seriously concerned about the drop in the standard of living of the lower and middle classes." These could be the words of a president of any nation. In fact, they were spoken by Mexico's President Miguel de la Madrid during his State of the Nation Address on September 1, 1984. For all practical purposes, Mexico is already a two-tiered society, with the vanishing "middle" clinging to its presumably comfortable status in vain. A likely consequence in the immigration area will be a growing influx of better-educated Mexicans into the United States, a trend that immigration researchers say has already commenced.

Since 1982, because of repeated devaluations of the peso, the average Mexican worker's hourly wage has dropped from about six times lower to fifteen times lower than that of the American worker in the same job. The pressure on Mexican workers is so grave, their job security so fragile, that many who formerly advocated unions now hesitate to do so. They are scared of being fired and have seen that the unions were unable to defend their jobs over the past decade. A survey of workers in the border city of Ciudad Juárez in 1978 showed 60 percent wanting unions; in 1983, of 5,000 workers interviewed in the same city, not one desired a union.[45]

These trends practically assure the means employers in both nations have been seeking to recover from the economic crisis: a growing international reserve army of labor, workforces experiencing declining real wages, and fading labor union strength—the ideal circumstances for increased immigration, runaway shops, and recovered *rates* of profit.

The Growing Need to Regulate the Flow of Immigrant Workers

One prominent economist, Clark W. Reynolds of Stanford University's Food Research Institute, has warned that curtailing immigration could produce "aggregate shortfalls of 18 to 33 million workers" by the year 2000, with the "brunt of the shortages" being borne by "the unskilled and semiskilled job categories." According to Reynolds, "Without substantial immigration, there will simply not be enough productive labor . . . to sustain even a modest 3 percent rate of output growth." Attributing at least 10 percent of the annual growth in the supply of

American labor in the early 1980s to Mexican immigration, Reynolds argues that the need for such migrant workers must intensify in coming years if the United States "is to maintain its position in the international economy." Thus, even disregarding the US interest in Mexico's abundant oil supplies (see Chapter 6), Reynolds concludes that quite possibly "in the future the United States will need Mexico as much or more than Mexico will need the United States."[46]

Assuming a century-long continuation of the present US fertility rate of 1.8, the effect of 1 million immigrants a year would be to create a labor force 70 percent larger than it would be without immigration, according to Leon F. Bouvier, director of the private Population Reference Bureau in Washington, D.C. "In other words," says Bouvier, "two out of every five persons in the US labor force would be post-1980 immigrants and their descendants."[47]

By the mid-1970s, therefore, many employers were pressing for measures to control the quantity and quality of temporary Mexican workers. They quietly got behind policy changes and new legislative proposals that would regulate the migratory flow and provide a reliable supply of pliant, low-paid Mexican immigrant labor.

Such regulation is not intended to stop the flow but rather to assure it. It is also designed to bring immigrant labor to heel and reduce worker militancy. The type of regulation begun in the 1970s under President Jimmy Carter—all in the name of "regaining control of our borders"—was meant to curtail spontaneous worker eruptions and possible economic chaos arising from the unpredictable migratory flow aggravated by Mexico's collapsing economy. Above all, it was designed to prevent immigrant workers from further organizing and converting "bad" jobs into "good" ones by means of unionization and strikes.

Thus, under President Carter, the Border Patrol began receiving military training in counterinsurgency techniques. The US started to construct what Mexican migrant workers dubbed the "tortilla curtain," a border fence many feet high made out of spiked steel wire but easily cut through. President Carter's secretary of labor, Ray Marshall, unrealistically proposed closing the border on the "liberal" premise that to avoid the exploitation of "undocumented" workers, they must be excluded or deported. These impractical "tough" tactics drew the predictable rhetorical and hypocritical wrath of the Mexican government while serving notice on the migrants. A special commission was named to draw up proposals that would more adequately deal with the problem of border regulation. From the work of that commission came the seeds of proposed legislation like the Simpson-Mazzoli bill, examined in Chapter 8.

Meanwhile, paramilitary units of the Ku Klux Klan roamed the border attacking Mexican immigrants. The INS in early 1981, and with greater intensity in subsequent years, stepped up the pace of factory roundups of alleged "illegals" for deportation. In May 1982 a major press fanfare was orchestrated from Washington around "Operation Jobs," when thousands of Mexicans were rounded up for deportation (most returning to work after a few days). Joaquin Avila, president of the prestigious Mexican American Legal Defense and Educational Fund (MALDEF, the US-citizen Mexicans' equivalent of the NAACP), told the press, "We're appalled at the raids. This will seriously affect the rights of Hispanics when they seek employment."

By September 1982 deportations of Mexicans were numbering about 1,000 a day and generating tensions in Mexican neighborhoods, whose older residents compared the deportation drive to 1954's "Operation Wetback." The historical comparison is significant: then, as now, mass deportations accompanied mass importations of Mexican workers—and, as we have seen, US business cannot prosper without both.

The situation in the United States was thus beginning to resemble the one in Europe, where immigrant worker groups spearheaded some of the most militant protest activities in labor's ranks while leading politicians and the press orchestrated a public racist outcry. But unlike the European scene, where deportations could more easily be made permanent and there was no immediate need for a fresh influx of cheap immigrant labor, the US situation centered on a neighbor group whose labor was sorely needed and whose destinies for almost 150 years had been inseparably linked to those of their relatives and other working people across a porous border in the "host" country (half of which was originally Mexico). The international ramifications of US immigration policy were therefore much more immediate and delicate than those of northern European policies on foreign immigrant labor.

The very resorting to Mexican immigrant labor while increasing the tempo of deportations—the accelerated spinning of the border's "revolving door"—inevitably led to strains in US relations with Mexico. Here too Mexican immigration became a pivotal concern affecting not just US-Mexico relations but the issues of war and peace rumbling from Central America, the Caribbean, and indeed all Latin America.

6

"Good Neighbors": The Migrant Worker Issue in US-Mexico Relations

"I think that people in the long run are less concerned about reports of [our] mining Nicaraguan harbors than they are about the danger of creating a wave of immigration into this country. . . . If we have another Cuba in Central America, Mexico will have a big problem and we're going to have a massive wave of immigration."
—William J. Casey, Director of the CIA, *US News & World Report*, April 15, 1984

"Nationalism is a phenomenon that exists throughout the world. As for the nationalism of Mexico, that nation opens its doors to foreigners, as it always has done in the past. So nationalism is no problem in Mexico."
—Henry Ford II, December 2, 1970

In spite of a long history of US military and other forms of intervention in Mexico's internal affairs, each new US president projects an image of united "good neighbors" by making a summit meeting with the president of Mexico his first order of diplomatic business in Latin America. Often he schedules this meeting even before he is sworn into office, and he repeats it frequently during his next four years.

More than other semi-industrialized giants like Brazil and Argentina or oil-rich nations like Venezuela, Mexico represents for US economic and political interests a veritable linchpin in the profitable edifice of global empire constructed since World War II. Mexico has

152

both industry and oil, as well as the most precious commodity of all—inexpensive labor power close at hand. From 1945 to 1978 US companies and banks invested an estimated $150 billion abroad, creating an overseas commercial empire that by 1980 was generating half a trillion dollars in sales, $20 billion in profits per year, and one-quarter of the world's GNP. Latin America's share of that investment is about 20 percent. Together with Brazil and Venezuela, Mexico accounts for over half of the investments in Latin America. The average 18.3 percent rate of return on US investments in Mexico remains the highest in all Latin America.[1] It is not mere cynicism that underlies Henry Ford's casual insult to Mexican nationalism in the quotation introducing this chapter; rather, it is the habit of years of profitable investment in the Mexican economy, of watching Mexico, in Ford's words, "open its doors to foreigners."

Not coincidentally, in light of the recent rise in importance of Mexican immigrant labor to the US economy and Mexico's growing need for an "escape valve," the two nations' presidents have chosen various significant border locations for their recent meetings. These border *abrazos* (embraces) have enriched the symbol of "good neighbors" while further disguising the border's porous quality. Border summit conferences have served to bring to the forefront of public consciousness the issues of immigration, drug smuggling, free flows of capital investment, and the importance of Mexico in America's future.

For some people, the sight of two presidents meeting at the border and exchanging gifts of pistols, saddles, or horses may overshadow the "tortilla curtain," Ku Klux Klan posses, and INS helicopters and loudspeakers. But in the eyes of many Mexicans on both sides of the border, presidential *abrazos* are as fraudulent as an embrace of the two Germanies' leaders at the Berlin Wall.

The United States wants Mexican oil, inexpensive Mexican labor power, a continued high rate of return on US investments, and Mexican acceptance of US foreign policy in the Caribbean Basin and the rest of Latin America. A lightweight power in the military and economic shadow of its big neighbor to the north, highly dependent on US trade and loans, Mexico has only a few bargaining chips to place on the table of bilateral relations: abundant reserves of oil and inexpensive labor power, potential constraints on foreign investment, and an "independent" foreign policy.

Mexico's space for maneuvering has diminished in recent years, particularly in the case of oil. Mexico's independent and anti-US-militarism foreign policy has not deterred increased troop deployments and stepped-up US military intervention in either Central America or the Caribbean. The other factors in Mexico's maneuvering—its debt, US investments, and Mexican migrant labor—are inexorably intertwined with the future of Latin America's revolutions and Mexico's oil. The fate of each bargaining chip affects that of the others.

On the international chessboard of Mexico's bilateral relations with the United States, the Mexican government would like to pin US capital's queen with its migrant labor pawn, oil queen, and foreign policy castle. Ultimately, Mexico would like to use the checkmating potential of migrant labor power by telling the US king that the migrant workers will no longer be allowed out of Mexico, thereby threatening to deprive the US economy of one of its main, if unrecognized, pillars of support. But Mexico's oil queen has been violated, its foreign policy castle has not stopped US aggression, and its migrant pawn has raced across the border in quest of economic survival.

For its part, the US government also would like to use the migrant workers as a pawn. It never fails to remind the Mexican government that without access to the US labor market, the migrants would remain in Mexico, where—their wages and employment opportunities being much worse—they might revolt. Unfortunately, as Mexico's space for diplomatic maneuver shrinks, the fundamental national and international issue of the migrants' human and labor rights gets swept aside by the false assumption that they are "an immigration issue" and therefore an internal US matter.

Mexico: The Threatened "Domino"

More and more Mexicans are becoming leery of President Reagan's repeated references to their nation as "the ultimate domino" in a vague row of nations positioned between "communism" and the "American way of life."[2] In his view El Salvador could "join Cuba and Nicaragua in spreading fresh violence to Guatemala, Honduras, even Costa Rica." From there, the violent tumbling of dominoes might lead to Mexico. And it is only a short distance from the Mexican border through the southeast corridor to Washington, D.C.—as Reagan again warned the American public in a nationally televised address in April 1984.

The hyperbolic vision of millions of immigrants and refugees flooding the United States provides one justification for a bellicose foreign policy in Central America—and a clarion call for an overhaul of US immigration law (see Chapter 8). As President Reagan said to a group of Central American businessmen in a major foreign policy address, March 25, 1985, he sees a real danger of "tens of millions of refugees streaming in a human tidal wave across the border."

Mexico's historical stance of semi-independence from the United States on foreign policy matters is subjected to extreme pressure by both Republicans and Democrats, who view Mexico as vital to US "national security interests" and who say they will not tolerate "another Cuba" in Central America. The phrase "another Cuba" is understood by most Americans to mean "communism." In actual practice, however, it means any nationalist revolution that undermines, or threatens to undermine, traditional US economic influence.

Intolerance of nationalistic revolutions is what produced the United States military invasions of Mexico in 1914 and 1915. At that time, President Woodrow Wilson's secretary of state, William Jennings Bryan, was honest enough to acknowledge that the goal of US foreign policy was "to prevent revolution," even though he sugared the interventionist pill with the humanitarian sentiment that the goal was also "to promote education."[3] With the former goal in mind, "to prevent revolution," the US military intervened again and again in other Latin American nations during subsequent decades, including Guatemala in 1954, Cuba in the 1961 Bay of Pigs invasion, the Dominican Republic in 1965, Grenada in October 1983, and Nicaragua several times, most recently during the not-so-secret "secret war" of the early 1980s.

The 1984 Kissinger Commission report on Central America and the Caribbean Basin acknowledges the United States' historic role against revolution. It points out the frequency of US interventions to quell popular revolt and adds that "the questionable practices followed by the [US] fruit companies in those early years, together with the power they wielded over weak governments, did a lot to create the fear of 'economic imperialism.' "

Mexico's attempt to maintain a semblance of independence from the United States by interpreting the Central American peoples' recent uprisings as only marginally connected to the so-called East-West conflict is a source of immense irritation to US policymakers, especially since the Mexican government's 1977 announcement of newly discovered oil reserves.

With the heating up of events in Central America, public attention given to the immigration issue has also increased. Almost two million political refugees from El Salvador, Honduras, and Guatemala have flooded into southern Mexico and in many cases all the way northward into the United States, usually "illegally." Mexico's 1981 recognition of Salvadoran guerrillas as a legitimate political force in El Salvador, together with its leadership in the Contadora group attempting to make peace in Central America, has focused its bilateral relations with the United States on the tides of battle in El Salvador, Guatemala, and other Central American hotspots. These conflagration points in turn have become powderkegs for wider regional use.

Both historically and today, Nicaragua and Cuba are good weathervanes of US will to intervene in Latin America. President Reagan has declared on several occasions that the United States is no longer bound by the international agreement ending the Cuban missile crisis of October 1962, which prohibits the United States from invading Cuba. Reagan's repeated rejections of the agreement strongly imply that he is considering a military adventure in Cuba. Indeed, like the Nicaraguans, the Cuban people have already begun constructing underground shelters and preparing for a long-term guerrilla war against an occupying army. Because the Soviets view the 1962 missile crisis agreement as still binding, any further spreading of regional war threatens to engulf the entire world in nuclear flames.

The Oil-rich Domino

Given the intertwining of all major issues in US-Mexican bilateral relations, the issue of Mexican immigrant labor is part of a larger whole. Inexorably, the immigrant issue is drawn into ever-widening negotiations on foreign policy matters that go far beyond it: US access to Mexican oil, warfare in the Caribbean Basin, and ultimately the survival of all humankind.

For the US government, the oil issue is paramount. In August 1980, in one of his last public addresses, Enrique Alvarez Córdoba, president of the Salvadoran Democratic Revolutionary Front, informed a group at the Riverside Church in New York City that during his just-concluded visit to Washington, D.C., officials of the Carter administration in the State Department had told him, "If El Salvador has a revolution, then the Mexican oilfields 150 miles away will be hit by revolution: we can't permit either." Three months later ultrarightist forces kidnapped

Alvarez and other members of the front's executive committee from a press conference in San Salvador and assassinated them, thereby eliminating the top civilian leadership of the Salvadoran revolution.

Secretary of energy and former CIA director James Schlesinger declared in 1977 that securing US oil supplies was "a *military* responsibility" (italics added). A CIA study entitled "The International Energy Situation: Outlook to 1985" anticipated that Mexico would provide the United States 4.5 million barrels of oil a day before 1985 (the actual figure in early 1985 was closer to 2 million). The proximity of Mexican oilfields to Guatemala and El Salvador soon became a cornerstone of the rationale for US military intervention in the Caribbean Basin. By 1980 Mexico was commonly acknowledged to be, in the words of American ambassador to Mexico Julian Nava, "a strategic and vital zone for US interests"—standard diplomatic language for an area subject to direct US military intervention.

The inner circle of Mexico's ruling political party, the PRI, had known since at least 1974 that Mexico was the Arabia of the Caribbean—but they realized that once the bureaucratic pirates broke open the oil treasure chest, the state, despite momentary stabilization, would soon be sacked of its cargo and drift toward disaster. They also recognized that US interference in Mexico's internal affairs would immediately intensify.

So they locked the oil story up in the presidential cabinet and chose instead, during the final years of the administration of President Luis Echeverría (1970–76), a rhetorical "nationalist" tack of verbally assaulting the TNCs for "looting" Mexico. Some of the business community, particularly large landholders and northern Mexico's powerful Monterrey Group of industrialists and bankers, along with key segments of the US investment and intelligence communities, took Echeverría's rhetoric seriously and mounted a "destabilization" campaign against his government. The resulting acts of US intervention, summarized in what follows, caused some Mexican authorities to suspect that the oil secret had leaked.

FBI documents obtained through the Freedom of Information Act show FBI director J. Edgar Hoover alleging President Echeverría to be "soft on communism." Operating through the office of the legal attaché in the American Embassy, the FBI carried out counterintelligence operations inside Mexico's trade unions, left-wing parties, and the government itself, infiltrating the Ministries of Interior (Mexico's equivalent of the FBI), Foreign Affairs, National Defense, and Public Education, and the attorney general's office. At one point, Hoover wrote the American Embassy's legal attaché of his "pleasure at the wave of night machine gunnings to divide subversive leaders" and congratulated him for the "detonation of strategic and effective bombs." Echeverría's attempts to build bridges with Mexican communities in the United States by currying favor with prominent Chicano leaders were partially countered by the FBI's routine planting of cocaine or other drugs in the leaders' cars in border areas.[4]

Aggravated by such "destabilization" tactics, polarization between Mexico's left and right increased. Prominent figures of the political establishment warned of the danger of Mexico's becoming engulfed in a process of gradual "Argentinization." The secretary general of the National University's center for political studies reported a struggle within the PRI between protofascist and democratic elements. During the final days of the Echeverría regime, many took seriously the unprecedented rumors of tanks moving in the streets of Mexico City in preparation for a military coup—a clear sign of the state's mounting crisis. (Similar rumors occurred again in 1982.)

At that point the PRI decided to play its "oil card." Announcing that he "found the nation on the edge of violence," incoming president López Portillo informed the world in 1977 that Mexico was sitting on not just ample reserves but a veritable sea of oil. The nation's economic and political problems were solved!

López Portillo planned to launch a campaign against corruption in government, finance economic recovery and develop heavy industry with oil export earnings, and bring Mexico into a bright new future of peace and prosperity. He promised the Mexican people that "their" state would never use its oil revenues to service its debt or to pay for corn imports. Yet by 1981 Mexico was doing just that, and by the autumn of 1982 the ship of state was keeling on the rocks of bankruptcy, unemployment was at an all-time high, and the winds of war were blowing hot from the south and the north.

Mexico's proven oil reserves are estimated at 72 billion barrels, its probable reserves at 90 to 150 billion, and its potential reserves at 250 billion, not far behind those of Saudi Arabia. In addition, Mexico has 200 trillion cubic feet of proven natural gas reserves and four times that amount of potential gas reserves. Prior to the bursting of the oil bubble in late 1982, PEMEX boasted of plans to provide Cuba virtually all its oil imports and to install distribution plants for gasoline and diesel fuel in California, Arizona, and Texas. Mexico eyed new markets for its petroleum and other products south of its border, moving boldly to develop favorable diplomatic relations with the Sandinistas in Nicaragua and the rebel FDR-FMLN in El Salvador. In 1980–81, Mexico defined Central America as its "natural area of influence."

These steps in foreign policy, like Mexico's earlier recognitions of revolutions in Latin America, served Mexico's ruling circles in their conflicts with domestic opposition forces of the left and right. The popular mass-based movements among Mexico's students, teachers, theologian-priests of "liberation," and underclasses could not easily criticize a government that recognized similar movements' triumphs in countries like Cuba and Nicaragua. Meanwhile, the ultraconservative, anticommunist forces of the right wing of the Catholic Church and the Monterrey Group of the bourgeoisie were finessed in their claim to be the true "nationalists" when the government showed its "independence" from US domination by criticizing US foreign policy.

In February 1982 the Permanent Conference of Political Parties in Latin America (COPPAL) issued peace proposals for Central America identical to Mexico's proposals. COPPAL incorporates Latin American social-democratic parties, Nicaragua's Sandinistas, and the PRI. It is an unofficial arm of the Socialist International, a minority political voice of the bourgeoisies of Europe that seeks to maintain economic systems and reform political ones without violent confrontation among social classes. By cooperating with the world's social democrats and Central America's nationalist revolutionaries, the Mexican government gains space for maneuver in its relations with the United States and refurbishes its "revolutionary" and "nationalist" traditions at home.

Mexico's foreign policy has also served to open up economic opportunities abroad. Throughout the Caribbean Basin, Mexico has worked out multimillion-dollar joint ventures with various governments. It has agreed to provide Central American and Caribbean countries with oil, 70 percent of it to be purchased at international market prices and the balance to be converted into long-term low-interest credits for the financing of high-priority development projects.

For Mexico, this arrangement offers a chance to establish an unprecedented industrial, technical, and financial presence in the region—one reason the government has been willing to accept new "developmentalist" revolutions there (which appear as inevitable as Mexico's did in 1911). Mexico has offered Central American nations new trade preferences, including a 25 percent reduction in import duties and new lines of credit worth $68 million for the purchase of Mexican products. Mexico has also offered to serve as guarantor of select syndicated loans to Nicaragua from foreign banks. For economic and diplomatic reasons, Mexico sends oil to the terrorist right-wing regimes of Haiti, El Salvador, and Guatemala on the same favorable terms as it does to the Sandinistas.

This does not mean that Mexico is independent of US economic interests. Through their influence in Mexican financial and industrial circles, US investors can, and upon occasion do, take advantage of the conduits that Mexico develops in the Caribbean Basin. Alternatively, of course, US interests can, and do, act to block these conduits for purposes of destabilizing governments that appear too nationalistic, as in the case of Michael Manley's Jamaica (Manley was replaced in 1980 by Edward Seaga, a friend of Reagan and the IMF) or the Sandinistas' Nicaragua. Indeed, growing US economic influence over the Mexican government has served to limit Mexico's supposed independence even in the area of state-owned oil.

Whether in production, marketing, or technological development, Mexico no longer has total control of the energy resources it owns—its oil, gas, and uranium. Even before US and other outside economic interests gained a stranglehold on the economy during the 1982–83 bankruptcy crisis (see Chapter 5), such TNCs as Occidental Petroleum and Dallas's Dresser Industries had established in Mexico oil-related operations generating tens of millions of dollars' worth of sales each year. Two other US concerns, Hercules and DuPont (the last-named moving strongly into the oil sector when it absorbed Conoco Oil in 1981 in history's largest corporate merger), had set up joint ventures with Monterrey's powerful big-steel ALFA group. ALFA also had negotiated a joint venture with Japan's largest corporate conglomerate, Mitsubishi.

In mid-1981 a group of eighty-two banks in eleven nations extended PEMEX a $4 billion short-term loan through Bank of America, with US banks accounting for 40 percent of the total and Japanese banks 30 percent. After the 1982 financial collapse, prices on automobile gas and home oil, tortillas, and other basic necessities were hiked as the government sought to pass the costs of crisis on to the consumer. Meanwhile, PEMEX continued to subsidize foreign and domestic industrial firms in Mexico by offering them reduced prices. Accustomed to exploiting the natural resources of poor peoples and to having a big voice in the formation of US foreign policy, US-based oil corporations assume that

Mexico's petroleum, gas, and uranium reserves are, in the long run, their own.

Besides having roughly one-third of all US overseas investments, US oil companies account for about 65 percent of the world petroleum industry's spending (capital investment), 80 percent of its expenditure on oil exploration, and 50 percent of its fixed assets. Over the years, executives, lawyers, and bankers associated with the giant Rockefeller-dominated Standard Oil of New Jersey have headed the CIA, occupied top posts in government cabinets, and determined many ambassadorial appointments. While the American ambassador to Mexico no longer can arrange military coups as easily as in 1913 or push a button on his desk and in a matter of seconds issue a command to the Mexican president (as one acting ambassador claimed to have been able to do as late as 1964), the American Embassy remains, as we have seen, a main conduit for US interventionist policies.[5]

The Role of US and Mexican Military Forces

Renewed US mass media attention to Mexico following the announcement of its oil discoveries in 1977 seemed to be preparing American public opinion for possible direct US military involvement in not just Central America but perhaps Mexico itself. A 1980 *Gallery* magazine article described an imaginary US invasion south of the border to secure oil supplies, while a 1982 CBS special news report portrayed Mexico as reeling on the verge of chaos and incoming President Miguel de la Madrid as a somewhat laughable incompetent. In response to the *Gallery* article, widely excerpted in the Mexican press, the Mexican army vowed "to defend the fatherland," which to date it has done by breaking up widespread peasant protests against PEMEX's raping of their lands.[6]

Oil is greasing an increased militarization of Mexican society. This meets the needs of US business interests, whose preferred strategy for securing Mexican oil is not direct military intervention (except as a last resort) but rather a combination of economic/diplomatic pressures and courtship of Mexico's police and military apparatuses.

As noted in Chapter 4, President López Portillo's director of federal security was the CIA's most important source of information in Mexico and Central America. A February 1977 story in the *New York Times* reported that ex-president Echeverría had accepted CIA monies when he served as minister of interior under his predecessor, President Gustavo Díaz Ordaz (1964–70). In October 1980 Mexico's director of police and transit announced a new agreement with the FBI "and other US security agencies" for an exchange of know-how, experience, and techniques.

The US-sponsored ideology of "the military coup [as] part of the democratic process in Latin America"[7] has not been excluded as a possibility in Mexico. US and Mexican security forces have conducted joint operations for years. Since 1946 US military and police aid to Mexico has totaled about $100 million. During the 1960s the Mexican military began cooperating with the Guatemalan and US militaries in combating Guatemalan guerrilla forces operating near the Mexico-Guatemala border.

In fact, the southern zone of Mexico and the northern area of Guatemala became a free-fire military theater of operations for the armed forces of Mexico and Guatemala and the US Rangers (Green Berets). The first major Guatemalan guerrilla leader, Yon Sosa, was killed by Mexican soldiers. The technology of the Vietnam War was introduced in Guatemala, along with the practice of massacring civilian populations—hundreds of Indian villages have since been destroyed. (The 1984 Kissinger Commission report candidly acknowledges that the Guatemalan dictatorship resorts to "the use of murder to repress dissent.") During the 1960s Mexico reportedly helped provide the US and Guatemalan antiguerrilla forces with napalm from its own napalm factory, along with tanks and other components from its burgeoning armaments industry.

Mexico's military and paramilitary forces have also utilized US-inspired counterinsurgency warfare to stamp out guerrilla bands in various parts of rural Mexico. During the 1970s the Mexican army beefed up its forces along the Guatemalan border in order to crush social unrest among the Indians there. Until late 1982, when Mexico's foreign ministry issued a formal protest, the army looked the other way each time Guatemalan soldiers crossed the frontier, allegedly to counterattack guerrillas but actually to gun down fleeing peasant refugees, most of them Indians.

In 1982 Mexico purchased its first supersonic jet fighters, seven F-5Es, from the United States. A military university inaugurated on the outskirts of Mexico City in the 1970s maintains an exchange program with such US military academies as West Point, and more than 1,000 Mexican army officers have been trained in the United States and Panama. Some of these officers constitute part of the elite counterinsurgency "White Brigade" (the 9th Army Brigade, based in Mexico City's Military Camp No. 1), which has been repeatedly accused by international human rights organizations of torture and other crimes, including the incarceration of some of Mexico's 500 "disappeared persons."

Mexico has built a complex power bloc of institutional force, including a 135,000-member military, a number of semiautonomous police units, various intelligence-gathering agencies linked to different branches of the government, paramilitary squads, and more. The degree of police autonomy is symbolized by the number of high-ranking officers accused of involvement in the drug-related assassination of an American DEA official in the spring of 1985 (see Chapter 4). Police chiefs and their subordinates have made fortunes from drug trafficking, bribery, and other forms of crime.

But even more than the police, Mexico's military retains a significant degree of autonomy and represents a political force to be reckoned with. The nation is divided into thirty-five military zones that receive their orders from the minister of defense (himself a military officer). No state governor can give orders to the *jefe* of a military zone, who retains a lot of power in matters of "social unrest."

Until 1964 the head of the PRI was usually selected from the army officer corps, and in the 1950s and 1960s almost 20 percent of presidential cabinets consisted of military personnel. Since the 1970s it has become common for generals to run for elective office, particularly at the gubernatorial and congressional levels—a trend generally assumed to have declined after 1940, when Mexico elected its first civilian president since the writing of the 1917 constitution.

For many decades Mexico's army and other military units have been called out to smash strikes or kill protesting peasants. In 1981, despite reductions in most of the federal budget, Mexico's defense budget was doubled. A reminder of the military's armed strength occurs each Independence Day, when a military parade passes down the capital's Paseo de la Reforma featuring Mexican-produced rockets, rocket launchers, tanks, and low-flying jet fighters. Besides the burgeoning home defense industry, the international weapons market arms the Mexican military to the teeth. The primary supplier is the United States, followed by France, Belgium, and Israel.

Although it advocates a nuclear-free zone for all Latin America, uranium-rich Mexico has ample potential to become a nuclear power. After the accident at Three Mile Island, when development of new nuclear energy plants in the United States ground to a halt, the United States began selling nuclear reactor systems to Mexico. In the late 1970s Mexico took bids from five countries for the construction of twenty nuclear reactors whose final sale price was estimated at more than $65 billion. Although two nuclear plants were built on Indian lands in Veracruz State, further nuclear energy projects were momentarily shelved in 1982 when Purépecha Indians successfully resisted construction of a nuclear facility in Michoacán and when the government declared bankruptcy.

The wide range of activities undertaken by the CIA, FBI, and US military in Mexico with the knowledge and cooperation of their counterparts in the Mexican state undermine the Mexican government's claims that it is independent of the United States. Yet in much of its foreign policy, Mexico *has* been able to establish a credible, though uneven and contradictory, independent posture built on the nonintervention doctrine that emanated from the Mexican Revolution of 1910–20. Indeed, Mexico's recognition of the Cuban Revolution in defiance of the United States and its recognition of the Salvadoran guerrillas whom the US government accuses of "trying to shoot their way into power" have caused many high US officials to express severe public criticisms of the Mexican government itself.

US ambassador John Gavin, for instance, reacted to Mexican dissatisfaction over his frequent meetings with the right-wing opposition National Action Party (PAN) by announcing his intention to end the historical pattern of Mexican attacks on the United States and its ambassador. "I am going to try to change it," Gavin reportedly said. "If I just succeed in turning it five degrees I'll have done something worthwhile."[8]

In February 1984 General Paul F. Gorman, chief of the US Southern Command, reportedly told the Senate Armed Services Committee that Mexico might well be the "number-one security problem" for the United States in the next ten years. He described Mexico as a "one-party state that has pursued a policy of accommodation with its own left and international leftist interests" and "the most corrupt government and society in Central America [*sic*]."[9]

As has become evident, larger US economic interests loom behind these crude characterizations of Mexico's less than perfect political system and threats "to change it." The fact that prominent American officials are speaking out with such passion about Mexico, however, suggests that the issues of war and peace, and not just oil and trade, are indeed becoming intertwined with the immigration question as part of a much larger, more explosive web of life-and-death matters straining US-Mexico relations.

The Kissinger Commission and Mexico's Role in the Contadora Process

The naming of the Kissinger Commission in 1983 and the issuing of its report on Central America and the Caribbean Basin in early 1984 were, in part, a response to rising US public protest against US interventionist policies in Central America. The Kissinger Commission's activities provided a kind of official counterpoint not only to the growing peace and anti-interventionist movements at home but also to the Contadora Group. Earlier, in January 1983, at a meeting on the Panamanian island of Contadora, the foreign ministers of Mexico, Venezuela, Colombia, and Panama had decided to mediate for a peaceful resolution of Central America's conflicts.

In the summer of 1983 the Contadora Group issued a general peace plan. It called upon the region's governments to take seven main steps: (1) end the arms race; (2) ban foreign forces, bases, or installations; (3) reduce and then eliminate foreign military advisers; (4) halt arms trafficking; (5) prohibit the use of their own territory for military or logistical support of groups intent on overthrowing other Central American governments; (6) oppose acts of terrorism and sabotage; and (7) commit themselves to promoting national reconciliation through the establishment of representative and pluralist institutions.[10]

It was clear that the Contadora Group had a reasonable peace plan that could demilitarize Central America and keep it out of the "East-West" conflict. Right after Nicaragua and other Central American nations expressed support for the Contadora process, the United States, through UN ambassador Jeane Kirkpatrick and Undersecretary of Defense Fred Iklé, publicly declared its policy of "military victory" in the region. As Iklé put it on September 13, 1983, "We do not seek military defeat for our friends. We do not seek a military stalemate. We seek victory." Six weeks later the United States invaded Grenada, a tiny Caribbean island it continues to occupy as this book goes to press.

The Kissinger Commission report concurred with the Reagan administration in proposing US intervention in any nation about to fall to "communism." But it cautiously commended the Contadora Group for its efforts toward peace—only to warn that it must, in the final analysis, have US approval of its finished product. The Kissinger Commission report served, in effect, to legitimize US intervention in the Caribbean Basin and increased US military aid, and, if need be, direct US military involvement.

It was during the Kissinger Commission's investigatory activities that the US-sponsored escalation in anticivilian warfare in Central America and the Caribbean was carried out: the mining of Nicaragua's harbors; the CIA's distribution of instructions for the assassination of civic leaders in Nicaraguan villages; the intervention of a "secret army" of American soldiers fighting inside Nicaragua on the side of the US-supplied "contras" (mostly supporters of the late US-imposed dictator Anastasio Somoza); the invasion of Grenada; the construction of immense airfields and military bases in Honduras; and the dropping of more tonnage of (nonatomic) bombs per square inch over a 200-square-mile area than ever before rained on a civilian population (on the 10,000 people living on the slopes of the Guazapa volcano outside El Salvador's capital city of San Salvador).[11]

In January 1984 the Contadora Group issued its Twenty-one Points, further elaborating the basic premises of the previous summer's peace package and attempting to overcome various US reservations about the plan. The United States officially stated that it continued to support the Contadora process. It claimed Nicaraguan intransigence as the only obstacle to Contadora's success. During that time the CIA was mining Nicaragua's harbors and directly coordinating the "contra" invasion of Nicaragua from Honduras and Costa Rica.

The harbor minings—described by prominent conservative ideologue Senator Barry Goldwater (R-Ariz.) as an "act of war"—and other direct and indirect acts of military intervention by the United States in Nicaragua were soon condemned by the International Court of Justice (World Court). Yet, for the first time in its history, the United States refused to acknowledge the validity of a decision by the World Court.

In late September 1984 Nicaragua announced it was ready to sign the Contadora peace treaty, the Twenty-one Points. Yet, as one high-up but anonymous US official said, "No one expected the Nicaraguans to accept it, so we didn't really worry about the [Contadora] treaty."[12] Quickly, the US brought pressure to bear on the other Central American countries and successfully blocked adoption of the treaty.

President Reagan promised Congress in May 1985 that he would resume talks he had earlier broken off with the Sandinistas if Congress voted in favor of humanitarian aid to the contras. Congress approved the aid, on the condition that neither the CIA nor the Defense Department would administer it. Reagan did not reopen the negotiations with the Sandinistas.

In July 1985, in bilateral talks that led to Mexican concessions on trade and other economic issues, Mexico's secretary of foreign relations pressed the US secretary of state to resume direct negotiations with Nicaragua. Mexico clearly preferred renewed US-Nicaragua talks to escalated warfare. But before year's end the Reagan administration was putting together a new proposed $100 million aid package for Nicaragua's "contras," most of it in military aid.

Mexico's Economic Nationalism vs. US Pressure

Growing US military involvement in Central America stirs Mexican nationalism and intensifies discussion of economic issues underlying the immense US stake in Mexico. Perhaps the main result of the bilateral negotiations between the two neighbors' foreign secretaries in July 1985 was their announcement of mutual satisfaction with the Mexican government's recent employee layoffs, budget cuts, and loosening of import restrictions. These measures both reflected and strengthened the ongoing "silent integration" of the two nations' economies.

But the question of Mexican migration continues unresolved, mainly because Mexico respects the US attitude that it is an "internal matter" of US law, when in fact it is an international matter of labor, economics, and human rights. Mexico's position is that whatever the fate of immigration legislation in the United States, it will go on doing all it can to "protect" the rights of its nationals abroad. Mexico is also considering two steps that would further integrate its economy with that of the United States: joining a possible North American "common market" and entering into GATT (the UN-sponsored General Agreement on Trade and Tariffs).

A North American Common Market, long a pet idea of President Reagan's in spite of earlier rejections by Mexican president López Portillo and Canadian premier Pierre Trudeau, would likely accelerate regional economic integration under US hegemony at a more visible cost to the national identities of the market's "junior" partners, Mexico and Canada. A kind of common market has been operating in the US-Mexico border zones for decades and has penetrated central Mexico through the *maquiladoras* (see Chapter 4). Official US acceptance of a large number of Mexican migrant workers could readily be converted into a "beachhead," or justification, for a further big step toward making the "silent integration" an actual common market. As an internal report for use by the US Congress stated, "Economic integration will be more complete if there is a free movement of workers."[13]

For many years powerful vested interests in the United States, led by the former president of Chase Manhattan Bank, David Rockefeller, have tried to persuade their friends in the Mexican business community that Mexico should join GATT. Mexico's participation in GATT would tie it more closely to the United States, make trade disputes between the two countries easier to resolve, and streamline a whole series of economic arrangements through GATT's clear-cut guidelines. Like the North American Common Market idea, it would strengthen the United States' hand in economic competition with the European Economic Community (EEC) and Japan.

David Rockefeller was the main founder and mover in the 1970s of the Trilateral Commission, a group of political and business leaders from North America, the EEC, and Japan that coordinates long-range economic and governmental policy formation affecting much of the globe. He and his long-time aide Henry Kissinger met with Mexican business leaders on the GATT issue shortly after the López Portillo administration was in place and the "nationalist" appointments of former president Echeverría were no longer an obstacle.

Rockefeller and the Trilateral hoped through GATT to "develop" Mexico in the direction of its "natural" oil-exporting advantages and to increase Mexico's imports of manufacturing and capital goods from the more industrialized nations. Responding to popular outcries against this scheme, President López Portillo announced in early 1980 that Mexico was postponing entry into GATT, but the Rockefeller group kept pushing the idea. In early 1986 Mexico succumbed to the pressure and formally applied for admission to GATT.

The Rockefeller family has long been central to US policy formation on Mexico and Latin America. Rodman C. Rockefeller, David's brother, is chairman of the US section of the Mexico-US Business Committee, an organization of business executives. This and similar organizations—such as the Commission of the Californias, various border area organizations, the American Chamber of Commerce (of Mexico), and the Rockefeller-sponsored, tax-free Americas Society, Inc.—are very influential in policy decisions emanating from Washington.

In 1981 the Reagan administration announced its intent to work closely with the newly created Americas Society, a merger of a number of Rockefeller-sponsored "nonprofit" organizations composed of corporation executives with heavy investments in Latin America. While not always agreeing on the details of Reagan's policy in Latin America, the Americas Society has backed its overall thrust and helped to formulate it.

These, then, are the behind-the-scene powers that end up influencing or even shaping US-Mexico bilateral negotiations and, in the case of the Americas Society, US foreign policy on Latin America in general. Their pressures on Mexico to join GATT, enter a hemispheric common market, cooperate on Reagan's Central American policy, stay out of OPEC, and so on, necessarily involve moving migrant workers from square to square on the bilateral negotiations chessboard.

It is hard for Mexico not to cave in under these pressures. The precedents are already set in the bracero and other bilateral negotiations with the United States. The foreign investment community's successful use of investments, loans, interest rates, and Mexico's resultant spiraling debt to gain greater control over oil and other resources has pointed up Mexico's relative weakness in bilateral negotiations.

Prior to Mexico's 1982 declaration of bankruptcy, the United States successfully withheld loans and investments and cancelled PEMEX contracts to force Mexico into lowering its oil price. One of the contract breakers, Exxon, was reputedly implementing a plan to break up the OPEC cartel by accumulating enough crude supplies in reserve to force producing nations into a price war. Mexico contributed to such a price war in 1981 when it slashed its oil export prices by $8 a barrel or more. Talk of a "world oil glut" soon became common, and there followed more reductions in the price of Mexican oil over the next few years.

The Mexican government has to deal with a powerful force among the populace, however—the force of nationalism. The 1981 oil price cut caused a national uproar and led to the firing of PEMEX chief Jorge Díaz Serrano, an associate of US vice-president George Bush's in Texas business enterprises. The succeeding administration of President Miguel de la Madrid Hurtado placed Díaz Serrano under house arrest for alleged corruption. Díaz Serrano thus served as a symbol to Mexico's nationalists that the government was serious about combating corruption in high places, even though most Mexicans recognized such gestures as a traditional charade carried out by each new administration.

In a similar effort to excuse itself and to assuage the forces of Mexican nationalism, the government claimed in early 1982 to have uncovered a secret US State Department briefing paper that allegedly said that Mexico's economic crisis might make it "less adventuresome" in foreign policy and lead it "to sell more oil and gas to us at better prices." During the same period and in subsequent months, Mexico did in fact slash oil export prices and provide new guarantees of oil shipments to the United States at bargain-basement prices.

The state's expropriation of private Mexican (but not foreign) banks in September 1982—most of which have since been re-privatized to a large degree—was also intended to rally nationalist forces around the government. In fact, it did. But it also caused foreign bankers to sigh with relief, for it meant that the government now stood behind both public and private debt obligations. Leading US bankers noted that the state's action saved the private banks from insolvency.

Mexico's debt represents about 10 percent of the combined debt of the less-industrialized countries and Eastern Europe, and 17 percent of US bank loans to third world countries and the Eastern bloc. A Mexican default might ignite a chain reaction of defaults elsewhere in the third world and lead to global financial panic. This threat has in turn led Mexico to collaborate more closely with other debtor nations, such as Venezuela, Brazil, Argentina, and Peru, in an effort to wield a modicum of leverage in its negotiations with the United States. In 1985, a so-called "Cartagena Group" of eleven Latin American debtor nations called for a "political dialogue" with the industrial powers— and many leading banks were reportedly proposing a dialogue of their own. Prospects for a successful "debtors' cartel" are slim, however, in light of members' needs for future credits and their lack of real power vis-à-vis creditor nations and banks.

On September 7, 1984, Mexico announced that it had reached an agreement with its foreign creditors to stretch out repayment of much of its $66 billion public sector debt over 14 years. For a substantial portion of the debt, Mexico was to pay only small amounts on the principal—as little as $1 billion by 1988—and to meet interest payments at lower interest rates. The approach was identical to that recommended by the US Federal Reserve Board chairman, banker Paul A. Volcker, who had long advocated "rewarding" Mexico for adopting strict IMF-dictated austerity measures with regard to wages and the federal budget.

Meanwhile, in the area of non-public debt, Mexico's largest private conglomerate Grupo Industrial ALFA S.A. (so-called ALFA group of the conservative Monterrey bourgeoisie) offered creditors up to 45 percent of the company as repayment of $350 million of debt. Having the approval of a negotiating committee consisting of Chase Manhattan Bank, Citibank, Morgan Guaranty and Bank of America, the plan reflected the continuing process of economic integration being led by key actors in both nations' economies. On balance, US bankers and corporate policymakers have seemed pleased by the López Portillo and de la Madrid administrations' economic policies and sophisticated attempts at assuaging the forces of Mexican nationalism. But the state of relations between the Reagan administration and the Mexican government continued extremely strained on the issue of Central America and the Caribbean.[14]

Migrant Workers, Political Refugees, and Detention Camps

In spite of frequent differences with foreign investors, the Mexican government obviously maintains a harmonious relationship with them. But its compromises with the foreign sector prompt the government to try to prove to an economically pinched and skeptical public that it remains independent of the IMF and foreign business interests. One way it does this is by emphasizing an independent foreign policy— whether in its claim to 200 miles of offshore fishing rights (a bone in the throat of US tuna fishermen), its verbal critiques of US intervention in the Caribbean Basin, or its advocacy of the human rights of Mexican emigrant workers.

Yet Mexico's repeated buckling under to external economic forces has weakened its ability to use migrant labor as a strong bargaining chip in its bilateral relations with the United States. Further reducing Mexican leverage are the government's own harsh dealings with the Central American immigrant workers and refugees residing in Mexico.

Mexican coffee growers in the southern states of Chiapas and Puebla need the immigrant labor to harvest one of the nation's main export crops. As in other sectors of Mexican agriculture, foreign capital is heavily involved. While Nestlé and General Foods dominate the domestic market for instant coffee, Folgers (Procter and Gamble), Coca-Cola, and Anderson-Clayton account for one-sixth of Mexico's huge coffee export trade (because of the Brazil frost in the late 1970s, Mexican coffee gained second place behind oil in exports).

Some 30,000 "undocumented" workers from Guatemala and El Salvador are paid $2 for thirteen-hour days to harvest the coffee. To help maintain these harsh economic conditions, the government keeps the border door with Guatemala "revolving." During the first half of 1984, Mexico's border patrol was deporting an average of sixty Central Americans a day from south Chiapas in the name of "protecting Mexican jobs"—an all too familiar slogan. It is obviously embarrassing for Mexican officials to insist that the United States guarantee the human rights of Mexican laborers when their government ignores or collaborates in the abuse of Mexico's own "undocumented" workers.

The conditions for Central America's political refugees residing in southern Mexico are no better. Behind the scenes, US government officials have pressured Mexico to deport political refugees fleeing Guatemala's and El Salvador's sanguinary military dictatorships. In the case of the Guatemalans, almost all of whom are Indians, US generals do not want Guatemalan guerrillas to have a rear base in southern Mexico.

The Mexican army has responded by sending thousands of the refugees back to Guatemala; initial reports indicate that most have been killed. The tens of thousands remaining in Mexican refugee camps near the Guatemalan border have been attacked by assailants wearing Guatemalan army uniforms, presumably the *kaibiles*, or anti-insurgency special forces responsible for most of the massacres of Indians in the Guatemalan highlands. Typical assaults include castration, rape, and cutting off ears. Commented one Mexican doctor sent to treat the wounded, "The skulls of the boy and the pregnant woman had been opened and their gray matter had been removed. Now, why on earth would they do something like that?"[15]

By late 1984 most Guatemalan refugees living in border area camps were being removed further into Mexico's rugged interior tropical forests, where their living and health conditions boded death by starvation or disease. Not surprisingly, many thousands were refusing to leave the camps, believing that the farther they were removed from their homelands, the less their chance of ever returning alive.

In the case of Salvadoran refugees, for many years the Mexican and US governments coordinated their efforts to detain them and deport them back to El Salvador. The Mexican airline Mexicana and the US airlines Pan Am and Western flew the detainees back to their homeland. The Salvadoran Human Rights Commission, based in San Salvador, has estimated that 30 percent of the returning deportees are killed within two months of their arrival.

In the greater Los Angeles–San Diego–Tijuana area, Central American refugee communities joined forces with organizations defending the rights of Mexican immigrant workers to launch boycotts of those airlines engaged in the "death flights." Chicanos, anti-interventionist groups, and civil rights, religious, and labor activists lent their support. This tactic forced Western, Pan Am, and Mexicana to end their trafficking in deportees. In 1984 the boycott was extended to the Salvadoran airline TACA, the only remaining one flying the deportees sent to them by the INS.

Mexico's treatment of Guatemalan immigrant workers and its compliance with US policymakers' wishes on the issues of Central American political refugees, together with other concessions to the United States, reduce its ability to use the issue of Mexican immigrant labor to advantage in bilateral negotiations. In addition, as a special report in *The Nation* pointed out, Mexico's bargaining power is undercut "by the Reagan administration's threat of economic sanctions and by Congress's wielding of the Simpson-Mazzoli big stick to stanch the flow of undocumented Mexican immigrants into the United States."[10] In other words, even though the Simpson-Mazzoli bill would ultimately guarantee a reliable number of Mexican immigrant workers to the US (see Chapter 8), it also carries with it the threat of closing the border.

And there are other grave pressures the US can apply. The same *Nation* special report stated, "The prospect of a large influx of 'feet people' from El Salvador and Guatemala has preoccupied the US National Security Council for the past year, and the INS has drawn up detailed plans for giant detention camps to be erected in remote areas of the United States." As Chapter 9 points out, such camps already exist and are rapidly being filled.

Another weapon wielded by US diplomats is the one used so often in American history—the threat to replace Mexican workers with other foreign labor. This threat is an integral part of the very US military interventionism that Mexico's diplomats criticize. For instance, first in the Dominican Republic after the 1965 invasion and then in Grenada after the 1983 invasion in similar circumstances, the United States expanded the US Farm Labor Program that extends visas to migrant laborers from the Caribbean. This pitted new inexpensive workers against other migrant labor and helped reduce the more than doubled unemployment rates that followed US military intervention. This easing of unemployment in turn made it easier for US-backed and US-financed candidates to win the "free" elections in the invaded countries. Mexican and other migrant workers have found their recent organizing efforts undercut by the influx of Vietnamese "boat people," Grenadians, and others.

Mexico can scarcely theaten to withhold its labor supply from the United States when it so desperately needs to export its own underemployment problem and to capitalize on the migrants' dollar remittances. Little wonder, then, that the Mexican government has responded mildly to the periodic news that the Simpson-Mazzoli bill is advancing through the US Congress. Its only reaction has been to repeat its standard vow to "protect" its nationals and demand for them "the full respect of their rights" while accepting the falsehood that US immigration policy in this case is strictly an internal US matter.

7

Organizing the Unorganized

"Today the global factory means the fate of a Mexican worker will in large part also determine what happens to a worker in Detroit."
—Harley Shaiken, *New York Times*, March 21, 1982

"I would say that one of the technical factors in the decline of the IWW was that the importance of the migratory worker was greatly lessened with the introduction of various farm machines. Then, when the automobile became common, freight trains were no longer ridden like they once were. That was unfortunate for the IWW, because the Wobblies had learned to control that situation."
—Art Shields, IWW veteran

"We look at workers as workers, not at their nationalities."
—Cesar Chavez, United Farm Workers leader

In spite of the immigrants' "bad press," growing numbers of Americans are beginning to sense that there exists a deeper, more complex web of issues beneath all the furor about Mexican immigration. Symptomatic of this growing public awareness is the emergence of new coalitions involving labor organizers, religious institutions, and established peace and anti-US-interventionist groups around the interrelated issues of US foreign policy, and migrant laborers' and political refugees' human rights. Significant elements of organized labor have begun to put their muscle behind the new coalition-building efforts.

This presence of representatives from organized labor—and workers in general—in the front ranks of new initiatives on the interwoven issues of immigrants' rights, labor rights, civil rights, US interventionism, and peace is a relatively new and important development. Given the immense barriers during times of economic crisis to organizing workers of any background on any matter, it is all the more surprising and significant.

Problems of Organizing the Unorganized

There are many problems associated with organizing immigrant workers, not the least of which is public ignorance or apathy. For decades at a time, Americans ignore the abuses suffered by the nation's poorest group of working people, farmworkers. Almost all of today's 5 million farmworkers are migrants, and more than half of these are "illegal" immigrants. Ordinarily, only when the migrants organize themselves, launch strikes, or otherwise rebel against their unfair treatment does the rest of the nation pay them heed. Usually, fresh waves of organizing activity build up, crest, and then fall back into reform efforts that do not accomplish much and may even help maintain the status quo.

Most farmworkers experience malnutrition amidst plenty. Many live in one-room plywood shacks on damp bare ground with no indoor plumbing. They suffer the effects of the toxic chemicals in pesticides, including water supply contamination from pesticide runoff. Few ever finish high school, and most stagger through filth and illness toward an early death. A farmworker's average life expectancy is forty-nine years, compared with the national norm of seventy-three.

The Farmworker Justice Fund said in a 1984 letter seeking financial contributions that "forty years after *The Grapes of Wrath* and twenty years after Edward R. Murrow's *Harvest of Shame*, we can finally do something about this injustice." The letter further pointed out that after more than thirty years of documentation of the unsanitary conditions under which seasonal farmworkers labor, a federal court ordered the federal Occupational Safety and Health Administration (OSHA) to issue "for public comment" a sanitation standard for fields and homes where farmworkers locate. One such piece of documentation that led to the OSHA request was the following:

Johns Hopkins researchers [have] found that almost half of migrant workers on the Delmarva peninsula, for example, harbor dangerous parasites. Remember that these same people are handling the fruits and vegetables that you eat every day and that the human wastes they deposit leach into the soil and eventually contaminate sources of drinking water.

While such reform pleas have obtained funds and kept the court system and politicians alive and well, the actual conditions of most farmworkers have remained unchanged or have grown worse, not better. There are still no federal regulations requiring employers to provide toilets and sanitary drinking and washing facilities for farmworkers. In September, 1985, Secretary of Labor Bill Brock gave states eighteen months to set toilet and water standards. Also, an agreement reached between the chemical industry and labor and environmentalist groups called for federal review of various deadly pesticides, while leaving unresolved how underground water supplies are to be protected. The last proposed sanitation standard issued by the Labor Department in 1976 "for public comment" drew 1,200 responses, almost all of them from agribusiness interests opposed to it. The absence of reform efforts, however unsuccessful they may be, would result in an even worse situation.

The pattern of periodic organizing endeavors by farmworkers, followed by modest reform and public neglect, goes far back in history. American populism, socialism, anarchism, and labor unionism are rooted in the revolt of farm laborers and immigrant workers. European and Mexican immigrant workers composed the backbone of the radical movements that produced many of America's first major labor unions in textiles, clothing, steel, and other industries. The 1905–21 labor movement, in fact, gave rise to an employer-sponsored hysteria against foreigners that culminated in the Palmer Raids, during which thousands of so-called aliens, anarchists, and communists were deported. Similarly, the 1921–24 immigration restrictions were a response— though not exclusively—to militancy and organization among previously unorganized "tractable" immigrant workers. It was during this period that American employers turned to importing and deporting Mexican laborers—from a shorter distance than Europe or Asia, at lower costs, and with fewer complications.

None of America's great labor upheavals of the past provided lasting gains for the people who harvest the nation's crops or do "unskilled" labor that most Americans refuse to touch. Mexicans on both sides of the US-Mexico border are rightfully proud of their role in labor's fight for decent wages and basic human rights over the past century and a half. As already observed, the word *huelga* was heard in many parts of the United States before the word "strike." Yet only a handful of Mexicans have received the fruits of their political and labor organizing activities all these years.

Organizing Mexican or any other immigrant workers has never been an easy task. The reasons usually cited are cultural or linguistic differences, the multinational ethnic character of the American workforce, and American nativism and racism. No doubt all of these (especially racism) are important causes of the ongoing failure of immigrant workers to achieve lasting organizational clout at either the union or political level. But three other reasons deserve special attention.

The first is that because of their vulnerability to racism and superexploitation, migrant farmworkers experience much harsher repression than that—admittedly severe—suffered by industrial workers who turn militant during a strike or organizing endeavor. Second, the desperate economic condition of these workers forces many of them to scab on other workers involved in a strike. In the case of "illegals," this economic desperation is compounded by their fear of deportation. Third, technological changes often undermine the character of the work performed by immigrants, as well as their manner of travel—as the IWW learned to its dismay when automobiles replaced freight trains. Given the obstacles it is surprising to find any organizing activity among Mexican immigrant workers.

Nonetheless, organizing activity, though intermittent and usually limited to a single region or group, does occur with frequency and strength. When it does, most people rarely, if ever, hear about it. Yet those more directly involved in the exploitation of these laborers hear and respond immediately with three tried-and-true techniques: repression; trucking in scabs; and controlling the news available to the public, either by preventing its transmission altogether or by distorting it. Anyone familiar with the history of the farmworkers' strikes and organizing drives launched by Filipino, Arab, and Mexican fieldhands and eventually coordinated by Cesar Chavez and the National Farmworkers Association (NFWA) in the 1960s can testify to this.

Farmworkers' Unionization in the 1960s and Early 1970s

The farmworkers' organizing campaign of the 1960s remains the *only* one since the days of the Wobblies that broke through the news blackout, challenged standard media distortions, and gained national public attention. But it took years and, as Chavez himself often pointed out, the first major turning point was the obtaining of outside assistance from Berkeley students involved in the civil rights movement. It was protesters already making noise on other issues (the Berkeley Free Speech Movement, civil rights, the Vietnam War), and not the official labor movement, farmworkers, journalists, or politicians, who helped Chavez break the wall of silence surrounding the repeated acts of brutality against his organization's rank and file. As important to the unionizing movement was the fact that the number of Mexicans residing in the United States, counting "illegals," had by 1966 reached 6 million—a force receptive to the examples of black civil rights militancy and anti–Vietnam War activism already sweeping the nation.

To the credit of the farmworkers and Chavez, additional creative tactics like marches on the state capital, fasts, folk church services, vigils, and the grape boycott further helped advance what soon became known as *la causa*—the cause. Their Teatro Campesino, directed by Luis Valdez and comprising farmworker-actors, toured the nation, spreading the word about the grape harvesters' strike and boycott and Mexican culture. People from Beverly Hills to Greenwich Village echoed the cries of *"Viva la huelga!"* emanating from California's Greater Delano area, where half of the world's table grapes are produced.

Born in 1927, Chavez was raised on his grandfather's farm near Yuma, Arizona. In 1937 his family was evicted for nonpayment of taxes and water bills. After that, Chavez spent many years following the migratory trail, picking the crops, before meeting Fred Ross, an organizer for the Community Service Organization (CSO). The CSO followed the nonviolent organizing philosophy and tactics of Saul Alinsky's Industrial Areas Foundation. Impressed with its methods, Chavez became a dedicated CSO organizer, eventually being named its general director.

But in 1962, when the CSO turned down a farm labor organizing program, Chavez resigned. He moved his family to Delano, where he began organizing an independent farm union rooted in three Mexican traditions: *mutualismo,* or cooperative credit and insurance programs; the family; and nationalism mixed with Catholic redemption, as symbolized by the farmworkers' carrying the banner of the Virgin of Guadalupe. Among Mexicans, the Indian Virgin of Guadalupe has traditionally symbolized not only the blessing bestowed by the mother of the gods upon suffering people but also an avenging spiritual force to be marshaled by the oppressed against the oppressor—first, against colonial Spain's Mary, Our Lady of Soledad, and later, against any exploiter, foreign or Mexican. The Virgin of Guadalupe thus combines the traditions of both the Indian and the radical Catholic cultures.

Chavez was not the only leader in those early days of 1960s militancy among America's farmworkers. Also present were Cesar's brother Richard and cousin Manuel Chavez; CSO alumni Dolores Huerta, Antonio Orendain, and Gil Padilla; rank-and-file leaders like Epifano Camacho; and others. These leaders collectively decided to put Chavez forward as a major spokesman for the movement. Another activist was Larry Itliong, who led Filipino farmworkers in some of the movement's first victories.

In early 1965 Camacho led a strike by rose grafters and nursery workers in McFarland, California. He obtained Chavez's support, and within a week the workers won their main demands. The union organizers' hand was strengthened by rising antiemployer sentiment in the farm fields, AFL-CIO protests against the wage-depressant impact of braceros, and Congress's repeal of the bracero program's main law, PL 78, in December 1964.

Encouraged by the McFarland victory and these other developments, Filipino grape pickers walked out in the spring of 1965 to protest braceros' obtaining 30 cents more per hour than they did. They were joined by nonbracero Mexicans, as well as by some of the braceros, and they won equal pay. Their movement, in turn, spread to the San Joaquin Valley.

On September 8, 1965, Itliong and the Agricultural Workers Organizing Committee (AWOC, founded by the AFL-CIO in 1959 after the collapse of the NFLU—see Chapter 3) called a strike against grape growers in the Delano area. Though Chavez protested that the fledgling National Farmworkers Association (1,200 members, $87 in the treasury) was not strong enough for a long strike, the mostly Mexican rank and file voted on September 16 to back AWOC's Filipinos in their strike against Delano growers. By then the strike had spread to nine ranches and involved 2,000 workers. *La huelga* had begun.

In only a few years the farmworkers put together one of history's broadest labor alliances. After the first grape strike faltered because of expected repression and widespread scabbing, a consumers' grape boycott took root and strengthened the *huelga*. Products of one of the world's biggest grape growers, the Gallo family, were also boycotted. By 1969 more than 17 million adult Americans had stopped buying grapes, Gallo wine sales had plummeted, and two-thirds of the Coachella Valley's grape ranchers went out of business. The "long march" from Delano, symbolized by mass marches of strikers and their supporters from Delano to the state capital, Sacramento, went on to triumph.

The first victory occurred in 1966 when the Schenley Corporation, a grower of wine grapes, signed a contract with the striking grape pickers of Chavez's NFWA. A boycott of Schenley products and the International Brotherhood of Teamsters' earlier refusal to cross a picket line turned the tide. After that, seeing a chance to recruit new membership from the rapidly expanding farmworkers' movement, Teamsters leaders began signing up farmworkers in competition with Chavez.

The Teamsters honored their corrupt tradition of big payoffs and "sweetheart" contracts (agreements between employers and union officials, on terms disadvantageous to union members) by siding with the Di Giorgio family in its contest with Chavez's NFWA. The Di Giorgios had long been one of California's largest, most prosperous, and most antiworker grape growers. When the aging patriarch Joseph Di Giorgio passed away, his nephew assumed the presidency of the corporation and attempted to clean up its public image by allowing union elections. But he did this in an underhanded way, by agreeing with Teamsters leaders to set up a "quickie" rigged union election, which the Teamsters handily won. The NFWA asked Governor Edmund G. Brown, Sr., a friend of Robert Di Giorgio's, to investigate the fraudulent election. Brown's investigator recommended a new election, which was set for August 30, 1966.

Thus began a long and bloody feud between the Teamsters and the NFWA that took much of the steam out of the farmworkers' originally independent movement, even though large numbers of farmworkers became unionized in the course of the interunion fight. The Di Giorgio campaign drained the NFWA's financial resources. Under these and other pressures, including the antipathy of old-guard AFL-CIO leaders who resented the new union's independence, Chavez reluctantly agreed to merge the NFWA with the AWOC into the AFL-CIO-affiliated

United Farm Workers Organizing Committee (UFW). This helped Chavez win the first major contest with the Teamsters, when the UFW took the state-monitored Di Giorgio union elections by 573 votes to the Teamsters' 425. After that, the Di Giorgio Corporation and the UFW signed a contract.

Other growers dug in to resist the UFW grape strike. They received support from the Pentagon, which increased its grape shipments to troops in Vietnam from 468,000 pounds in 1966 to more than 4 million pounds in 1969, all at taxpayers' expense. The red-and-black UFW flag, with its distinctive eagle, appeared on crates containing union grapes, and union grape sales jumped as scores of markets requested "the thunderbird." Faced with declining sales, rotting grapes, and newly strengthened UFW pickets, growers of California's Coachella Valley finally signed a contract with the UFW in mid-1970. Before the end of the strike's fifth year, the farmworkers' victory in grapes was assured.

Also in 1970 Chavez's UFW commenced its strike in the Salinas lettuce fields of California. Once again acts of violence were perpetrated against the nonviolent strikers; farmworkers and their lawyers were beaten up by the growers' hired goons. The Pentagon started buying up "scab" lettuce for troops in Vietnam. Chavez was arrested for refusing to obey an injunction and visited in jail by national dignitaries. A consumers' lettuce boycott was initiated. Chavez's personal, Gandhi-like fast was taken up by thousands on a symbolic one-day or weekend basis in churches and neighborhoods throughout the nation during the Thanksgiving holidays.

Yet Chavez's group still had to deal with the Teamsters, who unleashed vicious physical and Red-baiting attacks on the UFW and its sympathizers in a wide-open jurisdictional war for new members from the farm labor force. The Teamsters' greater economic resources, augmented by under-the-table deals with some of the growers, placed the UFW at a distinct disadvantage. So did the Teamsters' informal alliance with President Richard Nixon, who supported a bill outlawing secondary boycotts for farmworkers, requiring them to give ten days' notice before striking, and allowing growers a thirty-day "cooling off" period before going to binding arbitration—plenty of time to bring in the harvest.

In the spring of 1971 the Teamsters and Chavez initialed a pact giving the UFW jurisdiction over field workers and the Teamsters jurisdiction over food-processing workers. The lettuce boycott became international, and the UFW eventually won its second historic strike victory.

But the sacrifices entailed by the struggle were high. The Teamsters union failed to honor its pacts with the UFW. As countless reports in the mass media confirmed, Charles Colson, special counsel to Nixon, pressured the Teamsters to break these periodic "peace" agreements. (When Colson later left the White House, he was given a $100,000-a-year retainer as a lawyer for the Teamsters.) In 1973 the Teamsters hired goons who beat up pro-UFW Mexicans for $67.50 a day. Two Teamsters were arrested on charges of assault, kidnapping, and attempted murder.

Police repression came down hard on Chavez's forces and resulted in some 5,000 arrests that year. On August 14, 1973, Nagi Daifullah, a young Arab farmworker, was fatally clubbed by a deputy sheriff, and two days later Juan de la Cruz, a 60-year-old farmworker and one of the first UFW members, was shot to death by a strikebreaker. Within two years UFW membership dropped from 55,000 to 6,000. This was no match for the 2.2-million-member-strong Teamsters. The widely reported intimidation tactics of the growers, the Teamsters, and the Nixon administration, combined with their superior economic clout, cost the UFW dearly.

The farmworkers' movement had in the meantime spread to other parts of the nation. Antonio Orendain, Gil Padilla, and others led a vigorous movement in south Texas's Rio Grande Valley, where most farmworkers were surviving on less than $10 a day (when employed). They first gained national attention with the "great melon strike" of 1966–67, which led to demonstrations at the state capital of more than 10,000. However, as a three-judge federal panel belatedly ruled in June 1972, the Texas Rangers "used their law enforcement powers to suppress the farmworkers strike."

This author was among the first contingent of "anglo" civil rights activists to visit Orendain and his followers and marshal support for the strike and subsequent consumers' melon boycott. Strike supporters broke the news blackout by documenting and reporting the violence unleashed on Mexican farmworkers by the Texas Rangers. Throughout south Texas they saw the evidence of destruction of farmworkers' homes and beating up of strike militants by the Rangers, sheriffs' deputies, and hired goons. During this time Ku Klux Klan vigilantism received new impetus, with the obvious approval of many Rangers and law officials. In subsequent years Orendain and farmworkers throughout the South and Southeast undertook "long marches" of their own to state capitals and eventually (in 1977) to Washington, D.C.

In 1975 the UFW was preoccupied with the passage of the Agricultural Labor Relations Act in California under Governor Jerry Brown. Orendain was told to call off strike actions in Texas, since resources were needed in California. On August 14, 1975, Orendain broke with Chavez and founded the independent Texas Farm Workers (TFW). This organization went on to ally itself with other "independents" in the labor movement and to become a leading voice in a new wave of internationalist organizing of "undocumented" workers (discussed in the next section of this chapter).

Meanwhile, UFW sympathizers won passage of the Agricultural Labor Relations Act in California. It provided legal guarantees for agricultural labor unions and farmworkers' rights. It established the Agricultural Labor Relations Board (ALRB), which conducted more than 200 union elections won by the UFW during the following year. In less than a year the UFW successfully negotiated 88 formal contracts covering 25,000 workers.

During the 1976 California elections, the UFW campaigned, against overwhelming odds, in favor of Proposition 14, which would have amended the state constitution to guarantee the future of the ALRB. But the proposition lost by a two-to-one margin, and the UFW thereafter went into steady decline, in spite of a 1977 agreement with the Teamsters ending competition between the unions in organizing agricultural workers.[1]

By late 1984, when the Teamsters announced they were not renewing their 1977 agreement with the UFW, UFW membership among 350,000 farmworkers in California was about 15,000. Only 15 of the Delano area's 70 grape growers were under UFW contract, and less than a dozen of the Salinas Valley's 150 vegetable producers had contracts. Important leaders had split off, accusing Chavez of a new labor conservatism, corruption, and undemocratic conduct. UFW members continued to suffer the growers' counterattacks. On September 20, 1983, Rene Lopez, a twenty-one-year-old dairy worker and UFW leader, was shot in the head by two strikebreakers imported by the rancher—the fourth union member murdered in ten years.

According to a fundraising letter Chavez issued in early 1985, "During the early '70s, grape workers were the best protected farm workers in the nation. Now their wages and conditions lag far behind other farm workers. . . . Most grape growers refuse to even bargain for contracts." The state agencies established under Governor Brown to resolve labor conflicts in the fields had become ineffective or counterproductive. "Under Republican Governor George Deukmejian," Chavez's letter pointed out, "corporate growers control the state agency which was created to protect farm workers. When Deukmejian took office, 46% of farm worker charges were dismissed; by the end of 1984, 90% of the charges were rejected."

Moreover, the court system remained a serious obstacle to enforcement of California's progressive 1975 labor law. Few cases made it to the courts and prolabor decisions were endlessly appealed by the growers' well-paid lawyers. The courts did not award one monetary settlement.

In July 1984, in response to Governor Deukmejian's veto of a $1 million appropriation for the creation of a compliance enforcement unit under the ALRB, Chavez announced a consumer boycott of grapes (except the 3 percent of grapes produced under UFW contract). Said Chavez, "We take this action because, under Deukmejian, the law that guarantees our right to organize has been shut down. . . . Deukmejian can protect the growers from the law, but he can't protect the growers from the boycott." The struggle had thus come full circle—back to a grape boycott, but now without a strike.

After twenty years of effort, the UFW could claim historic—if modest and easily eroded—victories: the average California farmworker salary of $5.16 an hour (1982) was at least 20 percent higher than the average for the rest of the nation's farmworkers; and California farmworkers, including "illegals," became eligible for unemployment benefits in 1979. On the other hand, mechanization of production and reliance on "illegal aliens" for more than half the labor force eliminated many jobs while raising California's annual agricultural sales to almost $15 billion, the highest in the nation. The living conditions for immigrant farmworkers in many parts of the state remained primitive—often worse than those for pet dogs or cats. Of the eleven US communities with the highest proportion of welfare recipients, six are in the UFW-organized San Joaquin Valley.

Perhaps the UFW's most lasting accomplishment was the raising of consciousness and national pride among the nation's more than 10 million Mexicans. Abuse of workers' civil rights, however common, is not as simple as it was prior to Delano. Inspired in part by the farmworkers' movement, younger Mexicans in urban communities began calling themselves "Chicanos" as a means of asserting a new nationalist militancy and the right to self-determination, in contrast to the hyphenated ambivalence of the traditional term "Mexican-American." In the late 1960s they launched a Chicano political party and Chicano caucuses in the established parties, founded a youth militia ("Brown Berets"), belatedly advocated the rights of Chicana women, and undertook a consciousness-raising campaign to locate their roots in *la raza*, or the race of Mexicans who have resisted subjugation since the Spanish Conquest. *La raza* also refers to the human race struggling to be free, and expressions of solidarity became common between the US farmworkers, welfare mothers, Vietnam war veterans, and youth of the Chicano movement on the one hand, and rebellious peasants, slum dwellers, workers, and students in Mexico on the other.

Because it built bridges to other disfranchised constituencies and groups, and because of America's virulent nativism and racism, the Chicano movement was savagely repressed. Nonviolent mass demonstrations were broken up by gunfire, and scores of protesters were killed or wounded, especially in the Southwest. The most publicized killings occurred on August 29, 1970, day of the Chicano National Moratorium against the war in Vietnam. The Los Angeles police violently broke up a peaceful picnic and rally in East Los Angeles's Laguna Park. During the confusion and melee that followed, three Chicanos were killed, the most prominent of whom was television journalist Ruben Salazar.

Police marksmen shot ten-inch tear gas projectiles into a bar where Salazar was having a late afternoon drink. After bar customers fled the haze of tear gas, a couple of Salazar's friends pleaded with police to go back in and pull him out. They refused, and two hours later Salazar's body was found—his death attributed to the impact of one of the tear gas projectiles against his head. At the time, Salazar had become quite unpopular with the police, who had asked him to "tone down" his coverage of inconsistencies in police reports. Alleging that he was inflaming TV viewers, they had threatened to "get him" if he continued his coverage. A federal grand jury indicted the officers involved in one of the day's deaths, but a federal court later acquitted them; prosecution of policemen involved in Salazar's death never occurred.

At least one police agent has confirmed that there were plots to assassinate Cesar Chavez. FBI agents and police provocateurs streamed into the ranks of the UFW and most other progressive movements. Some of these agents later told the press the details of their underground work, showing that the aim was always to create violence, divide or kill leaders, and crush the democratic efforts by Mexicans and Chicanos to achieve their basic rights. The grand jury system was used to incarcerate or harass many leaders and activists of all US progressive movements, some of whom, especially Chicanos, were accused of having links with "terrorists" struggling for Puerto Rican independence.

Repression did much to slow the momentum of the Chicano/Mexican antiwar and civil rights movement. So did the end of the Vietnam War, when many felt that the main goal had been achieved and so ceased further political activity. With the advent of the Carter-Reagan social welfare cutbacks, the Chicano movement lost much of what little economic base it had achieved. Living standards plummeted, and more than a few of the Chicano "middle-class" militants who had gained employment inside the state and federal welfare bureaucracies were laid off.

In spite of the forces aligned against a Chicano/Mexican movement unprecedented in its vigor and depth, the "Vietnam syndrome" would not fade away. During a fresh upsurge of protest marches against the draft and US intervention in Central America in the 1980s, the most notable development was the emergence of Latinos as leaders and the participation of large numbers of Mexicans who had organized in their churches, schools, or *barrios* (neighborhoods).[2]

The UFW's herculean accomplishment of winning the right to unions and union contracts among farmworkers is being steadily undermined by two forces, only the second of which seems reversible: mechanization of farm production, and right-wing political reaction marked by a well-financed offensive not only against Mexican immigrant workers but against labor unionists in general.

Included in this offensive is the campaign to extend antiunion "right-to-work" laws from the Deep South into other states. These laws prohibit workers from negotiating union shop agreements with their employers (a union shop is a workplace in which only members of a labor union are employed). Traditional in low-wage parts of the country, especially the South and West, "right-to-work" laws were made possible by the 1947 Taft-Hartley Act as part of the government's "Red scare" witch-hunting of union activists. During the Reagan presidency, proposed "right-to-work" laws gained favorable attention in economically depressed areas of traditionally "unionized" states in the Midwest and Northeast.

Employers favor "right-to-work" laws because they guarantee the opportunity to hire and fire anyone at will, including cheap immigrant labor. With labor unionism having been given a bad name by much of the press, and by inadequate self-policing of union corruption and the failure of union leadership to sustain gains or uplift the living standards of the unorganized, more workers than ever before are apparently taking seriously the proemployer arguments behind the slogan "right to work."

In a dispute related to this antiunion atmosphere, the UFW launched in 1984 a new lettuce boycott in support of a strike against the Bruce Church lettuce company. The union's principal demand was the right to determine which of its members would work for the company and to dismiss any who did not adhere to union discipline.

Since the days of Delano, membership in American labor unions has declined markedly. In spite of population growth, union membership fell from 20.7 million in 1968 to 19.8 million in 1982. In the 1980s alone, the percentage of the workforce belonging to unions plummeted from around 21 percent (1980) to an estimated 16 percent (1985). More than a "trend," these figures represent a veritable breakthrough for union busters and offer nothing but intensified grief for the nation's growing numbers of migrant workers, as well as for the workforce as a whole.

Scapegoating Mexican immigrant workers fuels the fires of nativism, racism, and class division among the US labor force that threaten to frustrate each new unionizing endeavor. Even third- or fourth-generation Mexicans with decent-paying jobs or small businesses are not immune to these divisions. Some are aware and proud of their Mexican roots and have long been in the forefront of the defense of the human rights of Mexican immigrants. But others, largely because of their own economic advance, have lost touch with that proud tradition and are more than willing to exploit or condemn the immigrants newly arriving from their original homeland.

Divisions are deep in the Mexican community, not along racial or ethnic lines, but *along class lines*—between some employers, bureaucrats, or foremen of Mexican descent and Mexican, Chicano, or other minority laborers. Yet between the two poles of "Chicano" and "Mexican migrant" extends a chain that keeps them connected. The many links of this chain include kinship ties, generational friendship networks involving longer or shorter US residency and more or fewer roots in the *barrio*, language, music, and other cultural traditions, and similarities of work and life situations in either the past or the present. In brief, there exists a social-psychological continuum that connects the fate and identities of all Mexican immigrant workers and all Mexicans who are US citizens.

A particularly strong link in that continuum is the very racism that confronts Mexican immigrant workers—for it also affects US citizens of Mexican descent, sometimes very directly. Frequently, for example, they themselves are taken to be "illegal" or "undocumented." Like the immigrants, they are subject to INS stop-and-search raids at their workplaces, in their cars, on buses, or on the sidewalks of American cities and towns.

What happens to Mexican migrants thus affects all US citizens of Latin American descent—one reason why their civic organizations invariably oppose deportations of "illegals" or sanctions against employers who hire them. They know at gut level that in the eyes of the authorities, the Ku Klux Klan, and racists, all Mexicans, Chicanos, and. Latinos are lumped together.

Under President Carter's human rights rhetoric and harsh immigration policies ("tortilla curtain," deportation drives), as well as under President Reagan's similar policies of mass deportations accompanied by talk of "amnesty," millions of the Spanish-speaking have faced the prospect of arrest or deportation and the daily terror of uncertain status.

According to unpublished census data submitted by the INS to the US Select Commission on Immigration, some 95 percent of people detained, arrested, and deported by the Border Patrol are of Mexican origin even though the Mexican component of the "undocumented" population is only 45 percent (1980 figures). As attorney Peter Schey of the National Center for Immigrants' Rights has confirmed, almost all those deported are psychologically or physically forced to sign voluntary departure forms—*and 35 percent of the deportees are not even legally deportable in the first place.* The potential deportee is given only three hours to react to the "proceedings," as the INS routinely circumvents laws protecting even minimal rights granted US residents. [3]In this way, Latin American neighborhoods housing significant numbers of recent immigrants are often terrorized, and those wishing to organize themselves into labor unions are intimidated. Further intimidating US Mexican communities are the paramilitary units of the Ku Klux Klan that periodically roam the border and openly boast of having shot, incapacitated, captured, or otherwise "delivered" to the INS "illegal aliens."

Fear is a two-edged sword that can generate either silence with surrender or anger with resistance. It usually produces a combination of both. In the short run, however, the current INS focus on harassing Mexicans seems to have hindered the organizing of immigrant workers.

Labor's Links across Borders

From their experiences in the 1970s and early 1980s, growing numbers of workers have learned an important lesson: the struggle for improved wages and working conditions cannot be won without taking into account the internationalization of capital and labor, of which immigrant labor forms an important part.

Often, however, American workers have understood only part of this international picture. For example, they tended to approve of the AFL-CIO executive council's initial support of the proposed Simpson-Mazzoli immigration reform bill, observing that employers' use of "illegal" immigrants held most other workers' wages steady or even pushed them down. They used the same logic in protesting the phenomenon of runaway shops—business's setting up of manufacturing or other operations overseas in order to exploit cheap labor. Having experienced layoffs, lowered pay, and employers' repeated threats to move operations abroad, American workers have welcomed any legislation that slams the door on cheap immigrant labor. What they do not realize, however, is that runaway shops tend to *increase* immigration to the United States and Simpson-Mazzoli *opens* the door to additional immigrant labor whenever employers request it.

Corporate moves into less developed countries like Mexico transform the agrarian and industrial systems of production in those countries in such a way as to release larger numbers of workers from the land, herd them into urban slums, and drive them to a greater out-migration in quest of survival.

Both runaway shops and increased immigration reduce the high wage structure that Americans fought for and won in earlier generations. In the heyday of US economic hegemony in the world, most American workers prospered from the benefits derived from the labor of highly exploited workers controlled by America's client states overseas. Now, however, US labor is suffering the long-term consequences. The "conglomeratization" of diversified industries into giant corporations that spread their production into the most distant low-wage corners of the globe, along with the improvements in transportation, automation, and use of new technologies and pools of unemployed and immigrant labor that make the "global factory" possible, have greatly weakened the position of American labor.

Since 1970 American wage levels have moved from first to seventh relative to other countries. Temporary employment and moonlighting have become widespread, and the shape-up has returned to the labor market. (The shape-up is the selection of a work crew, usually on a day-to-day basis, from a fairly large number of persons assembled for a work shift or task.) In order to comprehend labor's weak position one has only to observe what happened in the 1983 Greyhound Bus employees' strike, when Greyhound lined up unemployed job applicants right next to the strikers' picket lines. Or one can note the return of low-wage, labor-intensive nonunion production "sweatshops" throughout the country (an estimated 3,000 sweatshops employing 50,000 workers in New York City alone) and the rapid growth of what economists call "the underground economy" of unreported income. A higher incidence of crime and increased worker exploitation have accompanied these trends.

But the new trends in America's economy also make corporations vulnerable and exposed in unprecedented ways. As labor economist David Montgomery has pointed out, "The type of specialized plant, computerized coordination, and low inventories that such [transnational] corporations now favor makes them highly vulnerable to sudden job actions."[4] A strike in the Mexican border town of Ciudad Reynosa, reported as a lead story by CBS Evening News, November 10, 1983, illustrates the point graphically. Some 8,000 mostly female Mexican workers walked off the job at the local Zenith plant and in so doing sent shockwaves through the American economy. Employers laid off workers at numerous US plants that depended on parts assembled at the Ciudad Reynosa plant. What the CBS newscast omitted was the fact that when Mexican workers win higher wages through their strikes, American workers benefit. Raising wage structures in one part of the world often contributes to lifting them elsewhere, just as lowering them (or keeping them low) tends to diminish the living standards of people everywhere.

US workers increasingly recognize the threat posed by runaway shops. In late 1983, for example, members of United Electrical Workers Local 332, in a congressional district having one of the Northeast's most conservative representatives, angrily walked off the job at General Electric plants in Fort Edward and Hudson Falls, New York, to protest GE's decision to eliminate 300 jobs by moving some of its capacitor production to Mexico. About 600 workers had already been laid off because of the recession. Said the local's vice president, Alric Lewis, "The federal government has deliberately done the bidding of the ruling conglomerates and set up sanctuaries for GE in Mexico and for other multinationals in Central America." He denounced "the conspiracy against working people in this country." Added Dorothy Danahy, the local's secretary, "The people down there [in Mexico] know they're being exploited. They're working people like us."5

When Mexican workers organize for higher wages, runaway shops are discouraged, as when unionized Mexican automotive workers (80 percent of whom have become independent of the PRI-dominated Congress of Labor in their decade-long struggle for union democracy) periodically win wage and other employment demands. In these instances Mexico looks less attractive to General Motors, Ford, and Chrysler, and other such companies who then move much of their production northward closer to the US border to cities like Ramos Arizpe and Saltillo, where there are fewer unions and lower wage structures. The auto companies have already left the US cities of Detroit and Pontiac, Michigan, which suffered severe unemployment as a result.

Once workers in the new locales of these companies' factories gain greater rights, all of labor stands to benefit. The US automobile industry's ongoing decentralization and restructuring has the potential of revitalizing workers' struggles for a better life on both sides of the border.

Labor's Current Strategies

But in the meantime, until recently at least, most union leaders in the United States have sought to stem labor's decline by making concessions to employers in the apparent expectation that these would keep the companies from "running away" or otherwise reducing the workforce and wages. Labor's concessions have included no-strike pledges (a pattern set by the pace-setting United Steelworkers of America in the 1970s) and other so-called givebacks written into contracts.

"Givebacks" typically are agreements to "give back" to employers part or all of earlier gains, such as cost-of-living wage increments, vacation time, higher overtime pay, and the like. They have the effect of either freezing or reducing workers' wages in comparison with the rates of inflation and corporate profit. For instance, the average first-year settlement in contracts covering 5,000 or more workers in 1982 and 1983 failed to increase wages plus benefits fast enough to keep up with consumer prices. In some 40 percent of the settlements workers accepted pay cuts or a freeze in pay (during 1984, the second year of so-called recovery, 27 percent accepted cuts or freezes).

This giveback strategy by organized labor only whetted employers' appetites for more concessions. They became increasingly bold in their crisis-spawned policies of asking for labor union concessions and encouraging union busting, robotics, and reliance on cheap immigrant labor, as well as shipping abroad assembly operations.

Wage givebacks do not necessarily save workers' jobs. Despite such givebacks, many firms continue to move abroad. Nor do wage givebacks necessarily "solve" the cost-of-labor problem. In the decade prior to the givebacks of the 1980s, labor costs as a percentage of total dollar sales had already dropped from 31.8 percent to 29.2 percent. Labor's additional givebacks after 1980 further diminished the purchasing power of most Americans and guaranteed only continued sluggishness in the demand for goods and services. American workers' *real* wages since 1970 thus dropped from $257 a week at the start of 1970 to $235 by the end of 1980 and $232 at the end of 1983 (in 1980 dollars). That decline in workers' incomes had a lot to do with the economy's prolonged lack of forward momentum.

Nor did the new contract signed by the United Auto Workers (UAW) with General Motors (GM) after a short-lived strike in 1984 offer real security for workers, in spite of its much-heralded billion-dollar job security fund. If GM carries out its plan to lay off 100,000 UAW members by 1987, the first few thousand will draw the promised compensation, while the remainder will get a pittance or nothing. The hotly disputed contract, which promised to become a benchmark for all industrial labor, included a wage giveback that would over a 3-year period deny each worker $2,200 that he or she would have earned had there been a return to the decades-old formula of a 3 percent annual wage increase.[6]

Further harming organized labor is the fact that "right-to-work" laws and other antiunion proposals are taking increasing precedence over more farsighted legislation, such as the Fair Labor Standards Act, the National Labor Relations Act, the Occupational Safety and Health Act, and the Federal Unemployment Tax Act, all of which were passed in response to earlier periods of labor insurgency. Genuine enforcement of these laws would vastly reduce the employment of inexpensive immigrant labor, since they require that all migrant workers be treated fairly, on a par with other workers. Such law enforcement, moreover, would facilitate the unionization and fair treatment of "undocumented" workers and "legal" workers alike. Separating the plight of the "undocumented" from the rest of labor and scapegoating them for all of labor's problems keeps workers from recognizing the commonality of their struggle, leaving them vulnerable to further givebacks.

Recent hard times for both organized and unorganized labor have led labor activists to pursue three contradictory and sometimes overlapping strategies concerning "illegal" workers: deportation, unionization tied to the AFL-CIO, and independent unionization accompanied by the creation of an effective international labor solidarity network. Each of these strategies was attempted in the aftermath of the farmworkers' organizing drive of the 1960s.

First, the AFL-CIO executive council endorsed the proposed Simpson-Mazzoli bill and the forcible removal of "undocumented" workers. The AFL-CIO's advocacy of deportation echoed its history of dissatisfaction with the bracero program and lack of consistent concern for the rights of minorities. But when popular and political pressures built up in the 1980s against Simpson-Mazzoli, the AFL-CIO was forced to rethink its position and to criticize the new legislation, even though it still supported some form of worker identity cards, employer sanctions, and "amnesty" (see Chapter 8).

A second strategy was undertaken by those within organized labor who saw unionizing as the only way to counter the harmful impact of cheap immigrant labor and maintain the previous gains of American unionism. These activists launched unionization drives among the "illegals" and rushed to defend them against factory raids and other unfair or abusive treatment. Some of the unions following this strategy were hoping to stem a decline in membership and dues payments that threatened their viability.

Locals of unions facing declining memberships and dues, such as the garment and textile workers' ILGWU, the auto workers' UAW, and the electrical workers' UE, moved to the front of a new drive to organize immigrant workers. A typical contract negotiated by one such local, for example, prohibits unreasonable search and seizure, obligates the employer to give the union notice of any valid INS search or arrest warrant, and calls for reinstatement of employees absent due to INS proceedings if they return to the workplace within seven days.[7] Sometimes, because of the difficulties encountered in union organizing among the "undocumented" and the employer's ownership of "sister" plants on the other side of the US-Mexico border, these locals have expressed international solidarity with workers attempting to unionize or on strike against employers in northern Mexico and have taken up collections for them.

A third approach was undertaken consciously and deliberately in the late 1970s by the Arizona Farm Workers Union (AFWU) and, on a less systematic, more spontaneous basis, by other organizers and workers involved in workplace disputes in services, industry, and agriculture elsewhere in the nation. The activists using this approach focused on organizing "illegals" into independent unions not beholden to the AFL-CIO. They stressed grass-roots participation and internationalization of labor's struggle. They sought and obtained support from progressive Mexican union leaders and radical "independents" who were infusing the Mexican labor scene of the 1970s with a new movement for labor democracy, often characterized as the "Democratic Tendency." The AFWU and occasional labor organizers elsewhere emphasized organizing workers not just on the job in the US but also in their hometowns in Mexico.

Although it emerged only by fits and starts during the 1970s, this independent approach consolidated fairly swiftly after 1978 when the AFWU merged with other independent unions into the International Coordinating Committee (ICC). The ICC incorporated both rural and urban workers, "legals" as well as "illegals." Since 1982 it has been known as the American Federation of Workers (AFW), whose principal affiliates are the AFWU, Antonio Orendain's Texas Farm Workers, the Florida Farm Workers Union, and José "Pepe" Medina's International Brotherhood of General Workers. This more independent and internationalist approach, sparked by the ICC, which claimed to incorporate 25,000 "undocumented" workers, helped generate the internationally sponsored Bill of Rights for the Undocumented Worker passed in Mexico City in 1980 (see Appendix III).

In October 1977 the AFWU's founders in Arizona's Maricopa County, then nominally affiliated with Cesar Chavez's UFW, launched a successful twenty-four-day strike at Goldmar, Inc.'s Arrowhead Ranch, owned by Senator Barry Goldwater's brother Robert and the Martori brothers. The first labor contract ever to be signed by "undocumented" workers marked the strikers' triumph, which occurred in spite of the deportation of 260 of Arrowhead's 300 workers and the jailing of an average of two AFWU organizers every day. The "deportees" kept slipping back across the border, and the frequent arrests only increased the strikers' determination.

The Maricopa County organizers' success was no fluke. It was built upon a consciously planned and implemented strategy that derived from earlier setbacks. Chavez's UFW had pulled out of Arizona back in 1973, and the only subsequent big organizing effort had produced an unsuccessful 1974–75 citrus strike in Yuma that had cost more than $1 million and ended with no contract. From that experience, however, organizers in Arizona recognized the need to bridge the divisions among Mexican workers who were US citizens, "green-card commuter" Mexicans with legal border passes, and Mexican "illegal" workers. Early in 1977, with Chavez's approval, a group of organizers founded the Maricopa County Organizing Project (MCOP), forerunner of the AFWU.

The MCOP earned the trust of many "illegals" by identifying and bringing to "worker's trials" various *coyotes* detested for purchasing workers at $20 each from Maricopa ranch foremen and later selling them to farmers in other areas for up to $450 a head (a sum deducted from workers' wages). In those days many workers made only $6 to $9 a day and were often deported by the INS on the last day of the week, before they could even collect their pay; today, AFWU members earn $60 a day.

Another innovative technique introduced by the MCOP was the organizing of the "illegals" in their home villages in Mexico. As two organizers later recalled,

> At first, we were afraid that our organizing in Mexico would encounter opposition from the Mexican authorities, but we soon found out that the migrant undocumented workers were usually the most prominent citizens of their communities and that they enjoyed the full respect of local authorities. In a period of three months, during the summer of 1977, these organizers trained 23 committees whose jobs were to infiltrate, organize, and take direct strike action in Arizona.[8]

When the Arrowhead strike broke out, the organized workers "took down the license plates of all *coyotes* in action, traced them and threatened them with legal action if they brought any workers to a ranch on strike."[9] This cut down scabbing at its source. The strikers' victory stunned people throughout the Southwest and put Maricopa County on the national and international labor map. It also led to further MCOP-organized strikes at other ranches by "undocumented" workers and by over 3,000 local "legal" union workers, who by then appreciated the commonality of their struggle. In fact, in Arizona the "undocumented" helped fund and organize the actions of the "legals."

For reasons that remain unclear, the AFWU split away from Chavez's UFW and became independent shortly after the successful Goldmar strike. Two of the AFWU organizers claim that Chavez ordered them to stop all organizing efforts—but they do not say why.[10]

Starting in 1979, AFWU-negotiated contracts stipulated that employers donate 10 cents per hour per worker (later raised to 20 cents) to a fund known as the Farmworker Economic Development Corporation. This fund (holding $45,000 in just the summer of 1980) plowed money back into some two dozen of the migrant workers' home villages in Querétaro State for the construction of water systems, schools, cooperatives, and the like. The states of Sinaloa, Guanajuato, and San Luis Potosí also benefited. In Querétaro, AFWU members organized a migrant workers' union known as the Sindicato Nacional de Trabajadores Migratorios and a marketing co-op called the Cooperativa sin Fronteras (Co-op without Borders). In those Querétaro areas most directly affected, migration to the United States dropped by 50 percent, apparently because the self-planned, self-financed development efforts of the migrants had made life at home more viable.[11]

A number of AFWU contracts with employers are bogged down in the courts, but by 1984 the union still had two contracts in force and had helped to raise wages and significantly reduce abuses in many of Arizona's farm fields. The AFWU claims a membership of between 10,000 and 15,000, two-thirds of whom are "undocumented" workers. The AFW, to which it is affiliated, has additional members in Washington, Texas, Arkansas, and Florida, as well as working committees in several other states.

Meanwhile, "undocumented" workers elsewhere were beginning to organize themselves in significant numbers, often with the assistance of independent labor organizers and progressive union locals. The heightened organizing and strike activities of the "undocumented" in the 1970s and early 1980s were a major cause of President Carter's anti-Mexican "tortilla curtain" and the new immigration legislation put forward by both Carter and Reagan (examined in Chapter 8). Employers and government officials felt the need to do something about the outburst of activism among immigrant workers, and concrete proposals to "regain control of our borders" multiplied.

Immigrant worker activism came at a time when most unionized workers were caving in to givebacks and the number of work stoppages involving 1,000 workers or more was in precipitous decline (down from about 440 in 1974 to only 62 in 1984). But this did not deter the activists among "undocumented" Mexican workers, who unionized themselves in the early 1980s into the National Coordinating Council of Mexican Workers in the United States.

A few examples reveal the depth and militancy of their little-publicized but high-impact movement:

· 1974: Some 4,000 garment workers (85 percent of whom were Chicana and Mexican women) won a twenty-one-month-long strike for union representation against Farah Clothing Company in the border towns of Texas and New Mexico. The strikers won the support of green-card commuters (potential scabs), the Amalgamated Clothing Workers, and eventually the AFL-CIO. They sponsored a nineteen-month boycott of Farah pants that drew international support from workers in Farah's Hong Kong plant, the Japanese Textile Workers Union, and garment workers in Cuernavaca, Mexico.

· 1975: A strike by 150 workers, mostly Mexican women, shut down Tolteca Foods in Richmond, California. The company granted the strikers' major demands. In Los Angeles, UAW Local 645 unionized Cyclone Automotive Products' 130 employees (all but 2 of them "undocumented") and obtained wage hikes. In 1981, when the company, renamed American Exhaust, moved to Mexicali, Mexico, the workers obtained excellent severance pay and fringe benefits.

· 1975–85: The UAW unionized "illegals" in Region 6, which includes California and a web of aerospace and automotive companies that employed 110,000 workers prior to 1981's layoffs (only 40,000 employed workers by end-year). "Undocumented" Mexican workers at General Motors' largest West Coast plant, in Van Nuys, organized by the UAW and interviewed by this author, were earning good wages plus handsome fringe benefits by the end of 1981. When General Motors threatened in 1985 to close the Van Nuys plant in order to maximize profits by consolidating production in the Midwest, the plant's workers (50 percent of them Latins) built a community-wide coalition that kept the plant open.

· 1978: "Undocumented" workers, labor organizers, and sympathizers organized the first National Workers Conference on the Undocumented, held in Washington, D.C., April 8–12.

· 1979: "Illegals" at Reflectolite Products, Inc., in Los Angeles, California, won a historic labor contract in spite of severe repressive measures unleashed against the independent International Brotherhood of General Workers. Responding to earlier pressures by organizers of Mexican "illegals," the AFL-CIO in December finally agreed to stipulate that its affiliates would protect the "undocumented" at workplaces against INS raids and other abuses.

· Late 1970s: United Electrical Radio and Machine Workers of America (UE) helped organize and supported strikes involving hundreds of "undocumented" workers at such southern California plants as Nissin (instant soup), Electrosound (records), Kraco (stereo sound equipment), Tigart Industries, and so on.

· 1977–81: The National Steel and Shipbuilding Company (NASSCO) at the West Coast's largest shipyard was rocked by independent rank-and-file organizing in Ironworkers Local 627 (3,000 workers); 42 percent of NASSCO's workers are minorities, who contributed to the organizing drive after five deaths in 1976–77 caused by unsafe work conditions and a 1976 protest against NASSCO's ordering Mexican "green-carders" to wear green stripes on their work hats. The local union was eventually placed in trusteeship by (and to) the Ironworkers' International, whose leadership had condemned the independent organizing; three of the independents' main leaders, "the NASSCO Three," were framed on charges of being "communists" and accused of planning "a terrorist act"; during their prolonged trial, a company-FBI-police plot to disrupt the union was exposed; and although the International narrowly won an election against the independents via intimidation, the independents continued their activities in hopes of winning a fairer union election and winning their court cases.

· 1980: The First International Conference in Defense of the Full Rights of Undocumented Workers was held in Mexico City, April 28–30, bringing together representatives of over sixty Mexican and US organizations, mostly labor unions. The conference issued a Bill of Rights (see Appendix III), recommendations, and a Plan of Action. Later, more than 200 women attended the First International Conference of Border Women. In Los Angeles, some 253 workers, mostly women, at Glydons (an underwear manufacturer) won a seven-month-long strike that forced the company to accept the union and pay lost wages to all the workers.

· Late 1970s, early 1980s: "Undocumented" farmworkers in Ohio, Florida, New Jersey, New York, and other states escalated organizing drives. Since August 1978 over 2,000 farmworkers, mostly Mexican migrants from Texas led by the Farm Labor Organizing Committee (FLOC), have been on strike in the tomato fields of northwest Ohio contracted to the Campbell Soup Company. Since 1979 they have gained support for their nationwide boycott of Campbell products from Cesar Chavez, the Committee to Organize Agricultural Workers (a mainly Puerto Rican farmworkers group from New Jersey), activists in the Nuclear Freeze Campaign, and countless unions and churches.

· September 1981: More than 400,000 workers mobilized in Washington, D.C., Los Angeles, and elsewhere on September 19, "Solidarity Day," to express the need to unify all workers against new threats to unions and minorities. Many banners championed the rights of the "undocumented."

· March 1982: Thousands of Mexican "illegals," Chicanos, and human rights activists marched in Los Angeles, California, in opposition to the Simpson-Mazzoli bill and in favor of the rights of "undocumented" workers.

· 1979–85: In greater Los Angeles, trade unionists from the International Longshoremen's and Warehousemen's Union, United Steelworkers of America, International Association of Machinists, and Retail Clerks International Union increased organizing efforts among "illegals"; unions were also doing brisk organizing of Mexican carpenters, upholsterers, furniture workers, shoemakers, metalworkers, and restaurant employees; and about a third of the Teamsters' Los Angeles membership were said to be "undocumented" Mexicans. Similar trends emerged in northern California, where the Hotel Employees and Restaurant Employees International Union was planning a vigorous new organizing campaign.

· 1983–85: Faced with drastic wage cuts and other givebacks, 2,900 workers led by the United Steelworkers of America launched a mining strike in Morenci, Arizona, against Phelps Dodge Corporation. This long, unresolved strike echoes the region's bloodstained history of the IWW and Rockefeller's "goons" (see Chapter 2). Many of the most militant strikers today, as previously, are Mexicans, as are many of the scabs. The prostrike Teatro Libertad, in fact, performs its play *La Vida Del Cobre* (The Life of Copper) on both sides of the US-Mexico border to make the historical point: "70 years later, same company, Phelps Dodge, same issue, survival of the union."

· 1984: Workers from both sides of the border founded the independent Border Agricultural Workers Union (UTAF) and went on to win strikes involving more than 500 farmworkers in southern New Mexico and west Texas.

· 1984–85: Union efforts to relate workers' economic demands to expressions of solidarity with laborers engaged in fierce fights against the forces of repression in Central America and South Africa received a boost. The UAW issued a fact pamphlet exposing US interventionism in Central America, and numerous top AFL-CIO leaders condemned US policies there and in South Africa. In September 1984 the UAW won the right to represent 1,200 workers, including many recently arrived Salvadoran refugees, at the Superior Industries auto parts plant in Van Nuys, California. The company refused to recognize the UAW's victory in the union certification election. Hundreds of San Francisco Bay Area longshoreman unionists participated in an eleven-day labor boycott of all goods to and from South Africa. In April, 1985, the National Consultation on Immigrants' and Refugees' Rights was held in Los Angeles, drawing labor groups from sixteen states and calling for an end to INS abuses of human rights. Responding to public pressure, police departments in Chicago, San Jose, and Santa Ana announced policies of noncooperation with federal immigration authorities.

New Tendencies in US and Mexican Labor Unions

During the 1974–84 decade, when American labor unions were on the defensive, their membership in decline, most unionists were agreeing to no-strike pledges, wage givebacks, and other concessions. But an altogether different effort was developing among Mexican and other immigrant workers: strikes, protest marches, national and international meetings, and organizing campaigns in city and field were all on the upswing among the "undocumented."

In addition, a number of rank-and-file union members in both Mexico and the United States, however much on the defensive, were questioning the strategies of their leaders, attempting to democratize their unions, and resisting the workplace speedups, social welfare cutbacks, and other hardships being imposed in response to the economic crisis. As Chapter 5 indicated, the labor insurgency in Mexico became quite strong. In the United States, in spite of much harassment and bureaucratic maneuvering, rank-and-file democratic candidates for the presidencies of such important American unions as the 1.2-million-member United Steelworkers of America and the 170,000-member Oil, Chemical and Atomic Workers' Union came within a hairsbreadth of being elected in 1976 and 1979/81, respectively.

However much separated by lack of information and distinct cultural and political milieus, the democratic reformers of the US and Mexican labor movements have increasingly expressed mutual support. Indeed, in recent years, expressions of solidarity for strikers in textiles, electronics, agriculture, and mining have flowed back and forth across the border.

In 1978–79, for example, ex-miners, young miners, and the unemployed led a militant strike at the huge Nacozari copper mine in northern Sonora, near the US border. The Confederation of Mexican Workers (CTM), which is the backbone of Mexico's official Congress of Labor (CT), opposed the action and attempted to break it up. The CTM considered the strike too independent of its control. Pointing out that many CTM leaders had been corrupted and were in cahoots with the employers, the strikers sought the support of the United Mine Workers (UMW). The UMW's rank-and-file democratization movement had itself succeeded in overcoming the power of an older and corrupted leadership clique (in part because of the repugnance caused by the assassination of reformist UMW leader Joseph A. Yablonski and his family in 1969), and UMW members responded to the appeals of their Mexican counterparts with messages of solidarity. Unfortunately, these were not enough to prevent the ruthless crushing of the Nacozari strike by army troops, police, and CTM's armed goons.

Though intensifying popular anger, the deepening economic crisis has made it hard for democratic labor unionism to achieve its goals. The two governments have usually sought to "solve" the crisis by siding with employers rather than unions. In Mexico the government's use of the army, police, and CTM goons to repress labor protest has been stepped up, while in the United States the Reagan administration broke the PATCO air traffic controllers' strike and has taken a variety of other steps to discourage union militancy or organizing.

For instance, in 1983 Reagan's appointees to the National Labor Relations Board (NLRB) reversed long-standing policy in declaring it necessary for a union to have the majority of workers' support to continue attempts to organize a workplace, *no matter what the working conditions*. This and subsequent antilabor decisions by the NLRB provoked AFL-CIO president Lane Kirkland to suggest that things might be better if the NLRB were to disappear and labor-management relations were to return to "the law of the jungle."[12] In addition, Reagan's economic deregulation policies in the name of free enterprise have made it easier for employers to turn to cheap nonunion labor on the grounds that increased competition brought about by deregulation makes payment of union wages nearly impossible.

Despite setbacks to unionizing, growing signs of support for the "undocumented" among Mexican and some US unions have caused concern among employers in both nations. Mexico's CT (the rough equivalent of the AFL-CIO) is one labor organization that has given strong, if delayed, support to the "undocumented" immigrant workers. It has done so in response to the ongoing advances achieved by the ICC and other independents involved in unionizing the immigrants.

In 1980 the CT endorsed the Bill of Rights for the Undocumented Worker passed by the ICC's First International Conference for the Full Rights of Undocumented Workers convoked in Mexico City. The CT established a "resistance fund" and protection agency for the "undocumented." A CT manifesto entitled "To the Mexican People" explained that the "Reagan Plan" on immigration "does not touch the causes of immigration, does not seek to stop it, but wants instead to use it under improved conditions to generate greater surplus value and reestablish the economy, pressuring Mexico politically with the threat of massive deportations." The manifesto ended with the warning that Mexican migrant workers, as the most vulnerable group involved in wide-ranging international negotiations, were being used as a weapon by the United States in "its economic recovery through an accelerated accumulation of surplus value [and] control of events in the Caribbean and Central America and of relations with Mexico."

The CT's support for Mexican immigrant workers in the United States helps the organization maintain a "nationalist" and "progressive" image in the face of repeated rank-and-file challenges to its aging leadership. As a powerful corporativist arm of the PRI (Mexico's ruling political party), the CT in the past fifteen years has faced serious erosion of its base among union members who in growing numbers were joining the strikes and demonstrations of the "Democratic Tendency" labor movement opposed to the corruption of the old CT leadership. Often, Mexican migrant workers returning from eye-opening experiences in the United States with a heightened awareness of the forces affecting their lives have supported this kind of grass-roots movement.

For instance, Ramón Danzós Palomino, a strong backer of the Democratic Tendency, returned from the United States in the 1960s to lead a mass-based independent peasant movement and, after being a political prisoner for several years, rose to a top leadership position in the Mexican Communist Party.

Cases of former migrants rising to leadership are more the exception than the rule, but because they bring to the ranks of labor a democratic and internationalist perspective, they assume an importance far beyond their numbers. Even in remote rural communities experiencing little radical politicalization after generations of emigration, such as Isauro Reyes's village in Michoacán (see Chapter 1), interview data reveal that 65 percent of the residents, most of whom never belonged to a union in the United States, view labor unions as useful and "a good thing." On the other hand, 22 percent either do not know what unions are or do not feel the issue applies to their situation, while about 2 percent think that unions are "dangerous." Only 10 percent consider unions "useless."[13]

Meanwhile, important elements of both the AFL-CIO and Mexico's CT in 1982 began making behind-the-scenes gestures to the main leaders of the "independents," who were promoting an internationalist working-class solution to the capital-labor conflict on both sides of the border—people like veteran Texas farmworker leader Antonio Orendain, Los Angeles labor leader José "Pepe" Medina, the activists of Arizona's Maricopa County, and Danzós and various other Mexican rank-and-file union spokesmen. The AFL-CIO and CT overtures demonstrated the strong impact of the recent independent organizing activities on the top leaders of both nations' official labor confederations. Although the details of the talks have never been made public, the agenda was to explore possible strategies concerning "undocumented" workers that might help turn back employers' attacks on labor in general.

While the consequences of these talks have yet to become clear, the fact that they occurred at all is significant. Such explorations of a coherent, international, and unified labor strategy will serve the interests of all labor, provided that the "independents" do not give in to the tradition of sweetheart contracts and to the corrupt and violent trade-union bossism (charrismo, as it is known in Mexico) that have periodically blemished organized labor's history. Unfortunately, the tension between independents and mainstream union leaders that surrounded Cesar Chavez's bringing of the UFW under AFL-CIO discipline has not disappeared, nor is it likely to as long as independent organizers act more efficiently and swiftly than do labor union bureaucrats.

Like the independents and democratic reformers in organized labor's ranks, many assembly-line workers and official labor leaders as well now endorse the sentiment expressed by Harley Shaiken, a labor and technology specialist: "The global factory mandates that unions have closer contact and communications."[14] Few nowadays in business, labor, or government think only in domestic terms.

Labor Broadens its Coalitions

A growing number of labor, human rights, church, political, and civil libertarian organizations are attempting to advance an "internationalist" perspective concerning immigration, border, labor, and related issues. A three-day regional meeting in Los Angeles in the fall of 1981, for example, brought together more than 600 trade-union, church, academic, political, and community organization representatives to deal with "economic dislocation" (runaway shops, layoffs, community decline, etc.). Among numerous Latin American delegates to the meeting were representatives of the Sandinista government of Nicaragua and El Salvador's Democratic Revolutionary Front. Large delegations were sent by Mexico's CT-affiliated telephone workers' and electrical workers' unions and workers of the independent and largely female Solidev electronic workers' union from nearby Tijuana.

Highlighted at the meeting was the experience of the Solidev independent trade unionists. In the late 1970s Solidev's 250 workers (they had numbered more than 1,000 before the mass layoffs during the mid-1970s recession) organized an independent union that won a contract with the powerful international electronics firm Solitron Devices Corporation, a semiconductor producer headquartered in Florida. The Solidev women, a tenth of whom had worked more than four years in the Tijuana assembly plant, won impressive wage hikes and the rehiring of dismissed workers. Moreover, by strengthening earlier alliances formed with national and international groups and friends, they held on to their gains against repeated efforts to destroy their independent union. In subsequent negotiations with the company, they established a wage level above the minimum professional wage offered by other border assembly plants, the right to exclusivity in contract negotiations, and an end to unjustified worker dismissals. These were unprecedented achievements for labor in border industry. In 1983, however, the company closed its Tijuana plant.

Linkages between issues and organizations like those manifested at the 1981 Los Angeles meeting have grown in number and kind since then. Church, labor, anti-interventionist, peace, and Latino and other minority groups have moved closer together in the 1980–85 period, culminating in such concrete practices as that of America's first "underground railroad" since slavery, providing transportation, housing, and protection for Central America's "illegal" refugees fleeing death squads and military massacres. The governing bodies of the United Methodists, the Presbyterian Church (USA), the United Church of Christ, and the American Baptist Churches, among other religious denominations, have endorsed the sanctuary movement and defended its militants, some of whom have been arrested, tried, and sent off to prison. Among at least a dozen city governments giving official support to the sanctuary movement are those of Berkeley, Burlington, Chicago, Los Angeles, Sacramento, and St. Paul.

Many Latinos who are US citizens have been in the forefront of organizing acts of solidarity with movements for democracy in Nicaragua, Honduras, El Salvador, and Guatemala. They have infused Latino nationalism with a strong internationalist flavor—in contrast to the more limited national-identity approach of the "Chicano" and "Puerto Rican Young Lords" movements of the 1960s and early 1970s. Representative of this new trend was the press release issued by a broad Chicano-sponsored coalition organized around the holding of the Olympic Games in Los Angeles in 1984:

> Most disturbing to us is that an extremely high percentage of the troops ready to invade Central America are US citizens of Latin extraction. We will not be forced to kill anyone, but especially people who are historically, culturally and racially our sisters and brothers. We are *un pueblo, una lucha*.

Latino labor leaders have been particularly active in linking the issues of immigrant labor, union rights, and peace in Central America. UE's Humberto Camacho and other former Mexican migrant workers have intensified their lifetime fight for the rights of "undocumented" workers. When the AFL-CIO executive council initially supported the Simpson-Mazzoli bill, Mexican labor leaders in the AFL-CIO like J. J. Rodriguez, Henry Lacayo, and Pete Beltran successfully pressured the leadership to reconsider its position and to come out against factory roundups and deportations of "illegals."

As union leaders and members have learned more about El Salvador death squads eliminating labor unionists and about AFL-CIO collaboration with right-wing labor union movements in Latin America through the American Institute of Free Labor Development (AIFLD), growing numbers of them have come out against US policy in Central America. AIFLD was founded in Mexico in 1962 by AFL-CIO anticommunist leaders, TNC executives, and the US government. Funded largely by the government's Agency for International Development but also by TNCs and AFL-CIO membership dues, AIFLD has worked closely with the CIA against many progressive or "nationalist" governments or labor unions throughout Latin America, protecting foreign capital in the region.[15]

An unusually large number of mainline American labor unions have banded together to form the National Labor Committee in Support of Democracy and Human Rights in El Salvador. This powerful organization successfully lobbied for and obtained the release of ten Salvadoran labor union leaders in the fall of 1984—nine of whom immediately went into exile in order to escape assassination.

Labor's resurgence in these areas of social protest may be a new birth or a dying gasp, but it is highly significant. Some 600 delegates, many of them from mainline labor unions, attended the First Emergency Conference on US Interventionism held in Cleveland, Ohio, in September 1984. Together with delegates from churches, schools, Latino neighborhoods, and anti-interventionist organizations like CISPES (Committee in Solidarity with the People of El Salvador) and antinuclear groups like Mobilization for Survival, they voted unanimously there and during subsequent meetings to build unity of the anti-interventionist forces with those of the peace (antinuke) movement around four common demands: end US intervention in Central America; end the arms race; money for jobs, not war; and end US support for apartheid in South Africa. This new move for unity helped produce the large demonstrations of April 20, 1985, that took place in Washington, D.C. (nearly 100,000 demonstrators), San Francisco (about 50,000), and other regional urban centers.

The active role of labor unions in organizing these actions is not unrelated to the issues of immigrant labor and economic crisis. Organized labor is—economically and politically—on the defensive. It needs new friends and allies. In earlier periods of history, it received impetus for growth and success from the organizing of immigrant labor. Now, for the first time since prior to World War II, organized labor has taken two new and bold steps. It has begun to organize the unorganized, and it has openly criticized the government on a major foreign policy issue—the war in Central America, where the AFL-CIO no longer backs the CIA's role, among other facets of US policy.

What are the solutions to many of the problems faced by immigrant and US workers? The examples of history suggest that workers in all sectors—industrial, agricultural, and services—cannot advance, or even maintain earlier gains, without paying attention to the international dimensions of their situation and the needs of the unorganized or nonunionized. The corporations' increased national and international mobility has put *all* workers (including farmworkers and slum sweatshop employees) at a distinct disadvantage. Securing economic gains for workers has come to depend more than ever before on building an international alliance among them. The recent upsurge in militancy among Mexican migrant workers on both sides of the border can vitalize other segments of the labor movements in both nations. Indeed, without the support of many of these newly organizing migrant workers, some of the older unions might well evanesce.

The constituency for future labor organizing is increasingly nonwhite, female, and immigrant. The Reagan administration's publicly declared intent to cut back bilingual education and rescind laws requiring federal contractors to set numerical goals to remedy possible job discrimination has weakened the position of minority-group workers at a time when they are entering the labor force at an unprecedented rate. Women make up an even larger portion of the workforce (less than 10 percent of mothers of young children now stay home as housewives). By AFL-CIO estimates, Latina women workers are entering the labor force at twice the rate of all US women. Studies show nearly twice as many women workers as men wanting a labor union. All this suggests that opposition to discrimination will be taking its place alongside traditional bread-and-butter union slogans if American labor unionism is to survive its current crisis.

Evidence of the possibility for uniting diverse groups showed itself recently in the founding in April 1983 of a coalition fighting for closures, the North American Farm Alliance (NAFA), made up of farmers, union members, blacks, women, and peace, church, and environmental groups, from twenty-three states and Canada. As NAFA chairperson Merle Hansen, a semiretired Nebraska farmer, put it, "Farmers feel that they've lost control of their lives, and it gives them a good feeling to work with Blacks, with labor and with other groups who have [organized]. There are a lot of people who . . . just don't see hope. . . . They're either going to be the base for mass fascism in this country or they're going to align themselves with the people's struggles and with peace and justice issues."[16]

8

Legislating
Immigrant Labor

"Illegal immigrants are a basic part of our workforce."
—President Reagan, introducing "guest-worker" proposal,
July 30, 1981

*"The [Simpson-Mazzoli] bill looks dead, but it moves every
time you beat it with a stick."*
—Anonymous member of Congress, quoted in *New York
Times*, October 12, 1984

*"The [Simpson-Mazzoli] bill is wrong because it is discrimi-
natory. The bill is wrong because it targets in on individuals
just because they are who they are. The bill is wrong because
it looks to deprive individuals of their ability to get jobs. The
bill is wrong, wrong, wrong."*
—Geraldine A. Ferraro, Democratic Party nominee for Vice-
President, 1984

At its July 1984 national convention, the Democratic Party issued an
open-ended call for reform of the nation's immigration laws—in the
context of the times, an implicit endorsement of the Simpson-Mazzoli
bill. The platform's stance on immigration reform weathered a threat
by Latino delegates to boycott the first presidential nominating ballot
in protest of Simpson-Mazzoli. At the convention, for the first time in
history, Latinos possessed sufficient strength to have a Mexican vice-
presidential candidate—Mayor Henry Cisneros of San Antonio,
Texas—taken seriously by a major political party.

The Democratic plank on immigration was proof of the high priority that the ruling circles of the nation's political parties give to Simpson-Mazzoli. During the 1984 presidential campaign, immigration was one of the most hotly debated issues. Both candidates called for immigration reform while reinforcing the idea that somehow "our borders are out of control." The irony of this rationale was well illustrated in a six-frame cartoon that appeared at the time in the weekly *Guardian*. The cartoon featured a plump man labeled "US industry" lamenting, "We moved our factories to Mexico to take advantage of the incredibly cheap labor but we pay less than the Mexicans could make for service jobs in the US so they leave our factories and risk crossing the border to compete for the service jobs with the workers we laid off when we moved to Mexico! Some people have no sense of national loyalty!!"[1]

In the summer of 1985, Simpson-Mazzoli, the oft-defeated immigration reform bill that can never say die, was back in the news with a few new teeth. Congressman Peter W. Rodino (D-N.J.), a veteran influential liberal, had decided to join Congressman Romano Mazzoli (D-Ky.) in an effort to see the legislation safely through to passage. This Simpson-Mazzoli bill is actually just a more sophisticated version of the same old laws that have governed the flow of Mexican immigrants in the past. Under its provisions, for instance, "bracero programs" will bear the modernized name of "guest worker programs."

In its final Senate-House conference version of 1984, the Simpson-Mazzoli bill opens the doors to *unlimited* numbers of "guest workers." It provides for an expanded, more flexible H-2 (temporary worker) program. It strengthens the Labor Secretary's powers to admit foreign workers when US workers "are not qualified and available." And it eliminates a ceiling on legal immigration. In sum, in the name of reducing the number of foreigners passing through the border doors, it opens them wider to potentially unprecedented numbers of immigrant workers.

Simpson-Mazzoli claims to protect the public interest by providing for sanctions against employers who hire "illegals," even though the most cursory investigation reveals that employer sanctions have never succeeded in the past. Furthermore, in a provision that has alarmed most civil libertarians (see Chapter 9), the bill calls for a "worker ID card."

To sweeten the pill, Simpson-Mazzoli promises "amnesty" for those "illegals" already here and who can prove at least four years of continuous residency. Yet, if one looks at this provision from a Mexican immigrant worker's point of view, one sees that proving residency after being in hiding, year after year, during seasonal trips to the United States, is nearly impossible.

While US officials often claim that the US must "stem the tide" or "close the valve" of illegal immigration, few admit that immigrants are both encouraged and needed. President Reagan during his reelection campaign said, "We have been the safety valve, whether we wanted to or not, with the illegal entry here." He was reinforcing the erroneous idea that no Americans are involved in bringing Mexican workers into the country. Yet all students of immigration history concur that US employers have always "wanted to" allow the "illegal entry" of Mexicans.

President Reagan himself stated on July 30, 1981, that "illegal immigrants are a basic part of our workforce," a point he made in presenting his administration's proposed "guest worker" program. Reagan's proposal, like Simpson-Mazzoli, opens the doors to as many or as few immigrant workers as the Labor Department deems necessary. As the bracero program proved, the Labor Department cooperates with employers requiring a steady, reliable supply of inexpensive immigrant workers. The Simpson-Mazzoli bill is actually a labor proposal disguised as an immigration law. Its promise of a return to forms of contract labor outlawed in the United States since the 1880s will do less to spur economic recovery than enforcement of existing labor laws like the Fair Labor Standards Act and the Migrant and Seasonal Agricultural Worker Protection Act.

The History of Legislating Immigrant Labor

The moving of immigration issues to center stage by the nation's principal political parties is not new in American history—it happens repeatedly during times of economic crisis, radical change in the technology or organization of economic production, or profound social or labor unrest.

The first national immigration statutes—other than the 1875 barring of convicts and prostitutes—were the Chinese Exclusion Act of May 6, 1882 (not repealed until 1943), and the Immigration Act of August 3, 1882. Effectively removing the states' power to regulate immigration, they forbade the entry of Chinese laborers, hundreds of whom had died alongside similarly exploited Irish immigrants in the heat and overwork of building the nation's railroads. At the time, the Chinese accounted for almost one-tenth of California's population and were the targets of frequent racist stonings, beatings, and killings. (Japanese laboring migrants soon replaced the Chinese in Hawaii and California, but during the 1907 depression they too were barred by President Teddy Roosevelt's "Gentleman's Agreement.")

The first federal acts regulating immigration according to national origin followed a major depression in the late 1870s. They came into effect in the midst of the economic change from slavery to full-scale wage-labor industrialization and the spread of the nation's first labor unions. Laws prohibiting the importation of foreign labor under contract were also enacted in the 1880s, in response to another depression, strikes, and the lobbying efforts of the Knights of Labor, the nation's oldest and largest labor organization at the time.

Those same years a century ago witnessed a "revolving door" practice. Supposedly to protect US labor, authorities restricted immigration on the grounds of individual qualifications and national origin. The main scapegoats were the Chinese. At the same time, they opened the borders to even more immigrants, whose cheap labor fueled economic recovery and increased production. As a result of these policies, the number of immigrants reached an astounding high of 5.25 million in the 1880s. This figure was not surpassed until the first decade of the twentieth century, when 8.8 million arrived, followed by 5.74 million in the second decade.

The Immigration Act of February 5, 1917, passed over President Woodrow Wilson's veto, established the Asiatic Barred Zone, which further restricted the entry of Orientals. It also established literacy requirements for entry into the United States—a measure aimed at intimidating Mexicans and Jewish and Catholic immigrants from southeastern Europe. In practice, these requirements, together with the mass administration of newly introduced and culturally biased "IQ" tests offered only in English to students, job applicants, and soldiers, were used to recruit cannon fodder for World War I. Those whose IQ scores were the lowest, usually because English was their second language, were the first to be sent off to war.

To these qualitative regulations, quantitative ones were added in the 1920s, starting with the temporary Quota Act of May 19, 1921, and continuing with the permanent Immigration Act of May 26, 1924, which lasted until 1952. These laws excluded Western Hemisphere immigrants from numerical quotas, while the Asiatic Barred Zone continued to limit the entry of Orientals severely. Based on an annual ceiling of 150,000 immigrants for all other nationalities combined, the annual quota for nations became fixed, as of July 1, 1929, according to a complex formula meant to assure a high proportion of whites. The number of a given nation's people to be allowed entry would bear the same ratio to 150,000 as the number of its inhabitants in the United States (as of 1920) to the white US population (with provision for a minimum of 100 entrants for each nationality).

The next major immigration legislation implemented the bilateral bracero agreement between Mexico and the United States (see Chapter 3), the twentieth century's first officially recognized and legally regulated "guest worker" program (1942–64). After World War II, Congress passed in 1948 the Displaced Persons Act, the nation's first refugee legislation, which provided for the admission of mainly Poles and Germans.

There soon followed the even more restrictionist and conservative McCarran-Walter Act, or the Immigration and Nationality Act of June 27, 1952. In addition to a family reunification program, it established a selection preference system emphasizing the admission of people with high education or exceptional abilities. Partly in response to "the loss" of China and other Asian nations "to communism" and a new wave of entry applications from the East, McCarran-Walter eliminated race as a bar to citizenship. It permitted Asians to become citizens, and it opened up new, if limited, quota allotments for most of south and east Asia. This curious modification of America's racist immigration policy was also a way of dealing with fresh demands for equal rights surfacing among Mexican, Asiatic, black, and other minority war veterans who had discovered nonsegregated societies during their overseas service.

The 1952 McCarran-Walter Act prohibited citizens' arrests of "wetbacks" but included a supposed concession to Texas congressmen, the Texas Proviso, which allowed the employment of "aliens"—a part of immigration law still in effect today. It also incorporated the exclusion of communists contained in the 1950 McCarran Internal Security Act, thereby reinforcing the Cold War and anticommunist atmosphere of the period (see Chapter 3). The 1950 McCarran Internal Security Act's Title II authorized the construction of "emergency" concentration camps, six of which had been built by 1952—an early precedent for the type of detention centers now overflowing with unwanted immigrants and political refugees (see Chapter 9).

President Harry S. Truman vetoed the McCarran-Walter Act on the grounds that the quota system interfered with US foreign policy or, in Truman's words, restricted the nation's ability to "succor those who are brave enough to escape from [communist] barbarism." Significantly, Truman also pointed out that "the basis of this quota system was false and unworthy in 1924 and is even worse now."[2] He further stated that the McCarran-Walter Act's provisions for "denaturalizing" naturalized citizens on political grounds created a group of second-class citizens by distinguishing between native and naturalized citizens.

Overriding Truman's veto, Congress passed the McCarran-Walter Act, including its "denaturalizing" provisions. This and subsequent legislation opened the doors wide to "refugees" and "escapees" from "communist-dominated" countries, and in doing so helped cement the conservative foundations of US immigration policy. The 1950 and 1952 McCarran acts were used to smash labor unions, break strikes, further intimidate immigrant workers, and harass the Mexican minority in the United States. But in 1965, as the civil rights movement began to sweep the nation, legislators approved amendments to the 1952 McCarran-Walter Act repealing the national origins quota system and replacing it with one based primarily on criteria of family reunification, skills needed in the US economy, and political refuge.

These amendments did not seriously reduce the restrictionist, racist, and anticommunist flavor of American immigration law, however. In fact, they established an annual ceiling of 170,000 immigrants from the Eastern Hemisphere, including a ceiling of 20,000 per country. They also established an annual ceiling of 120,000 for the Western Hemisphere as a whole while retaining the ban on per-country quotas for the Western Hemisphere.

This Western Hemisphere ceiling was meant to stem the tide of hundreds of thousands of Mexicans accustomed to migrating northward under the just-terminated bracero program. The "illegal" flow, however, continued unabated. In 1972 and 1973 Congressman Rodino, who later co-sponsored the Simpson-Mazzoli bill, introduced legislation that would penalize employers for hiring "undocumented" persons. Each year Rodino's bills passed in the House but stalled in the Senate, where agribusiness interests held considerable power. A similar bill in 1977 got stuck in the House Rules Committee.

The Refugee Act of March 17, 1980, redefined "refugee" to conform with the definition used in the United Nations Protocol and Convention Relating to the Status of Refugees. It provided for the annual admission of as many as 70,000 additional people having a "well-founded fear of persecution" on account of race, religion, nationality, membership in a social group, or political opinion. It permitted the emergency admission of refugees and provided federal assistance for resettlement.

In practice, however, the 1980 Refugee Act did not alter the traditional high politicization of immigration policy. Shortly after its passage, some 125,000 "boat people" from communist Cuba were admitted and given a rousing welcome while thousands of refugees escaping the violently repressive right-wing dictatorship of Haiti, all of them nonwhite, continued to be detained, deported, or otherwise harassed. Similarly, refugees from the sanguinary US-backed dictatorships of Guatemala and El Salvador were ushered home by federal authorities, in many cases to their deaths.

This double standard in the application of the refugee clauses of US immigration law gave rise not only to the "sanctuary" movement for Salvadorans but also to new legislative proposals to protect them. In 1985 Senator Dennis DeConcini (D-Ariz.) introduced a bill to grant Salvadorans "illegally" in the country the same status as refugees from Poland. DeConcini's bill would suspend deportation hearings against Salvadoran refugees for about two years. His proposal, coupled with another little-known bill introduced in the House by Congressman Joe Moakley (D-Mass.), would allow as many as 850,000 Salvadorans residing in the United States to come under its protection. (The DeConcini-Moakley bill was still in congressional committees as this book went to press).

In 1976 a major change in immigration law affecting Mexicans was passed at the last minute during the closing session of a lame-duck Congress. It placed a 20,000 annual ceiling on each Western Hemisphere country, *including Mexico*. Thus, for the first time in history a numerical restriction was placed on "legal" Mexican immigrants. Not since the death of the "Box laws" (see Chapter 2) in the 1920s had such an effort even come close to succeeding.

The 1976 change reflected a new upsurge in anti-Mexican bigotry in the United States. During the previous decade (1967–76), North and Central America, including Mexico, Cuba, and the West Indies, had led all other regions in legal immigration—1.51 million. Mexico had accounted for a third of that total. Asian immigration for the same period, swelled by an influx of Vietnamese and Cambodians after the US defeat in Vietnam, had totalled 1.05 million.

In brief, Europe was no longer the main source of America's immigrants. Whereas in 1959 some 61 percent of immigrants had come from Europe, by 1979 the percentage had dropped to only 13.4. The corresponding 1979 figure for Latin American immigrants had doubled to 38.6 percent, while that for Asians had quintupled to 41.4 percent.

This radical shift led to a rapid intensification of the nation's historic pattern of anti-immigrant sentiment, a process typically aggravated by economic crisis, technological change, and social discontent. Violent acts of bigotry were reported on the upswing against not only Mexicans and Latinos but also Asians.[3] The new wave of anti-immigrant feeling echoed the pattern set in the nineteenth century by the attacks against Catholic, German, and Irish immigrants and the formation by mid-century of the nativist Know-Nothing movement. There are, however, four notable differences today.

First, the groups targeted by today's nativists are different. Now Latinos, Asians, and Middle Eastern peoples in general—and Mexicans in particular—are the main focus of attack.

Second, the targeted groups, especially Mexicans, have fought back with considerable success and on an international scale. This fight-back led to the passing of a Bill of Rights for the Undocumented Worker at an international emergency conference held in Mexico City in April 1980 (see Appendix III). It has included numerous other emergency conferences, mass mobilizations in the streets of cities heavily populated by Latinos, a coordinated national lobbying effort, and a national call for a day of protest on behalf of "the undocumented" (October 12, 1985). Representative of the new resistance was the National Chicano Immigration Conference held in May 1980, which joined hundreds of Mexican and Latino organizations in a united front against all forms of contract labor, for the abolition of the INS/Border Patrol, for an "open border" for workers and a "closed border" for transnational corporations, and for recognition of "the fact that we are a people without borders with full rights to self-determination."[4]

Third, the preconditions for a fresh outbreak of anti-immigrant bigotry today are *all present simultaneously and have developed over a longer stretch of time.* A prolonged economic crisis has been accompanied by a radical economic change characterized by the dividing up, internationalizing, and mechanization of production systems, *and* by signs of profound social unrest, particularly in the ranks of immigrant labor itself.

Fourth, the structural depths of the economic crisis are more hidden, multidimensional, and intense than at any previous time, giving rise to more complicated strategies for solving it. The persistence of the crisis is concealed by short-lived spurts of "recovery" or by lethargic blips of slow economic growth accompanied by high unemployment, described by some economists as periods of "growth recession." For example, the first two quarters of 1984 typified a short-lived spurt heralded as "recovery," while the third quarter was a blip called "growth recession." A more or less identical pattern emerged during the first three quarters of 1985.[5]

The crisis is also far more complex, having grown out of a number of major events: defeat in a foreign war (Vietnam); far-reaching changes in the character of production; collapse of the dollar's global hegemony; heightened competition between major capitalist powers; a potential global debt crisis; threatened collapse of key sectors of the economy in the absence of cheap immigrant labor; a sharp rise in the number of runaway shops; intensified racial and ethnic divisions; and the leapfrogging (not "domino-falling") spread of nationalist (not "communist") revolutions. In light of all these more or less simultaneous occurrences, the means for controlling crisis and recovering from it become correspondingly more complex and more difficult to coordinate.

One of the strategies is to speed up the revolving of the border door, to escalate attacks on Mexican migrant workers while continuing to call upon their inexpensive labor power. The emergence of a Latino minority outnumbering American blacks and the likelihood of its rapid growth during the spread of turmoil in Latin America adds to an ever more assertive bloc of voters anxious to affect national and foreign policies in ways not necessarily compatible with the goals of recent presidents and the transnational corporations. The threat of a strong Latino population, in turn, leads the government to attempt further control over immigration.

Deepening economic crisis at home, political crises in neighboring Mexico and Central America, and an unprecedented upsurge in the organizing of immigrant labor have prompted a full-scale effort to control Mexican immigrant workers and have taken legislative form in the Simpson-Mazzoli bill.

A New Anti-Immigrant Offensive: "Guest Workers" and the Simpson-Mazzoli Bill

The opening salvo of the attempt to control immigrant workers occurred August 4, 1977, when President Jimmy Carter asked Congress to prohibit the hiring of "illegal aliens" and to give legal status to those residing in the United States since 1970. Carter was unsheathing the two-edged sword that would be made the *public* centerpiece of subsequent immigration proposals: the deportation of many Mexicans as "illegals," on the one hand, and a tightening of control over those remaining in or entering the country, on the other.

When it became clear that Carter's proposed measures could not be enacted without upsetting too many groups and creating new political problems, Congress established in October 1978 a Select Commission on Immigration and Refugee Policy, headed by the Reverend Theodore M. Hesburgh. The commission was asked to investigate the problem and propose some solutions as quickly as possible. The problem was presented as an immigration issue involving international borders and national security rather than as a matter of corporate practices and labor recruitment.

When the Simpson-Mazzoli bill was introduced in Congress on March 17, 1982, supporters made it appear patriotic, restrictionist, and in the interests of labor. The bill was presented as a means of regaining control of the nation's borders, of slamming the door on unwanted Mexican "wetbacks," of stemming a potential tidal wave of Caribbean and Central American "boat people" and "feet people," and of preserving the nation's culture. At the same time, it was said to live up to the nation's "melting pot" tradition by granting "amnesty" to long-term resident "aliens." The bill's sponsors claimed it was fair and even-handed. On the one hand, employers knowingly hiring "illegal" immigrants would be fined up to $10,000 a violation. On the other hand, "amnesty" would be granted for "illegal aliens" who arrived before January 1, 1980, and had been living in the country continuously since then.

The central provision of the legislation—a "guest worker" program laid out in Section II-B (see Appendix IV)—established special procedures for an expanded H-2 program for seasonal workers in agriculture and allowed the hiring of immigrant workers ("visitors") who had "nonrefundable roundtrip tickets." The "guest worker" provision was quickly covered up by assertions—which soon became publicly accepted assumptions—that the migratory flow would be curtailed, not continued or increased.

Yet in fact Simpson-Mazzoli provides legal admission for almost double the present annual ceiling of 270,000 people (maximum of 20,000 from any single country) and for *unlimited* numbers of temporary "guest workers." It also doubles the number of routine annual visas allotted Mexicans and Canadians, from 20,000 to 40,000 in each instance, while permitting either Mexico or Canada to make use of the other's unused quota. In effect, this means more than tripling the Mexican quota to at least 70,000 visas, since Canadians rarely use up more than 10,000.

The media mostly reflect the above-mentioned assumptions. On July 8, 1985, *Time* magazine's "Special Immigrants Issue" failed to mention the "guest worker" provision but instead defined Simpson-Mazzoli's "dual centerpiece" as employer sanctions and "amnesty." A September 3, 1985, CBS television prime-time special program, "Whose America Is It?," focused almost entirely on provisions for employer sanctions, without noting their past failures. It further gave the impression that Mexicans are taking Americans' jobs, even though it pointed out that they are paid wages substantially below what most Americans are willing to accept. The same program devoted a quarter-hour segment to a burgeoning campaign to make English the nation's "official" language.

The CBS program scarcely mentioned "amnesty" and said nothing about "guest workers." Indeed, the issue of employer sanctions has come up repeatedly in all public debates and mass media coverage, while Simpson-Mazzoli's core "guest worker" provision, a giant loophole that adds to the meaninglessness of employer sanctions, gets little or no play—except by Latino organizations, whose access to the media remains limited.

Recent world events helped heat up the immigration issue and steer public opinion toward acceptance of legislation like Simpson-Mazzoli. Revolutions swept Iran and Nicaragua in 1979; El Salvador witnessed its death squads' horrendous deeds and the rapid growth in the guerrillas' popularity in late 1979 and the early 1980s; 125,000 Cuban "boat people" arrived on US shores in April 1980; and in 1980–81 the nation was jolted by the deepest recession yet in the prolonged economic crisis. All stimulated popular discontent with foreign "job-takers," some of whom were labeled "revolutionary fanatics," "spics," and "communist-inspired unionizers." Many elements in the media contributed to a crisis atmosphere by means of "yellow journalism"[6] that encouraged what soon became an informal, only partially organized national campaign to "regain control of our borders." The media effectively laid the groundwork for public acceptance of this obviously unenforceable demand.

In this charged atmosphere, the Reverend Theodore Hesburgh's Select Commission on Immigration and Refugee Policy recommended, on February 26, 1981, legislation to provide a one-time "amnesty" for most "illegal aliens" and an *increase* in legal immigration for a few years to absorb some of the migratory flow. A "guest worker" program, preferably an expanded H-2 temporary visa system, was mentioned as a possible further means of "legalizing" and regulating the influx of Mexican laborers. A more open-ended guest worker program, the commission pointed out, would increase illegal immigration in the long run.

The commission's report was an early indication, for those willing to see it, that "regaining control of our borders" meant, not keeping Mexican workers out (even though presented that way), but making sure Mexicans would continue to migrate to the United States on a more controlled and regularized basis. Later in 1981 President Reagan's attorney general, William French Smith, acknowledged that the goal was not to *cut off* but simply to "reduce and regulate this flow" and to channel foreign workers "into jobs where they are needed."[7]

In other words, by 1981 it was obvious to informed observers that the American economy *needed* Mexican migrant workers as cheap, highly productive labor power, and not just as scapegoats. It was evident that Mexican workers were heading north in larger numbers than ever before and that the border area was far too immense to police, so there was no real prospect of cutting off the migratory flow there.

Talk of a possible "guest worker" program had been heard as early as the late 1960s. Ever since the termination of the bracero program, agribusiness and other sectors dependent on Mexican migrant labor had made headway in overcoming labor and liberal opposition to legislation that would create a "guest worker" program. Discussion of the "guest worker" idea in the Select Commission report helped make it an acceptable option.

President Reagan's immigration proposals, made public on July 30, 1981, closely resembled those of the Select Commission. They included a "guest worker" program allowing up to 50,000 workers for stays of nine to twelve months, and they gave the Labor Department authority to *expand the number of guest workers whenever it liked.* There was no hint that such a program would do anything other than allow employers—operating through their associations and the Labor Department—to control and regulate the migratory flow in their favor, much as they had done in the days of the bracero program.

Nor was there mention of the fact that the Reagan "guest worker" program would tend to force American workers' wages down in the same way they had been forced down under the bracero program. Both the 1951 President's Commission on Migratory Labor and the 1959 panel of experts appointed by the secretary of labor had documented this and other adverse effects on labor. Reflecting on the fact that Reagan's "guest worker" program was proposed as part of a "good neighbor" relationship, several commentators in Mexico referred to its workings thus: "They [US citizens] are the neighbors and we are the goods."

From its inception, Reagan's immigration program has served to divide workers. The likely scenario is that the Reagan "guest worker" policy, like that proposed by Simpson-Mazzoli, would expand the Mexican migratory flow to the United States. It would also attract to US consulates or contract centers in Mexico tens of thousands of new job-seekers, each of whom would demand an increase in "guest worker" quotas. Those not finding a place within the quota would most likely find their way into the United States anyway (without legal entry permits), where they would compete for the same jobs for which the "guest workers" had been contracted. Employers in states like California and Texas would use the legal presence of cheap Mexican labor as an excuse (and a scapegoat) for holding all workers' wages down. Chicanos would protest the Mexican government's tolerance of such a program, and in doing so they might also aggravate "anti-Chicano" tendencies among Mexico's citizenry. Any movement toward "pan-Mexican" and international working class unity to achieve better treatment of all workers on both sides of the border—an idea with a long history going back to the Flores Magón brothers' PLM (Mexican Liberal Party), the Debs Socialists, and the IWW ("Wobblies")—would be seriously undermined. Specific employers in US agribusiness, industry, and services would benefit.

Reagan's immigration proposals at first elicited widespread bipartisan support. They were, after all, in line with the earlier Carter and Hesburgh commission proposals, as well as the entire history of US immigration policy. Consequently, the Simpson-Mazzoli bill, introduced into Congress in March 1982, incorporated the substance of the Hesburgh commission and Reagan programs.

Underlying nativism was apparent in the words Senator Alan Simpson (R-Wyo.) used to present the legislation:

> If language and cultural separatism rise above a certain level, the unity and political stability of the nation will, in time, be seriously eroded. A common language and a core public culture of certain shared values, beliefs, and customs make us distinctly "Americans."

Senator S. I. Hayakawa (R-Calif.) added a "sense of Congress" clause to the bill making English "the official language of the US." This would have the effect of undercutting various bilingual programs—including bilingual education and ballots—required in many states, as well as imposing a kind of de facto "Jim Crow" discriminatory bar against Latinos. Bilingual programs are already under attack. In Greater Miami's Dade County, Florida, for instance, an ordinance prohibits the transaction of business in any language but English.

As more and more amendments were added to Simpson-Mazzoli in the course of congressional committee work and debate over the next two years, it became almost impossible to tell what the final details of the bill would be. Indeed, so many special interests were lobbying around the bill's multifaceted contents and so many touchy political issues concerning human, civil, and labor rights were involved that Simpson-Mazzoli experienced a number of apparently fatal setbacks from 1982 to 1985. But the bill kept rising from the ashes, each time with an apparently better chance to pass. As the issues it addressed heated up, Simpson-Mazzoli had an increasingly chilling effect on the organizing activities of Mexican immigrant workers, who feared the bill's presumed prohibition of their entry or employment.

Rather than present the Simpson-Mazzoli bill in dense detail, it is more useful to concentrate on its legislative history and major themes—a "guest worker" program, employer sanctions, and "amnesty"—together with the opposition they have evoked. Since the Senate and House versions contained various minor differences, and since an alternative bill was offered in early 1984 by Congressman Edward R. Roybal (D-Calif.), all three bills—Simpson, Mazzoli, and Roybal—are compared in Appendix II. The Roybal bill differed from Simpson-Mazzoli mainly in its reliance on current labor law rights to be applied to temporary farmworkers and in its omission of employer sanctions, worker ID cards, and a "guest worker" program. All three bills called for significant increases in the INS budget and a beefing up of the US Border Patrol. In 1985 Roybal introduced a new bill that differed from his earlier one by providing for employer sanctions and a three-year transitional "guest worker" program for agricultural interests.

The Senate first approved Simpson-Mazzoli on August 17, 1982, by a vote of 80 to 19, but the bill died on the House floor on December 18, 1982, as time ran out with nearly 300 amendments pending. Then, on May 5, 1983, in a new Congress, the House Judiciary Committee approved the immigration bill by a vote of 20 to 9, making it likely that before year's end the full House would reach a vote. Two weeks later the Senate again approved Simpson-Mazzoli, this time by a vote of 76 to 18.

But by then the bill had become a political hot potato, in large part because of a public campaign of protest led by Latino and immigrant worker organizations and civil rights groups. On October 4, 1983, House Speaker Thomas P. O'Neill, Jr. (D-Mass.), blocked action on the bill, saying he could find "no constituency" for it. Once more, Simpson-Mazzoli appeared to be dead.

The Democrats reportedly feared that President Reagan would veto Simpson-Mazzoli to gain voting strength among Latinos. But on October 19, 1983, Reagan reaffirmed his strong support for immigration legislation. Then, on November 22, 1983, Speaker O'Neill, claiming he had assurances from Senator Simpson that there would be no presidential veto, reversed himself and announced he would bring the bill to the floor soon after Congress reconvened in January 1984. The seemingly dead bill was alive after all.

On February 22, 1984, Representative Roybal, with the support of some but not all "Hispanic" groups, introduced his alternative to Simpson-Mazzoli, apparently aiming to derail the durable bill. To elicit support for his bill as a passable alternative, Roybal included a call for increasing the financing, training, and numerical strength of the US Border Patrol. A press release issued by groups backing the Roybal bill explained on February 16, 1984, "Without an aggressive grassroots effort pushing an alternative bill, it is safe to say that Simpson-Mazzoli will most probably pass the House."

But some grass-roots organizations, such as the San Diego–based Committee on Chicano Rights (CCR), set up pickets in front of the local offices of pro-Roybal groups like the American GI Forum, an antidiscrimination group founded in 1948 by Mexican-American World War II veterans. Explained CCR chairman Herman Baca,

> For the first time in the 15-year immigration struggle, we have persons of Mexican American ancestry agreeing with the racist and the Anglo political establishment that immigration is a law enforcement problem and not a social, economic and political issue. . . . [The Roybal bill's] 1600 new Border Patrol agents at the US/Mexico border and in the Chicano/Latino communities is not an alternative, but a sell-out. . . . What the Roybal Bill is saying is that "the US Cavalry" should take responsibility for resolving the "Indian problem."[8]

Whatever the differences among Latino organizations on the Roybal bill, the Mexican and Chicano community was *not* divided on the issue of the need to reduce or eliminate, rather than strengthen, the US Border Patrol, or on the fact that immigration is a social issue rather than a law enforcement problem. In general, the community backed Baca's view.

At the request of candidate Mondale, obviously aware of the strong Mexican voting bloc, Speaker O'Neill postponed action on Simpson-Mazzoli until after the June 5 California Democratic presidential primary. On June 8, 1984, the House Rules Committee cleared the way for debate on Simpson-Mazzoli and sixty-nine amendments. Later that month, after a week of impassioned debate, the House narrowly passed its version of Simpson-Mazzoli, 216 to 211.

Reaction was intense in some cases. The more sensational tabloid newspapers featured headlines like, "Amnesty for Criminals!" White House spokesman Larry Speakes announced that President Reagan, preferring the more conservative Senate version, found the House version of the bill "too expensive" and "unacceptable." In a joint Senate-House conference committee meant to bring a single, unified Simpson-Mazzoli bill to final congressional approval, the question of the amount of money states would receive as reimbursements to cover the costs of naturalizing "undocumented" workers blocked all compromise.

The other sticking point, less publicized, was the so-called Frank amendment, named after Representative Barney Frank (D-Mass.) and approved in the House by a vote of 404 to 9. It sought to create a special civil rights unit within the Department of Justice to investigate and prosecute alleged job discrimination against newly documented "aliens" and US citizens. The discrimination issue was central for not only all major Latino organizations but also groups like the American Civil Liberties Union, the NAACP, and the Church World Services. While the 1964 Civil Rights Act already forbade discrimination on the basis of "national origin," the Supreme Court had ruled in 1973 that the statute did not forbid discrimination against aliens. Senator Simpson, a staunch conservative, adamantly rejected both the Frank amendment and a subsequent watered-down version of it offered by Congressman Mazzoli.

Meanwhile, opposition to Simpson-Mazzoli gained momentum as every major Chicano/Mexican organization put muscle behind preventing its passage. The usually moderate, cautious, and restrained League of United Latin American Citizens (LULAC), founded in 1927 by middle-class Mexicans emphasizing the rights of US citizenship and the need to learn English, called for a boycott of the Democratic Party convention's first presidential ballot in protest of Simpson-Mazzoli. (LULAC, sometimes compared to the NAACP, had been an early backer of the Roybal bill.) After considerable arm-twisting by Mondale forces and Mondale's promise to oppose Simpson-Mazzoli, a Latino caucus vote taken a day later broke the tie and defeated the first-ballot boycott idea.

Once the political hoopla of conventions had died down, House and Senate conferees returned to work to hammer out a final version of Simpson-Mazzoli. In October 1984 they reached a compromise on the Frank amendment and other issues. They agreed to bar discrimination against a specific group of "legal aliens," namely those who signed a "declaration of intent to become a citizen." This effectively overlooked the largest and most important group covered by the legislation, temporary Mexican migrant laborers, and left them unprotected against discrimination.

The conferees also decided to eliminate a ceiling on legal immigration (opening the doors to *unlimited* numbers of "guest workers"); to maintain the current availability of visas for brothers and sisters of US citizens; to drop the "sense of Congress" section about English as the official language; to drop the House version's "sense of Congress" section allowing Salvadorans facing deportation to stay in the country until their safety in El Salvador could be determined; to establish a verification system for worker ID cards, involving a three-year pilot project with a toll-free number for employers to call to validate an applicant's Social Security number; and to impose (token) fines upon employers who knowingly hired "undocumented workers."

The only issue on which the conferees could not reach a compromise was the question of imposing a limit on federal payments to states for welfare benefits to "illegal aliens" who would gain legal status under the bill. Once more, Simpson-Mazzoli could not make it through the final stages of congressional approval. Simpson's new bill of 1985 placed a $1.8 billion limit on federal reimbursements to states and municipalities for services extended to those benefiting from an "amnesty"—a figure previously rejected by many in Congress as too low.

Even though the "guest worker" program gained strength through almost every stage of the bill's progress, some employer groups, including the 3.3-million-member American Farm Bureau Federation, felt the bill did not give enough emphasis to farmers' needs for workers during the harvesting of perishable crops. They made this objection even after a successful lobbying campaign led by the newly organized Farm Labor Alliance (FLA) had won House approval of a "guest worker" program allowing the admittance, on just three days' notice, of unspecified numbers of workers to pick crops—terms never before achieved. The FLA was organized by Thomas J. Hale, a former president of the Grape and Tree Fruit League, whose 300 members grow most of California's table grapes, peaches, plums, and pears. Corporate farmers like league members Tenneco West, Inc., and Sun-Maid Growers of California financed the FLA's lobbying campaign.

To direct Republican strategy, FLA growers hired James H. Lake, a veteran agribusiness lobbyist and a top aide in three of President Reagan's campaigns, including that of October 1983. To help influence Democrats, they hired the law firm of Robert S. Strauss, the party's former chairman.[9]

On the other hand, some AFL-CIO lobbyists considered the Simpson-Mazzoli bill *too generous* to agribusiness and began to echo Latino complaints about "legal peonage in America's fields" and "government-sponsored union-busting." Never mind that during the August 1984 Democratic Party convention the AFL-CIO had issued a policy statement in favor of employer sanctions, an ID system, and a "generous" amnesty for "illegal aliens" already in the country.

The 1985 version of the bill introduced by Senator Simpson was more, not less, conservative on the questions of amnesty, labor rights, and federal funding. For example, it would provide for "amnesty" only after a presidential commission certified that the new law's provisions had resulted in a "substantial" reduction of illegal immigration—a highly unlikely development under any circumstances.

The Senate passed the bill on September 19, 1985, by a vote of 69 to 30. The powerful farm lobbies secured an amendment to the bill that went beyond the Simpson provision (which granted farmers an additional three years in which to stop hiring "illegal aliens"). The farm lobby amendment provided for a guest-worker program allowing as many as 350,000 "aliens" to harvest perishable fruits and vegetables for up to nine months a year. The Senate bill also called for the passing of a new law extending the guest-worker program after thirty-three months (as the PL 78 had provided for the renewal of the bracero program a generation earlier). Congressman Rodino, chief sponsor of the House bill, told the press he was "deeply disappointed" by the Senate's action, saying he was "adamantly opposed to any massive importation of foreign agricultural labor."

A critic of Simpson-Mazzoli, Linda Wong of the Mexican-American Legal Defense and Educational Fund (MALDEF), a moderate civil rights organization having considerable political influence in Washington, D.C., suggested a policy alternative that addressed the core labor recruitment question of Simpson-Mazzoli: raise Mexico's quota from 20,000 to 60,000 and enforce existing fair labor laws that regulate wages and working conditions. Some of these laws are: the Fair Labor Standards Act, affording equal protection to all employees regardless of citizenship status; the National Labor Relations Act, prohibiting unfair labor practices; the Federal Unemployment Tax Act; the Occupational Safety and Health Act; and the Federal Insurance Contributions Act (FICA), which withholds income taxes of all employees and thereby extends equal protection to workers.

The main opposition to Simpson-Mazzoli continued to come from MALDEF, LULAC, the American GI Forum, the CCR, and other Latino organizations, in spite of misleading public opinion polls purporting to show a majority of Latinos in favor of Simpson-Mazzoli.

Public Reaction to Major Provisions of Simpson-Mazzoli

Opinion Polls

Supporters of Simpson-Mazzoli repeatedly refer to public opinion polls to back their cause. In some instances the results of these polls allege that the overwhelming majority of Americans, including Latinos, support most, or even all, of the bill.

These polls are, in fact, superficial and misleading. To expect the average citizen to respond to·questions on a matter as contradictory and esoteric as the Simpson-Mazzoli bill is almost as farfetched as expecting the public to be able to answer questions about plant genetics. Most Americans remain either uninformed or confused about Simpson-Mazzoli.

Furthermore, most polls miseducate Americans as to what the Simpson-Mazzoli bill is all about. They omit, for instance, the bill's core: its provision for a "guest worker" program. They make it appear that the bill will exclude foreign workers when in fact it will let in more. Moreover, by focusing on immigrant labor as the problem, the polls confuse Americans about the deeper problems of immigration law and about the real causes of the economic crisis, thereby reinforcing the scapegoating of foreign workers. When those polled are asked if they support fining or otherwise sanctioning employers who hire immigrants, the implicit message behind a "yes" answer is obvious: immigrant workers are to blame, so don't hire them. Lastly, by raising the issue of "control of our borders" and "national security," the polls indirectly contribute to possible support for US military aid and intervention in Central America. They do this by suggesting the idea that more and more "feet people" are swarming into the United States.

Pollsters often ask rhetorical questions that invite only one answer. For instance, the question "Do you support amnesty for illegals?" invites a "no" from people opposed to all "aliens" in the first place. But it invites a "yes" from most Latinos and recently naturalized citizens. There is no room in such a question for an amnesty's requirements or its consequences.

Similarly, few Americans would respond negatively to the idea of "employer sanctions," a concept that correctly implies that employers are responsible for hiring immigrant workers, yet falsely implies that sanctions will work. With this in mind, President Reagan expressed concern for oppressed migrant workers in the second 1984 presidential debate by stating that Simpson-Mazzoli would sanction employers and thereby prevent the abuse of immigrants hired "at starvation wages and with none of the benefits that we think are normal and natural for workers in our country."

A highly dubious 1983 poll commissioned by one of the main pro-Simpson-Mazzoli lobbying groups, the conservative Federation for

American Immigration Reform (FAIR), is frequently cited to bolster the argument that a majority of "Hispanics" favor Simpson-Mazzoli. Based on an unusually select and supposedly random sampling of only 800 Latinos and 800 blacks reached by telephone (many Latinos do not have telephones), the FAIR poll claimed to show that 69 percent of Hispanics and 51 percent of blacks believe "illegal" immigrants take jobs that Americans would otherwise fill. As we have seen, this does not usually happen. Almost every major study—including those conducted by the Urban Institute, numerous university research teams, and the Hesburgh commission itself—has pointed out that *immigrant workers probably create more jobs than they take away.*

More than two-thirds of FAIR's telephone interviews with Latinos were conducted in English, a language many Latinos either do not really understand or else manage haltingly, deferentially, and in response to the speaker's tone of voice. Most Hispanic respondents predictably favor legalization of "undocumented aliens," without necessarily having any idea of the onerous preconditions established in the Simpson-Mazzoli bill for such an amnesty (see below). But because so many Latinos favor legalization and the word "amnesty" sounds so unqualifiedly generous, a number of Latino respondents to the FAIR poll may have been inclined to support Simpson-Mazzoli on this basis alone.

FAIR has billed its biased poll as "objective proof" that leaders of Hispanic organizations, by opposing Simpson-Mazzoli, are "totally out of step" with their constituencies. Yet it must be pointed out that FAIR's poll is seriously flawed on many counts. Its questions are loaded to elicit responses favorable to Simpson-Mazzoli and to cover up consequences detrimental to minorities.

Moreover, FAIR is a well-known ally of the INS, supporting anything that will strengthen the US Border Patrol. FAIR chairman Roger Conner is an outspoken advocate of Simpson-Mazzoli; his letters appear regularly in the nation's leading newspapers. Founded in 1979 and claiming to be a nonpartisan organization with 15,000 members, FAIR is a preeminently partisan political body. Typical of FAIR's political activities was its organizing of a pro–Border Patrol rally billed as "a tribute to the troops on the line," held on August 29, 1982, in San Ysidro, California.

Arnold Torres, chief Washington lobbyist for the nation's oldest Latino organization, the fifty-eight-year-old LULAC, has noted that FAIR's poll "doesn't address what we believe will be the adverse effects of the Simpson-Mazzoli bill."[10] What are some of those adverse effects? First and foremost, the "guest worker" component of the bill brings back a form of contract labor outlawed a century ago and as bad as the bracero program of 1942–64. It runs counter to the needs and rights of all working people in the United States. In directing the president "to develop and implement a new, secure system to verify work eligibility within three years" and to limit any ID card's use to "verification of work eligibility," Simpson-Mazzoli opens the doors to America's first-ever requirement of an identification system for getting a job. Such a system could ultimately channel into government computers information on all workers. But the bill has other ominous components.

Employer Sanctions

The extra burden placed on nonwhite workers by the presence of Mexican "guest workers" and the threat of employer sanctions is obvious. Employer sanctions force nonwhite workers to "prove" they are not Mexican or "illegal." Every Latino organization, whatever its politics or focus, has come down foursquare against employer sanctions, seeing in them (and worker ID cards) a potential "apartheid" system. In the words of Herman Baca, employer sanctions, enforced by a beefed-up Border Patrol, will "only lead to an increase in violence and to the creation of an apartheid-type system for Chicanos."[11] LULAC's José Treviño thinks Simpson-Mazzoli will increase "the likelihood of discriminatory actions against Hispanics. It institutes identification practices comparable to Nazi Germany and South Africa."[12]

Largely unenforceable, sanctions are more a proemployer provision of Simpson-Mazzoli than a check on employer abuses. In fact, if history is any guide, employer sanctions will have no such beneficial effects for labor. Not a single person has ever been convicted under the California sanctions law passed in 1971, although in 1982 some Los Angeles homeowners were arrested for allegedly holding Mexican and Indonesian "slaves." Nationwide, only five very minor convictions have been recorded in the eleven states having employer sanction statutes. A 1982 survey conducted by the US General Accounting Office concluded that in twenty countries with employer sanction laws, the laws "were not an effective deterrent to illegal employment."[13]

Sanctions offer employers an excuse for unfair labor practices such as refusing to hire a nonwhite or arbitrarily firing a union organizer. Employer sanctions provide a cover for increased employer discrimination against Latinos, Asians, other "foreigners," minorities in general, and union activists—the excuse being an employer's implied duty to "screen" employees.

Sanctions can also be used as an excuse for lower wages, on the ground that an employer's costs are increased because of the time spent on checking documents. Because of the pressure to screen new employees, labor unions might find themselves policing members instead of expanding membership. Employer sanctions give the INS and other police forces a pretext for factory raids to round up "illegals"—a further intimidation of employees interested in organizing their workplaces.

Dr. Kitty Calavita, of the University of California–San Diego's Program in United States–Mexican Studies, has pointed out that employer sanctions lead to the "double criminalization" of Mexican migrant workers: first the migrants have to cross the border without papers, and then they must present bogus documents to employers. Their "crimes" make them even more susceptible than otherwise to employer blackmail and discipline. Indeed, Dr. Calavita envisions a situation in which "many undocumented workers, and in some cases the documented, will literally have to pay the price for the legislation. In the initial stages, layoffs, wage reductions, and up-front payments at the time of employment will be the price that unknown numbers of workers will pay for the 'risk' their employers assume in hiring them."[14]

Calavita labels this "the kind of worker approach" (as opposed to an approach based on decent wage and working conditions) that underlies the acceptability in Congress of legislation like Simpson-Mazzoli. Because it is supportive of anti-immigrant ideology and does not significantly alter economic reality, such an approach gets politicians' votes. But if a more prolabor approach were followed, such as enforcing existing protective labor laws and thereby reducing the possibilities of hiring low-wage "undocumented" workers, Congress would react very differently.

Amnesty

Simpson-Mazzoli's provision of "amnesty" for "undocumented" workers has, predictably, provoked outrage in reactionary circles. But it also has angered many Latinos, since it offers no guarantee that any noncitizen will meet all the necessary qualifications during the long, complex process of receiving amnesty. Moreover, the amnesty provision places an applicant at risk of deportation at any stage without fair judgment or due process. Rather than satisfy Latino organizations, Simpson-Mazzoli's version of "amnesty" has only incensed them. A broad-based coalition of Latinos protesting the Los Angeles Olympic Games stated in a June 1984 press release,

> Democrats are hypocritical in their championing of amnesty for undocumented workers. They know that they are forcing workers to gamble with the lives of their family members. If their applications are denied they are subject to deportation. Significantly, Mayor Tom Bradley spent much more time lobbying for the Olympics than he did in fighting the racist Simpson-Mazzoli bill. . . . While it pretends to give amnesty, in reality it forces undocumented workers and their families to play chicken. If they lose they are deported. Already, even before Simpson-Mazzoli becomes law, unscrupulous employers are laying off workers.

Because the "amnesty" provisions agreed upon by the House-Senate conferees in September 1984 require proof of four years or more continuous residency, few Mexican migrant workers qualify. Most of them are temporary immigrants who return to Mexico frequently.

Those applying for "amnesty" would have to pass various tests to qualify as permanent residents, including demonstration of a "minimal understanding of ordinary English and a knowledge and understanding of the history and government of the United States," or enrollment in courses approved by the attorney general to achieve such knowledge. *This would be the first time in US history that an English language test would be a requirement for permanent residence.* To become actual citizens they would have to show five years of legal permanent residency—twelve years for those who entered the United States prior to January 1, 1977. And, of course, the applicants would get no guarantee that the laws or requirements would remain the same along the way.

Moreover, in contrast to the "family reunification" foundation of past US immigration policy, the Simpson-Mazzoli amnesty proposal would force the long-term division of nuclear families, since it allows only the individual "undocumented" worker to apply for residency and citizenship. In the meantime, he or she would have to pay taxes like any other US citizen and yet would not be eligible for the public services paid for by the taxes.

Amnesty is a process by which criminals or political prisoners are pardoned by the state. It should be inapplicable to workers—since when in the United States is it a crime to sell one's labor power cheaply to an employer?

The so-called amnesty is no guarantee at all of full human rights; on the contrary, it ultimately helps cement the economic institutionalization of second-class status for the more than half of the US workforce that qualifies as "minority." It practically assures (while disguising) a temporary worker program within which foreigners will be discouraged from asserting basic rights because of the threat of termination of status. Reinforcing the marginal status of such a subclass necessarily threatens all labor, particularly those minorities most vulnerable to accepting substandard wages and poor work conditions (nonwhites, women, high school dropouts, etc.).

A worker who applies for "amnesty" would be placed in a tenuous "probationary" situation tantamount to an "indentured alien" program. The term first coined by a former director of the bracero program, "legal slavery," is the practical effect of both the "guest worker" *and* the "amnesty" provisions of Simpson-Mazzoli.

Yet for most Mexican "undocumented" workers, conditions already resemble bondage. They are in far too vulnerable a position to demand the basic rights granted them by existing labor and constitutional law, although growing numbers of them have taken the risk of speaking out. Consistent with its history of collaboration with employers of Mexican migrants, the Department of Labor looks the other way when it comes to enforcing the Fair Labor Standards Act and the Migrant and Seasonal Agricultural Worker Protection Act. Even these acts only partially extend to farmworkers the rights other Americans enjoy.

Among those rights is that of having a union eligible for collective bargaining. But by making it illegal for "undocumented" immigrant workers to be employed in the first place, the Simpson-Mazzoli bill guillotines the unionizing activities already undertaken by the AFL-CIO and AFW among Mexican immigrant workers (see Chapter 7). On the other hand, by keeping the doors open for a regular and dependable flow of these workers, Simpson-Mazzoli makes it that much easier for employers, in collusion with the Department of Labor (as during the days of the bracero program), to use them as an antiunion, antistrike force in their conflicts with labor. Thus, rather than serving the interests of organized labor, Simpson-Mazzoli is preeminently an antiunion measure.

Further placing immigrant workers at a disadvantage is the fact that they pay into the system but are afraid to file for refunds or benefits. Contrary to the prevailing stereotypes about Mexican migrant workers "draining taxpayers' resources" for social services, numerous studies have shown that about 75 percent of the migrant workers contribute monies they neither recover nor see benefits from to the Social Security Administration and to state and federal tax systems. *Newsweek* magazine estimates they contribute $80 billion every year to Social Security, a financially pinched service that already faces difficulties surviving and therefore depends heavily on the contributions of the "undocumented."

A 1977 San Diego County study showed $48 million in "illegal" workers' contributions (pay deductions for taxes, Social Security, etc.), against $2 million in benefits received. The ultraconservative Heritage Foundation reportedly has found that only 4 percent of "undocumented" workers' children receive free schooling and just 1 percent collect food stamps or welfare. A 1982 survey by the pro-Simpson-Mazzoli FAIR found that in most states "illegal aliens" are not eligible for general assistance.[15]

According to the *New York Times*, "In general, programs supported wholly or in part by the Federal Government deny benefits to illegal aliens, although some states provide benefits, generally such aid as hospital insurance and workers' compensation, but not unemployment insurance."[16] As the Hesburgh commission has confirmed,

> All the partial sub-samples of illegal migrants indicate that illegal migrants pay taxes consistent with their earnings levels. Data on social service usage from these studies, as well as fragmentary administrative records, show no large amounts of utilization of taxpayer-financed services.

Recent Abuses, Court Decisions, and the Future of Legislation

Over the last fifteen years, reports of physical abuse of Mexican migrant workers have grown in number. A notorious case in 1976 involved the robbing, torturing, shooting, and hanging of three Mexican farmworkers by the Hanigan brothers in Arizona. During a subsequent trial, one of the brothers was found innocent and another guilty.

In 1979 CCR chairman Baca repeated accusations that US Border Patrol agents were guilty of "documented cases of illegal and unconstitutional acts" during the past ten years, including rape, physical abuse, and murder of Mexican migrant workers. Calling upon Senator Edward Kennedy (D-Mass.) and Representative Elizabeth Holtzman (D-N.Y.) to investigate his charges, Baca concluded that the Border Patrol "is now totally out of control and is nothing but a lawless agency which is accountable and responsible to no one."[17] Yet no congressional investigation has been forthcoming.

On the contrary, in spite of numerous documented cases backing Baca's allegations, the response from Washington has been a deafening silence combined with annually augmented budgets for the INS, including monies for the training of the Border Patrol in "counterinsurgency" techniques. In 1985 the INS enforcement budget totaled $366 million for a staff of 7,599. The Simpson-Mazzoli bill calls for further increases in the INS budget, up to a quarter of a billion dollars.

During the 1980s the Ku Klux Klan has frequently roamed the US-Mexico border looking for "illegals." Its vigilante activities, widely reported in local newspapers, have not been deterred by law enforcement agencies. Meanwhile, the INS (or in the Latino vocabulary, *la migra*) and the Border Patrol have stepped up their helicopter and automotive patrols, rounding up more "illegals" than ever before in history.

By September 1982 deportations of Mexicans were numbering about 1,000 a day; they frequently doubled or tripled that in 1983, 1984, and 1985. The reference in the 1984 film *El Norte* to the border as "a war zone" was not far off the mark. "Operation Jobs" in 1982, analyzed earlier, was just one of many nationwide sweeps undertaken by the INS. These raids continued in spite of momentary legal victories won by some of their victims in the US court system.

In January 1982 US district judge Prentice H. Marshall of Chicago ruled that the INS can no longer surround or enter factories and residences and harass, detain, or forcibly interrogate all persons of "Hispanic appearance." On July 15, 1982, the Ninth Circuit Court of Appeals in California ruled that INS "area control" operations in factories violated the Fourth Amendment to the US Constitution. But the raids continued unabated while legal appeals carried the "factory raids" issue all the way to the US Supreme Court.

After reviewing these and related cases, the Supreme Court ruled, on April 17, 1984, that immigration officials may conduct unannounced raids on factories and businesses to look for "illegal aliens." This struck down any right to privacy and annulled the Fourth Amendment's prohibition against unreasonable search and seizure. As dissenting justice William J. Brennan, Jr., observed, the Court's ruling perpetuated "a frightening picture of people subjected to wholesale interrogation under conditions designed not to respect personal security and privacy, but rather to elicit prompt answers from completely intimidated workers."[18]

The real, unstated result of the Simpson-Mazzoli bill will be to further undermine the few democratic rights "undocumented" workers already have or to which they can lay claim. For instance, a recent US Federal District Court decision recognizes the right of children to get an education regardless of the status under immigration laws of the parent(s). The US Supreme Court ruled on June 15, 1982, that a Texas statute authorizing public school districts to deny enrollment to children who were not "legally admitted" into the United States violated the Equal Protection Clause of the Fourteenth Amendment. And on June 25, 1984, the Supreme Court ruled that "illegal aliens" are entitled to the protections of federal labor law.

In its June 25 ruling, the Supreme Court stated that it is an unfair labor practice for an employer to report "illegal aliens" to the INS in retaliation against their efforts to organize a union. The National Labor Relations Act protects a worker's right to organize and/or strike without reference to citizenship status. As already noted, the Simpson-Mazzoli bill would make the Court's decision meaningless since it would prohibit employers from hiring "illegals" in the first place. Efforts by "illegals" to unionize would thus become nearly impossible.

Under Simpson-Mazzoli, the entire recruitment, employment, and disciplining of "illegals" would be driven further underground. Indeed, under the bill's amnesty program, the freedom of an "undocumented" worker to escape detection, send the children to school, or unionize would be placed in extreme jeopardy.

As a result of the courts' failures to protect immigrant worker rights and because of the stepped-up harassment Latinos have suffered at their workplaces and in their *barrios*, tensions in Latino neighborhoods have been approaching the boiling point. Widespread unemployment has aggravated these tensions. Unemployment among Latinos has risen to more than 15 percent, with the rate among teenagers around 30 percent. A 1983 Census Bureau study showed 30 percent of Latinos living below the poverty line—double the national average, and 14 percent more than when President Reagan took office.

Older residents in the nation's deteriorating urban *barrios* have compared the stepped-up deportation drives of the 1980s to 1954's

"Operation Wetback." This historical comparison is appropriate, for then as now, mass deportations accompanied mass importations of Mexican workers—and US business cannot prosper without both.

In early 1982 more than 10,000 people marched in Los Angeles in the largest demonstration concerning immigration issues ever held. It brought together not only Latinos but scores of "anglo" labor union and civil liberties advocates to protest recent deportations and the Simpson-Mazzoli bill. The immediate spark igniting the demonstration was the federal government's decision to begin deportation proceedings against an estimated 100,000 Mexicans holding temporary visas (known as "Silva letters") that allowed them to remain pending regularization of their status. The granting of the letters authorizing temporary visas had stemmed from a 1977 class action lawsuit filed and won in the US Supreme Court by Refugio Silva, charging that quotas for people in the Western Hemisphere who wished to immigrate had been applied in a discriminatory fashion—Mexican quotas had been used to let in Cuban refugees. Then, in January 1982, the government demanded that the "Silva letter" people report to the authorities, thereby threatening some 20,000 US citizens (US-born children of the letter holders) with immediate deportation—clearly an illegal and unconstitutional act.

The parents' refusal to report to the INS and the unified response of Mexicans/Chicanos and their Latino and anglo allies, together with messages of international support from Mexico,[19] showed how strong the resistance to US immigration policy had become. But it did not alter the precarious situation in which "Silva letter" holders had been placed. Nor did it keep Simpson-Mazzoli from coming to a vote in Congress.

What is the future of immigration reform legislation? Proposals like Simpson-Mazzoli will likely continue to command the nation's attention until one of them is finally approved by Congress or unless the balance of political forces shifts. More fair-minded proposals aimed at righting the imbalances of existing laws and eradicating the nativist biases of immigration law and policy are unlikely to succeed in the absence of a continued growth of political alliances supporting the rights of immigrant workers and political refugees.

Opposition to the Simpson-Mazzoli bill has come from major civil rights and Latino organizations, as well as many labor, church, lawyer, and student groups. Among the more influential anti-Simpson-Mazzoli lobbying groups have been the American Immigration Lawyers, the

110-organization-strong National Immigration and Refugee Network, and the National Committee for Fair Immigration Reform (composed of representatives of AFL-CIO labor unions, churches, and Latino organizations).

The threat of Simpson-Mazzoli has united Latino organizations throughout the nation, including ones as diverse as LULAC, MALDEF, the National Council of La Raza, the Los Angeles–based Hermandad Mexicana and Comité Pro-Derechos y Visas, the American GI Forum, the San Antonio–based Southwest Voter Registration Project, the Cuban National Planning Council, the Texas Coalition against Simpson-Mazzoli, the Mexican American Republican Council, the Houston-based Unión para la Defensa y Educación Latino (UDEL), and the Conference on Immigration and Refugee Advocacy (CIRA, a southwestern regional grouping). The alliances these groups built with non-Latino organizations temporarily beat back Simpson-Mazzoli in 1982, 1983, and 1984.

But some of the Latino organizations that had initially backed the Roybal bill in 1984 were taken by surprise when Representative Roybal modified his bill in 1985 to incorporate employer sanctions and a transitional three-year "guest worker" program for agricultural interests. They could not easily reverse their positions against these measures without losing credibility among their constituencies. Roybal explained his own reversal as an attempt to obtain "a responsible immigration bill that was also fair and balanced."[20]

Clearly, neither the Simpson-Mazzoli bill nor the anti-immigrant wave has subsided. Nor have their consequences. For as the next chapter shows, the attacks on one group's civil liberties and human rights erode the democratic way of life for all Americans. The ultimate "domino" may be US democracy itself.

9

Immigrants and the Ultimate Domino: US Democracy

"In the 131-year history of the Chicano/Mexicano people in the US there have been two repressive agencies whose only job has been to insure that our community does not organize and begin to enjoy the same rights, wages, and working conditions as the Anglo majority. One of them was the Texas Rangers. The other, since 1924, is the US Border Patrol."
—Herman Baca, Chairman, Committee on Chicano Rights, 1979

"Aliens, even aliens whose presence in this country is unlawful, have long been recognized as 'persons' guaranteed due process of law."
—US Supreme Court in *Plyler* v. *Doe*, 1982

"How apt that the welcoming lamp has been hauled down from the Statue of Liberty. Its disrepair is greater than anyone knew."
—*New York Times*, November 20, 1984

The preceding chapters have suggested some of the ways in which the government's treatment of immigrants, along with proposed immigration bills like Simpson-Mazzoli-Rodino, threatens traditional American civil liberties. Proposed sanctions against employers who hire "illegal" immigrants will discriminate against all nonwhite workers, as well as workers whose English is less than standard. Such penalties imposed on workers and employers will undermine the wages and union organizing

239

rights of all American workers. The creation of a national ID card system to verify eligibility for employment will create a massive national databank of personal information about all workers. Until now an ID system for employment and a national databank have never been authorized or even accepted as a legitimate subject for public debate in the United States.

As so often happens, attacks against one group of workers soon spread to others, affecting even high-placed union officials. The *New York Times* reported on February 19, 1985, that possible administrative action would be taken by the federal Office of the Special Counsel of the Merit Systems Protection Board against the president of the American Federation of Government Employees, the president of the American Postal Workers Union, and the president of the National Association of Letter Carriers for violations of the Hatch Act (limiting political activities). All three men had been on union leave while supporting the Mondale presidential campaign. Noting the Reagan administration's "antiunion biases and its implacable hostility to the rights of unions and their members," the AFL-CIO's thirty-five-member executive council accused the Reagan administration of trying to "silence free speech."

One of the most laudable yet fragile features of American society's evolution has been the government's uneven but generally expanding recognition of popular democratic rights when people mobilize to demand them. Yet since Vietnam, this society has displayed a deepening "anticommunist," racist, nativist, and class-biased character in its treatment of immigrants and in its immigration policy. More troubling, as suggested by the AFL-CIO's recently expressed concern about attacks on "free speech," it has also experienced a wave of legislative, administrative, and court decisions that may curtail the basic civil rights of not only immigrants but of all US citizens.

American democracy may well be the ultimate "domino."

Peeling Away People's Rights

In the last several years Americans' civil liberties have been steadily eroded. Taking a decidedly conservative turn under the stewardship of Chief Justice Warren E. Burger, the US Supreme Court has peeled away many rights on the dangerously open-ended grounds of "overriding considerations of public safety." These grounds were used to justify the Court's approval of police questioning of suspects without first advising them of their right to remain silent. Public safety was also cited in the Court's 7-2 decision in *Nixon* v. *Williams* to admit at trial illegally obtained evidence if the prosecution can prove that the evidence would have "inevitably" been discovered by lawful means.

"Public safety" and "national security" also prompted the Court to signal that CIA operations are too sensitive to be monitored by judges—implying that the CIA is beyond the law. On April 16, 1985, the Supreme Court invoked the National Security Act in giving the CIA broad discretion to withhold the identities of its sources of intelligence information from public disclosure under the Freedom of Information Act.[1]

With five justices over seventy-seven years of age and nearing the ends of their careers, the Supreme Court might very well be "packed" by a conservative President Reagan during his second administration. This, then, is the conservative Court that will likely uphold any new legislation or presidential actions that threaten to neutralize or eliminate what is left of Americans' basic rights.

Many challenges to measures undertaken by the Reagan administration are already in process. They include both foreign and domestic affairs—from White House involvement in military actions against the Nicaraguan government in defiance of the so-called Boland Amendment (and other congressional acts) to the constitutionality of parts of the omnibus crime bill passed by Congress that portend preventive detention and other acts normally associated with undemocratic regimes. In addition, numerous cases dealing with increased denials of equal rights to women, blacks, political dissidents, and other minorities, including immigrants, are making their way to the Supreme Court. A class action lawsuit based on the Fifth Amendment's due process clause has been filed by the Los Angeles–based National Center for Immigrants' Rights. It challenges INS regulations and policy providing that arrested persons shall only be advised of their right to counsel *after* they have been interrogated.

Using "public safety," "national security," and the specter of "terrorism," the Reagan administration has expanded the budgets and vastly extended the power of police and intelligence agencies to interfere in the lives of citizens not even suspected of criminal activity. For example, Reagan's 1981 Executive Order 12333 allows the CIA to spy on people in the United States by tapping their phones or homes and by infiltrating groups like the Committee in Solidarity with the People of El Salvador (CISPES) that have alleged foreign connections. In other words, under Executive Order 12333 the CIA now has the legal authority to conduct domestic operations, including monitoring US-citizen organizations like CISPES and conducting secret surveillance of American citizens.

Under its 1983 revised guidelines, the FBI similarly has the authority to spy on legal organizations and to infiltrate political or human rights groups in a manner that seriously undermines rights protected by the First Amendment. The FBI may follow people, spy on them, and collect information on them if it has merely "grounds for suspicion." According to the *New York Times*, an alleged Puerto Rican terrorist cell in Chicago was broken up in 1984 after the FBI observed its activities in a private home through a closed-circuit television camera that had been secretly installed.[2] The new FBI guidelines have made a mockery of all those constitutional protections reaffirmed during the Watergate and Cointelpro scandals of the 1970s, when so many citizens' basic rights were found to have been violated by the CIA and FBI.[3]

Within the FBI's National Crime Information Center, a special computer file has been activated to keep track of people who are described by the Secret Service as "anti-authority or anti-law enforcement." The file reportedly includes the names of civil rights activists like Coretta Scott King and pediatrician Benjamin Spock. Another national computer file has been proposed to track people not expected to commit a crime but "believed" to be "associated" with people suspected of being "terrorists." This kind of technique was used earlier, when the FBI placed the Reverend Martin Luther King, Jr., in their files because someone "believed" he was "associated" with "communists."[4]

The targets of these surveillance measures are strictly left of center on the political and cultural spectrum. They are not proven right-wing terrorist groups like the Ku Klux Klan, which the FBI denies is terrorist. The FBI also excludes from its definition of terrorism the bombings of abortion clinics—of which more than twenty occurred in 1984 alone.

A number of more recent executive orders have further eroded Americans' fundamental rights. On April 3, 1984, for instance, President Reagan signed National Security Decision Directive 138, a presumed "antiterrorist" preventive that allows US military units and intelligence agents to use force against persons or groups who are thought to be planning operations against US targets at home or abroad.

In addition, the Reagan administration has introduced a number of bills in Congress that could be used to suppress any domestic opposition to government policies under the guise of "fighting sabotage and assassination." These bills have the potential to criminalize the work of many individuals and groups who declare their "solidarity" with Mexican immigrant workers facing the daily threat of deportation or with victims of repression and torture in Central America. Perhaps most threatening of all is the open-ended and vague language of Reagan's proposed legislation.

For instance, the Prohibition against the Training or Support of Terrorist Organizations Act of 1984 (HR 5613, S 2626) makes it a crime to "act in concert with," train, or serve in any organization designated by the secretary of state as an intelligence agency or armed force of any foreign government, faction, or international terrorist group. Penalties are a fine of up to $100,000 or ten years in prison. Under this legislation, the secretary of state would have the unilateral power, independent of judicial review, to determine that a particular group or government is "terrorist," based on "acts or likely acts." The inclusion of "likely acts," or probable conduct, can readily be construed to sanction FBI, CIA, or grand jury investigations into the lawful and peaceful activities of any American. Moreover, the accused (or merely observed) is prohibited from arguing that an organization or government on the list has been wrongly included. In effect, then, the executive branch of government would assume powers belonging to the judicial system. Like the attorney general's lists of "subversive" organizations of the 1950s, like the Smith Act, which entitled the government to jail anyone for "conspiracy to teach the overthrow of the government," these proposed laws could make it illegal to protest US government policy anywhere.

Immigration legislation fits into this new legal framework, as it has in the past (recall the McCarran-Walter Acts, passed during the height of McCarthyism). In September 1982 the American Civil Liberties Union (ACLU) responded to Senate passage of the Simpson-Mazzoli bill by alerting the public to the fact that the bill "would sweep away broad areas of legal and constitutional protection, such as due process of law and judicial review." In addition to the proposed employer sanctions and the worker ID system, the ACLU singled out for criticism what it called the bill's "court-stripping" features.

Simpson-Mazzoli, the ACLU pointed out, would limit judicial review of political asylum and other immigration cases, including the refusal of a visa to so-called undesirables like homosexuals or suspected "communists." Once a potential immigrant's request was turned down, his or her access to the federal judiciary would be denied. Not only that, but a hearing by an independent Immigration Board would also be denied. The public forum offered by the court system for civil rights advocates defending the rights of Salvadorans, Guatemalans, Haitians, and others seeking political asylum would thus be removed.

As it is, tens of thousands of these political refugees have been not only speedily deported whenever possible but even, in the case of the Haitians, intercepted by the US Coast Guard in international waters *before* their arrival in US territory. This interdiction policy violates both the US Constitution and international law.

The present immigration laws and their enforcement are restrictive enough without the "reforms" of new legislation like Simpson-Mazzoli. Under the 1952 McCarren-Walter Act, the INS claims it excluded 8,000 people in 1983 on the grounds that they were "subversives." Some observers of US immigration policy believe the true figure was closer to 23,000. Among those excluded were French author and cabinet member Régis Debray, Colombian novelist Gabriel García Márquez, and Hortensia Allende, the widow of Chile's slain president. The INS also acknowledges that under the same act it continues to bar more than 3,000 Canadian citizens believed to be Communist Party members or sympathizers.[5]

Carrying on a tradition that continues to cause the United States embarrassment overseas, Simpson-Mazzoli would exclude those persons who "the government has reason to believe seek to enter for activities inimical to the welfare, safety or security of the US." It would also exclude those who "are, or have been, anarchists, communists, or who advocate the overthrow of the government, are Nazis, or would engage in subversive activities." This approach to immigration policy has its roots in the Chinese exclusion acts, the Palmer Raids, "Operation Wetback," and the like.

Detention Camps or Concentration Camps?

On October 22, 1981, the Reagan administration formally proposed legislation that would give the president "broad new emergency powers to deal with a 'mass migration' of illegal aliens." The president sought authority to: (1) seal "any harbor, port, airport or road to prevent unwanted aliens from getting into the country"; (2) "restrict travel by Americans, both domestically and to a country named in an emergency declaration"; (3) put apprehended aliens "into detention camps," from which "they could only be released at the discretion of the Attorney General," who also "could transfer the immigrants from one facility to another at will"; and (4) "exempt the government from virtually all environmental laws . . . in setting up the detention camps." Under these proposals, overnight all Americans could be denied the freedom to travel to another designated city or country or even to visit designated areas, including the detention camps.

"Detention camps" is a euphemism for concentration camps. The last time concentration camps violated all known or imagined "environmental laws" was in Hitler's Germany (the United States still has not signed the international genocide convention that resulted from that experience). But one does not have to look abroad for the terror of midnight knocks on the door and sudden transferral to concentration camps. After all, tens of thousands of Japanese Americans were put in concentration camps during World War II, and their property was confiscated by the government. Later, the McCarran Act of 1950 included a provision establishing "emergency" concentration camps— a section of the law sponsored by the late vice-president Hubert Humphrey.

Even though they are probably aimed at specific groups, especially Latinos, blacks, and other so-called minorities, these existing and proposed laws violate the rights of all Americans and the democratic premises of American society. Thousands of Haitians have already been housed unlawfully for up to a year or more in detention camps in Puerto Rico, southern Florida, Georgia, and upstate New York.

Earlier, from 1954 to 1981, the government granted aliens parole pending hearings at which their status in the country would be determined. But in 1981 President Reagan ordered that aliens be detained pending their hearings, a policy that was applied with particular ferocity and selectivity to Haitian refugees, of whom there were some 40,000, with up to 1,000 more arriving by boat every month. *Newsweek* and other sources have described the detention camps housing the Haitians as tantamount to concentration camps.[6]

With increasing frequency in 1985, television cameras began photographing some of these "detention camps" for unwanted political refugees and "illegal" immigrant workers. Although newscasters did not call them "concentration camps," they did acknowledge the abominable conditions—while the cameras rolled.

Moreover, the proposals submitted to President Reagan by his 1981 Task Force on Immigration and Refugee Policy included legislation "to establish an emergency mass migration fund for *domestic crises* [sic] of $35 million, and to provide, in an emergency, for reprogramming of existing immigration and refugee and other funds."[7] The words "domestic crises" could refer to urban riots or other domestic protest. They could conceivably apply to the rounding up and packing off to "detention camps" of large numbers of protesting blacks, Latinos, or even anti-interventionist and antinuclear groups. For the fiscal year 1982, the administration requested the task force's recommended sum of $35 million for the development of permanent detention centers—in effect, concentration camps whose conditions have already provoked riots and hunger strikes by Haitian immigrants in Florida. The Reagan administration task force itself noted that "detention could create an appearance of 'concentration camps' filled largely by blacks."[8]

On April 12, 1983, a three-judge panel of the US Court of Appeals for the 11th Circuit in Atlanta found the federal government guilty of "discriminatory" and "unconstitutional" practices in its Haitian detention policy. But in 1984 the same Court overturned this ruling by an 8 to 4 vote. On December 3, 1984, the US Supreme Court agreed to take up the question of whether Haitian refugees seeking political asylum can challenge the constitutionality of their confinement in federal detention centers (its decision is still pending).

At issue, of course, is not only the human rights of the Haitians but issues related to racism and the right to political asylum. When predominantly white or mulatto Cubans are granted political refuge but black Haitians, if not interdicted on the high seas by US authorities, are seized and thrown into camps, an obvious double standard is being applied. All major US-based and international human rights groups have condemned ongoing violations of human rights by the recently deposed Duvalier dictatorship in Haiti, conditions that forced the flight of tens of thousands of Haitians. But because the US government supported the Duvalier regime, it claimed it was unable to grant political asylum to its victims.

Consistent with this traditional double standard, the US government announced in December 1984 that it was granting 125,000 Cubans of the 1980 Mariel boatlift the right to apply for permanent residence status, the first step toward citizenship. The government assured them they would receive permanent residence status under the 1966 Cuban Adjustment Act. This, in turn, would allow their relatives to emigrate to the United States.

Meanwhile, many Haitians languished in detention camps like Miami's Krome Detention Center, their status unchanged. More than 7,000 of the Haitians had arrived the same year the Cubans did, 1980—yet unlike the Cubans they received no amnesty or right to apply for permanent residence status. Even educational background seemed to make no difference for the Haitians—doctors, lawyers, students, and workers alike were unwanted. Not since the anti-Jewish policy of World War II, when tens of thousands of Jewish refugees were refused permission to enter the United States, had such a clear-cut case of discrimination appeared in US immigration policy.[9]

The overthrow of Duvalier in early 1986 was preceded by reports from Washington that the US government was considering cutting off the flow of aid to Haiti on the grounds of human rights violations. The US government flew Duvalier to France, therby culminating his overthrow. Where this left the detention-camp Haitians remained to be seen. Some argued that had not their claims to political refuge now been exposed as valid by the very government holding them captive?

Haitians were not the only victims. Estimates of the number of Salvadorans who "illegally" entered the United States by the end of 1984 exceeded half a million. Since about 1980 more than 400 Salvadorans a month had been arriving in flight from the "death squads" and military dictatorship governing their country. Under the new civilian government of President Duarte in 1984, the number of Salvadoran arrivals underwent a sharp increase in response to the stepped-up bombing and napalming of peasant villages. In equal numbers, Guatemalans—mostly Indians—escaped to the United States from Guatemalan army attacks that wiped out more than 200 Indian villages in 1983–84. A pastoral letter of the Guatemalan Conference of Bishops called this "genocide." Human rights activists have repeatedly protested the deportation from the United States and Mexico of these obvious political refugees.[10]

A more fair, humane, democratic, and nondiscriminatory refugee policy would recognize the needs of victims of oppression even when the government responsible is allied with the United States. Temporary political asylum was granted by the Carter administration for nearly half a million Nicaraguans fleeing the death-dealing National Guard during the final months of the Somoza dictatorship. Most of them returned to Nicaragua when the Sandinistas took power, while National Guardsmen responsible for their original flight came to the United States and Honduras to receive US arms and training.

Detention camps being created throughout the United States not only serve to hold Central American and Caribbean refugees prior to their deportation but also serve as actual and potential holding pens for growing numbers of alleged "illegals," particularly Mexican immigrant workers. The *New York Times* reported that 372 "illegal entrants" were being held in El Centro, California, at a camp among "the lush fields of the Imperial Valley, where summer temperatures top 100 degrees." Of these, 180 announced a hunger strike to protest inadequate food and medical attention, poor sanitation facilities, physical abuse, lack of access to lawyers, and being forced to stand outside in the desert sun fourteen hours a day. After six days, an antiriot squad of fifty guards forcibly broke the strike, in which a large number of Central American detainees and a broad coalition of churches, lawyers, and concerned citizens were involved.[11]

Existing detention centers are filling up so fast that the INS has begun subcontracting out to private security firms arrangements for detaining suspected "illegals." Federal courts and other critics have argued that the INS's detention facilities are overcrowded and unsanitary. Of detained "aliens," 7 percent have been held for four months or longer.[12]

Those released have encountered the INS's controversial "no-work" rule, implemented December 7, 1983, forbidding them from taking jobs while trying to prove their legal right to remain in the country. Immigration attorney Peter Schey has described the "no-work" rule as a "catch-22": aliens must prove they are self-supporting while in the country, yet they are barred from supporting themselves while proving it. In 1984 the National Center for Immigrants' Rights won a nationwide injunction on behalf of about 100,000 refugees and immigrants, allowing them to continue working while their deportation hearings were pending.[13]

The Simpson-Mazzoli bill would add to the overcrowding of existing detention facilities. Its proposed increase in the Border Patrol by almost one-third would add nearly a half million apprehensions a year to the already escalating trend in detentions (up from 910,361 in 1980 to 1.25 million in 1983). As Yale Law School professor Peter H. Schuck has pointed out, senators and representatives who vote for Simpson-

Mazzoli "must also face squarely the human implications of transforming the INS into a long-term jailer of noncriminals whose values most Americans admire."[14]

Jailing innocent people by the thousands is not a hallmark of democracy, nor is having private enterprise carry out the task. But that is what is happening. In Houston, Texas, for instance, the Olympic Motel is actually a detention center jointly operated by the INS and the private Corrections Corporation of America. It holds 140 "illegal aliens" behind a twelve-foot cyclone fence topped with coiled barbed wire. A larger detention camp capable of holding up to 450 "undocumented" workers is under construction south of Houston's Intercontinental Airport, for which the INS will pay the same private company $2.2 million the first year of its use. Other such camps are under consideration in Oklahoma, New Orleans, and Roswell, New Mexico. The INS already has a detention camp in Pasadena, California, operated under contract by a private security agency. For the year 1984 Congress approved a supplementary INS budget request of $93 million to finance an "enhanced enforcement" package that includes funds for 200 detention and deportation officers.

The INS is not the only federal agency involved in imprisonment for profit. The US Bureau of Prisons has announced that it plans to contract out to a private security agency the operation of a minimum security prison at a former military installation in Mineral Wells, Texas. The ACLU has undertaken legal action to stop the prison, which it views as part of an ominous and unconstitutional trend. According to ACLU lawyer Stefan Presser, "There are instances in Arizona and New Mexico in which small towns in the backwater are saying, 'Look, we think private business can do this cheaper than government.' So they're hiring these private security firms who are going to hold traffic violators, felons, whoever needs to be held."[15]

The *New York Times* has reported that "incarceration is a growth industry."[16] Private companies, which already own or operate more than two dozen major correction facilities, can look forward to more business based on just two trends: the more than doubling of the nation's imprisoned population in the last decade, to half a million; and the fact that an estimated 60 percent of the nation's correctional centers are under federal court orders to remedy overcrowding and other inhumane conditions.

Until new law is created to govern them, private operations have more leeway to commit abuses. So far, to this author's knowledge, only one court case has come to a decision, and it is being appealed. It involved a private firm known as Danner in Houston, Texas, to which the INS had dispatched some "undocumented" workers. In *Medina* v. *O'Neill*, Chief Judge John Singleton of Houston's Federal District Court found that "because both immigration and detention are traditionally the exclusive prerogative of the state, it is evident that the actions of all the defendants were state action within the purview of the public function doctrine." The "actions" included a Danner guard's murder of one of the inmates during an attempted escape with other inmates from a windowless twelve-by-twenty-foot cell holding sixteen people but designed to hold no more than six.[17]

James K. Stewart, director of the National Institute of Justice, the research arm of the Justice Department, signaled the legal future for prisons run by private enterprise when he told the *New York Times*, "Chief Justice Burger is very supportive of the idea that, instead of having warehouses, we ought to have factories with fences."[18] Given these trends and possibilities, there are ample grounds for Americans to recall the common saying that "a threat to one is a threat to all."

Basic Rights of Americans Threatened

The mistreatment of Mexicans in the United States affects all Americans. In light of the negative impact of the bracero program in the 1940s and 1950s and of employers' use of "illegal" workers to break strikes and drive wages down, it makes sense for most Americans to support the basic rights of these workers, who are not about to go away. The rights they seek are outlined in the Bill of Rights for Undocumented Workers drafted and approved by the well-attended First International Conference for the Full Rights of Undocumented Workers (see Appendix III).

The bill's thirteen articles grant legal residency or full rights to a tax-paying wage earner; demand due process; ban unreasonable search; prohibit raids on factories; allow immigrant workers to adjust their status without having to return to their country of origin; grant immigrant workers the right to organize or to join a union; reject English proficiency as a requirement for a job or resident status; and bestow on immigrants the right to vote both in federal elections in the country of origin and in local and state elections where they work and pay taxes once their immigration status is legalized. The simple fact is that these rights encompass rights already protected by the US Constitution and various existing US laws guaranteeing due process, civil rights, and bilingual ballots and education.

Yet even these guarantees are being stripped away—not only from Mexican immigrant workers, but from US Latino citizens and all other minorities. In November 1984, for example, California voters approved an advisory measure that would prohibit bilingual election ballots. Prior to that, the federal government had more than halved the number of counties requiring bilingual ballots for Latinos and other minority groups per the Voting Rights Act (from 384 in 1976 to 160 in November 1984). In Los Angeles County, where more than half the schoolchildren speak Spanish, the ballot exists only in English. Texas and Arizona are the only remaining states fully covered by the bilingual ballot requirement.[19]

Similar attacks have been undertaken against bilingual education. In San Diego, California, for instance, a nineteen-member grand jury requested on April 23, 1984, that a ban be issued against bilingual education in the city's public schools.[20] Located only a few miles from the Mexican border, San Diego houses countless Mexican children whose first or only language is Spanish. Denial of the right to an education for those still learning English—a right assured by bilingual education laws won in the 1960s by the civil rights movement—has gained impetus from proposals before the Congress that would for the first time by law make English the official language of the country (see Chapter 8). These proposals come, as we have seen, at precisely the historical moment when the Spanish-speaking are emerging as the nation's largest ethnic minority.

These and related measures have established a climate of bigotry, separatism, demoralization, or fear in many urban communities of America. On June 12, 1984, the Supreme Court decided by a vote of 6 to 3 to prohibit the protection against layoffs of recently hired minorities, including women. This and other decisions have strengthened the legal basis for the old practice of "last hired, first fired" and for the double and triple rates of unemployment and lower wages for all minorities. NAACP executive director Benjamin Hooks said about such practices, "To uphold the 'last-hired, first-fired' doctrine in a nation that has a history of excluding classes of people because of race, creed or sex is to turn our backs on the reality that such discriminatory practices have had and continue to have upon excluded groups."[21]

In a climate of heightened intimidation, INS and Border Patrol abuses of Mexican and other Latino immigrants, already described in Chapter 8, have escalated. In 1984, for example, the National Center for Immigrants' Rights and El Rescate, a legal service center, filed suit in San Diego's Federal District Court against the INS for using some 200 rounded-up youngsters as "hostages" to lure "undocumented workers" out of hiding. According to the lawsuit, the children were held against their will and asked to reveal their parents' whereabouts without being informed of their constitutional right to remain silent. No one was allowed to pick them up except their parents. In an earlier case (1982), the National Center for Immigrants' Rights won an injunction in California stopping various counties from requiring "undocumented" mothers who applied for Aid for Dependent Children (AFDC) for their US-citizen children to sign affidavits stating that they would give up custody of their children if expelled from the United States.

The INS holds some minors for months at a time, including an estimated 2,000 Central American refugee children. It routinely deports other minors, some of whom are legal residents and/or US citizens, often after they sign, under pressure, voluntary departure forms. Federal court judges periodically issue temporary restraining orders or injunctions against the INS in these matters, but to little avail. In the worst of cases, INS Border Patrolmen gun down minors, as in the highly publicized case of a twelve-year-old Mexican boy critically wounded near San Ysidro, California, April 18, 1985; other minors have drowned with their parents during periodic INS "herdings" of farmworkers toward waterways, forcing them to choose between surrender or an attempt to swim across.

Also deported without proper consideration are the sickly. For example, a Mexican woman who fought deportation for fear she would not receive in Mexico kidney dialysis treatment she was "illegally" obtaining through a federally funded program in Dallas, Texas, died two months after being sent back to Mexico in November 1984.[22] The rate of detention and deportation has risen so sharply that a Houston-based Latino civil rights organization, La Unión para la Defensa y Educación Latina (UDEL), has introduced a "*migra* insurance" program to help protect disrupted families.[23]

In 1985 the INS instituted a new immigrant arrest program called "Operation Co-operation," by means of which it carries out its traditional practices of cooperation with employers. The INS informs an employer of an impending sweep, giving the employer time to find legal replacements for "undocumented" employees before moving on the plant. Alternatively—as this writer was informed in 1981 by a plant owner who had recently sold his operation to a larger corporation but had remained to manage the plant—an employer calls the INS and requests it to launch a sweep when workers are in the midst of a union organizing drive or a threatened strike action. The INS has also increased its cooperation with state and federal social service agencies, seeking to identify the "undocumented" and deny services.

Also in 1985, word leaked out about a new, heavily armed "SWAT team" being trained to police the US side of the border with Mexico. According to CBS News Anchor Dan Rather, reporting on the evening news, March 8, 1985, "The US government has put its border SWAT team on alert. CBS News has learned [that] for almost a year the US Border Patrol has secretly been training a special 100-man unit. This elite group is known as the Border Patrol Tactical Team. BORTAC is trained to use heavy fire power." A spokesman for the Border Patrol said that BORTAC would be ready to deal with a sudden influx of "illegal aliens."

Concentration camps called "detention camps," heavily armed "SWAT teams," child "hostages," escalated rates of detention, deportation, and factory raids, Supreme Court decisions and grand jury recommendations undermining earlier civil rights victories, proposals to make English the official language of the nation—these are the stuff of civil strife. An early sign of what could result occurred in Lawrence, Massachusetts, in August 1984. Widespread fighting erupted between Latinos, on the one hand, and descendants of French Canadians and whites, on the other. At least fifteen people were injured and twenty arrested—mostly Latinos. Property damage was extensive.

The question for Americans, then, is whether they will tolerate injustice, ethnic and racial hatred and violence, and severe threats to their civil liberties. Unfortunately, one area where Americans readily assume bigoted attitudes and make the wrong decisions is precisely immigration and language rights. The fate of Mexican immigrant workers, the core around which the nation's immigration and language policies will continue to be made, becomes central to the future of American democracy.

CONCLUSION

"Once, walking through his apricot orchard, a California grower was asked what would happen if Congress reformed immigration law, sharply curtailing illegal farm workers. 'I'd go out of business the next day,' he said."
—*New York Times*, Sept. 22, 1985

We have seen how discussion about Mexican "undocumented workers" and the Simpson-Mazzoli bill has moved toward center stage of political debate. This renewed public attention has been a product of economic hard times, intense unionizing and strike activity among Mexican immigrant workers, and accelerated internationalization and technification of economic production.

Employers have sought to reverse falling profit rates and to find scapegoats for the prolonged economic crisis by both employing and blaming cheap Mexican labor. In daily practice, the border's "revolving door" has illustrated this dual role Mexican "illegals" have been called upon to play.

In the legislative arena, the annual resurrection of the Simpson-Mazzoli bill has facilitated the same process. Simpson-Mazzoli seeks to assure, regulate, and control the expanding pool of immigrant labor, while denigrating it in the name of national security.

Once again in history, US immigration policy and lawmaking are not solely internal matters. Like the economic and political forces to which they respond, they involve questions dealing with transnational corporations, an internationalized work force and system of produc-

254

tion, and, ultimately, other governments and peoples caught up in the tide of human rights abuses—from Guatemalan refugee camps in southern Mexico to newly constructed detention centers in Florida and California.

In the end, the future character and even survival of American democracy is at stake. Immigration is not merely a legal issue. It is preeminently a social, economic, and political one.

Socially, the nation's immigration laws and policies reinforce an institutionalized racism that has long been a worldwide shame. The often publicized attacks on Mexican immigrants heighten racist fears and activities and contribute to divisiveness and disunity in the labor force. Economically, the importation and abuse of Mexican immigrant workers help employers to hold back labor's demands for better wages and work conditions, and facilitate the breaking up of labor unions. Politically, a double standard on refugees and enforcement of undemocratic "anticommunist" criteria turn immigration policy into a club of US foreign policy that strains relations with other governments and peoples.

The kind of new immigration law that should be introduced to rectify this is epitomized in the Bill of Rights for the Undocumented Worker, which in fact incorporates what exists in the US Constitution and in labor laws already on the books. The refugee policy that should be enforced is the 1980 Refugee Act that adopts the single standard of the United Nations' definition of a political refugee.

Questions that still go to the heart of labor legislation posing as immigration law are: Why is a guest-worker program needed? Is the problem one of there not being enough US workers? Do foreign workers deliberately come to the United States to "take our jobs"?

Why aren't there enough jobs for everyone? Couldn't we be putting the nation's unemployed to work rebuilding our deteriorating cities, railroads, and industrial plants? Couldn't skilled workers gain more employment and satisfaction training unskilled ones as carpenters, electricians, plumbers, and welders, helping to put unemployed adults and youth back to work building much-needed housing? Couldn't college graduates in urban planning also have their talents put to better use this way?

With all the work that is needed to be done to clean up the environment, rebuild the cities, reindustrialize America, and regenerate economic growth and prosperity, there is obviously enough work for every US citizen and twice the number of "illegals" already here. Why couldn't the US government stop supporting ruthless dictatorships and other US-propped governments that enforce labor discipline on behalf of TNCs and local oligarchs, fuel popular revolt, and increase the flow of desperate refugees into the United States?

Whether to introduce non-discriminatory and fair immigration law or to make possible full employment in the rebuilding of America, a new social agenda is demanded. To shape and implement it requires a new social movement, for profound changes are never made in the absence of independently marshaled social forces.

▼

NOTES

Note: When background or frequently documented information is available in a variety of primary and secondary sources, specific references are not offered in these notes.

CHAPTER 2

1. Cited in Ferdinand Lundberg, *The Rich and the Super-rich* (New York: Bantam, 1969), p. 890; and Scott Nearing and Joseph Freeman, *Dollar Diplomacy* (New York: Monthly Review Press, 1969), p. 273.

2. Cited in Kitty Calavita, *U.S. Immigration Law and the Control of Labor: 1820–1924* (Orlando: Academic Press, 1984), p. 49.

3. Theodore Lothrop Stoddard, *The Rising Tide of Labor Against White World Supremacy* (New York: C. Scribners' Sons, 1920), pp. 107–08; Dr. Laughlin's testimony cited in Joyce Vialet, *A Brief History of US Immigration Policy* (Washington, D.C.: Library of Congress, CRS, December 22, 1980), p. 17; C. M. Goethe, "Immigration from Mexico," and other articles in Madison Grant and Charles S. Davidson, eds., *The Alien in Our Midst, or, "Selling Our Birthright for a Mess of Pottage"* (New York: Galton Publishing Co., 1930). Fashionable in the 1920s and 1930s, such racist arguments were "backed" by many other books and articles.

4. Colby made this claim in widely quoted interviews granted to *Playboy* magazine and the *Los Angeles Times* in June 1978.

5. Cited in R. W. Van Alstyne, *The Rising American Empire* (New York: Oxford University Press, 1960), p. 81.

6. James M. Callahan, *American Foreign Policy in Mexican Relations* (New York: Macmillan, 1932), p. 34; Lewis Hanke, ed., *History of Latin American Civilization: Sources and Interpretations* (Boston: Little, Brown, 1967), p. 25.

7. The most comprehensive of a number of books on this sanguinary history is Rodolfo Acuña's *Occupied America: A History of Chicanos* (New York: Harper & Row, 1981). Others include Mario Barrera, *Race and Class in the Southwest: A Theory of Racial Inequality* (Notre Dame, Ind.: University of Notre Dame Press, 1979); Arnoldo De Leon, *They Called Them Greasers: Anglo Attitudes Towards Mexicans in Texas, 1821–1900* (Austin: University of Texas Press, 1983); Roxanne Dunbar Ortiz, *Roots of Resistance: Land Tenure in New Mexico, 1680–1980* (Los Angeles: UCLA Chicano Studies Research Center, 1980); Mario T. Garcia, *Desert Immigrants: The Mexicans of El Paso, 1880–1920* (New Haven: Yale University Press, 1981); Robert J. Rosenbaum, *Mexicano Resistance in the Southwest* (Austin: University of Texas Press, 1981); and Julian Samora, Joe J. Bernal, and Albert Peña, *Gunpowder Justice: A Reassessment of the Texas Rangers* (Notre Dame, Ind.: University of Notre Dame Press, 1979).

8. For further elaboration on these changes affecting the labor force, consult James D. Cockcroft, *Mexico* (New York: Monthly Review Press, 1983), Chapters 2 and 3.

9. Cited in Acuña, p. 133.

10. Juan Gómez-Quiñones, "Notes on an Interpretation of the Relations Between the Mexican Community in the United States and Mexico," and Rodolfo O. de la Garza, "Chicanos and US Foreign Policy: The Future of Chicano-Mexican Relations," in Carlos Vásquez and Manuel García y Griego, eds., *Mexican-US Relations, Conflict and Convergence* (Los Angeles: UCLA Chicano Studies Research Center, 1983), pp. 406, 421; Acuña, pp. 46–48; Cockcroft, *Mexico*, p. 78.

11. Marta Loyo Camacho and Javier Rodríguez Piña, *Historia de la migración mexicana a los Estados Unidos*, Universidad Autónoma Metropolitana-Azcapotzalco Reporte de Investigación no. 82 (Mexico, 1982), pp. 15–16.

12. Cited in ibid., p. 17. The PLM program is reproduced in James D. Cockcroft, *Intellectual Precursors of the Mexican Revolution, 1900–1913* (Austin: University of Texas Press, 1976), pp. 239–45.

13. Rafael de Zayas Enríquez, *Porfirio Díaz, la evolución de su vida* (New York: D. Appleton & Co., 1908), pp. 216, 234.

14. Cockcroft, *Intellectual Precursors* and W. Dirk Raat, *Revoltosos* (College Station: Texas A & M University Press, 1981). See also notes 7 and 15.

15. Ibid.; Loyo Camacho and Rodríguez Piña, p. 23; Carlos H. Zazueta, "Mexican Political Actors in the United States and Mexico: Historical and Political Contexts of a Dialogue Renewed," in Vásquez and García y Griego, pp. 447–49; Dan Georgakas, *Solidarity Forever: The IWW Reconsidered* (Chicago: Lakeview Press, 1985); Juan Gómez-Quiñones, *Development of the Mexican Working Class North of the Río Bravo* (Los Angeles: UCLA Chicano Studies Research Center, 1982); Juan Gómez-Quiñones and Luis Leobardo Arroyo, *Origenes del movimiento obrero chicano* (Mexico: Ed. Era, 1978); John M. Hart, *Anarchism and the Mexican Working Class, 1860–1931* (Austin: University of Texas Press, 1978); Salvador Hernández, "Tiempos libertarios: El Magonismo en México—Cananea, Río Blanco y Baja California," in Ciro R. S. Cardoso et al., eds., *La clase obrera en la historia de Mexico: De la dictadura porfirista a los tiempos libertarios* (Mexico: Siglo XXI, 1980), pp. 101–248; *New York Times*, July 30, 1984.

16. See note 3.

17. Zazueta, pp. 451–55.

18. Cited in Acuña, p. 136.

19. Manuel Gamio, *The Life Story of the Mexican Immigrant* (New York: Dover Publications, 1971), pp. 127, 180.

20. Loyo Camacho and Rodríguez Piña, p. 24; Gómez-Quiñones, pp. 426, 430; Marcos Cazares, "Organización y lucha de trabajadores indocumentados en Los Angeles en la coyuntura actual," *Revista 'A'* 4, no. 8 (January–April 1983): 104; Acuña, pp. 157–67.

21. Cited in Zazueta, p. 458.

22. Ernesto Galarza, *Merchants of Labor: The Mexican Bracero Story* (Santa Barbara: McNally & Loftin, 1964), p. 39.

23. The use of immigrant workers to combat economic crisis is examined further in Chapter 5. The tendency of the rate of profit to fall derives from the growth in the organic composition of capital, or the ratio of constant capital (instruments and raw materials of production) to variable capital (labor power, the only source of surplus value and hence profit). Although modified by monopolies' ability to control prices, this tendency is one component of the occurrence of periodic crises in capitalist accumulation. For elaboration, consult Manuel Castells, *The Economic Crisis and American Society* (Princeton, N.J.: Princeton University Press, 1980), Chapter 1.

24. Loyo Camacho and Rodríguez Piña, p. 28; Acuña, pp. 137–43; Mercedes Carreras de Velazoo, *Los mexicanos que devolvió la crisis* (Mexico: Secretaría de Relaciones Exteriores, 1974), p. 38.

25. Archivo de la Secretaría de Relaciones Exteriores 41-26-139, IV/241 (73) (03)/1 (January 27, 1932).

26. Carreras de Velazco, pp. 38–40; Loyo Camacho and Rodríguez Piña, p. 40.

27. *Uno Más Uno*, October 2, 1979.

CHAPTER 3

1. The most detailed account of the bracero program remains Ernesto Galarza, *Merchants of Labor: The Mexican Bracero Story* (Santa Barbara: McNally & Loftin, 1964). Other highly informative accounts include Jorge A. Bustamante, *Mexican Migration to the United States: Causes, Consequences and US Responses* (Cambridge: MIT, 1978); James D. Cockcroft and UAM-Azcapotzalco Migration Research Team, *Trabajadores de Michoacán: Historia de un pueblo migrante* (Mexico: imisac, Ediciones Contraste, 1982); Rosalinda Méndez González, "Capital Accumulation and Mexican Immigration to the United States" (Ph.D. diss., University of California–Irvine, 1981); Richard H. Hancock, *The Role of the Bracero in the Economic and Cultural Dynamics of Mexico* (Stanford: Institute of Hispanic American and Luso-Brazilian Studies, Stanford University, 1959); David R. Maciel, *Al norte del Río Bravo (Pasado inmediato) (1930–1981)* (Mexico: Siglo XXI, 1982); Javier Rodríguez Piña and Martha Loyo Camacho, "El movimiento perpetuo: la migración reciente de trabajadores mexicanos a estados unidos, 1942–1982," *Revista 'A'* 4, no. 8 (January–April 1983); and Julian Samora, *Los Mojados: The Wetback Story* (Notre Dame, Ind.: University of Notre Dame Press, 1971).

2. US President's Commission on Migratory Labor, *Migratory Labor in American Agriculture* (Washington, D.C.: GPO, 1951).

3. Méndez González.

4. *Dallas Morning News*, April 30, 1980.

5. Galarza, pp. 222–23.

6. US Department of Labor, *Employment Security Manual* (Washington, D.C., November 1956), Part 6, p. 9123.

7. Cited in Rodolfo Acuña, *Occupied America: A History of Chicanos* (New York: Harper & Row, 1981), p. 216.

8. See Tom Miller, "Class Reunion: *Salt of the Earth* Revisited," *Cineaste* 13, no. 3 (1984); and Michael Wilson, *Salt of the Earth: A Screenplay* (Old Westbury, N.Y.: Feminist Press, 1978).

9. US President's Commission on Migratory Labor, p. 50; Galarza, pp. 126, 199, 203.

10. Cited in Galarza, p. 129.

11. Cited in ibid., p. 153.

12. Cited in ibid., pp. 154–55.

13. Acuña, p. 174. The full story is revealed in Ernesto Galarza, *Spiders in the House and Workers in the Field* (Notre Dame, Ind.: University of Notre Dame Press, 1970).

14. Galarza, *Merchants*, p. 218.

15. Cited in ibid., p. 169.

16. Ibid., p. 225.

17. Cockcroft, *Mexico* (New York: Monthly Review Press, 1983), pp. 172–73.

18. Galarza, *Merchants*, pp. 258–59.

19. TNCs are corporations that have their base in one country but draw much of their income, raw materials, labor, and operating capital from several other countries, through ownership of foreign subsidiaries, joint ventures with foreign governments or investors, and a host of other means. The compelling force behind the rise of TNCs is the need for corporations to grow and maintain their profitability, as well as to gain control over as much of the world's resources and capital as possible. The TNC, a logical outgrowth of monopoly capital that has outgrown nations, constitutes the economic heart of modern imperialism. The term "transnational" is preferable to "multinational" because it is a less ideological and more accurate concept, combining the control aspects implicit in "national" with the global aspects of "trans." On the other hand, "multinational" implies a shared power among various investors of two or more nations—obviously not the case for TNCs' wholly owned foreign subsidiaries.

20. Ernest Feder, *Imperialismo fresa* (Mexico: Ed. Campesina, 1978).

21. Cockcroft, Chapter 5.

22. Jorge A. Bustamante and James D. Cockcroft, "Unequal Exchange in the Binational Relationship: The Case of Immigrant Labor," in Carlos Vásquez and Manuel García y Griego, eds., *Mexican-US Relations: Conflict and Convergence* (Los Angeles: UCLA Chicano Studies Research Center, 1983), pp. 309–23.

23. Because the migrants come and go with such frequency and are difficult to count, their exact numbers are unknown. All empirical studies concur that the size of the Mexican "undocumented" population in the United States at various mo-

ments during the years 1975, 1976, and 1977 was at least 235,000 and no more than 2.9 million. See Manuel García y Griego and Leobardo F. Estrada, "Research on the Magnitude of Mexican Undocumented Immigration to the US: A Summary," in Antonio Rios-Bustamante, ed., *Mexican Immigrant Workers in the US* (Los Angeles: UCLA Chicano Studies Research Center, 1981), pp. 51–70.

CHAPTER 4

1. See James D. Cockcroft, *Mexico* (New York: Monthly Review Press, 1983), Chapters 3, 4, 5, and 7.

2. Ibid., pp. 93–94; Jorge Basurto, *El proletariado industrial en méxico, 1850–1930* (Mexico: Universidad Nacional Autónoma de México, 1975), pp. 25–27.

3. Alonso Aguilar and Fernando Carmona, *México: riqueza y miseria* (Mexico: Nuestro Tiempo, 1967), p. 65; Alonso Aguilar, "La burguesía no sólo manda, gobierna," *Estrategia* 28 (July–August 1979): 2–32.

4. Cockcroft, *Mexico*, Chapter 5; state control of worker and peasant organizations is illustrated throughout Part II of that work. In 1966 Cockcroft and sociologist Bo Anderson developed an analysis of Mexican cooptation techniques in the article "Control and Cooptation in Mexican Politics," which Cockcroft later expanded and refined as "Coercion and Ideology in Mexican Politics"; both articles appear in James D. Cockcroft, Andre Gunder Frank, and Dale L. Johnson, *Dependence and Underdevelopment: Latin America's Political Economy* (New York: Anchor Books, 1972), pp. 219–268.

5. Clark W. Reynolds, *The Mexican Economy: Twentieth-Century Structure and Growth* (New Haven: Yale University Press, 1970).

6. For illustrative examples, see María Guadalupe Acevedo López and Gilberto Silva Ruiz, "Análisis de las situaciones de clase de los trabajadores mexicanos" (Tesis de Licenciatura en Sociología, Universidad Nacional Autónoma de México, 1973).

7. José Luis Ceceña, *México en la órbita imperial* (Mexico: El Caballito, 1970); Fernando Fajnzylber and Trinidad Martínez Tarrago, *Las empresas transnacionales: expansión a nivel mundial y proyección en la industria mexicana* (Mexico: Fondo de Cultura Económica, 1976); Peter Baird and Ed McCaughan, eds., *Beyond the Border: Mexico and US Today* (New York: NACLA, 1979).

8. Quoted in Richard S. Newfarmer and W. F. Mueller, *Multinational Corporations in Brazil and Mexico: Structural Sources of Economic and Noneconomic Power*. Report to the Subcommittee on Multinational Corporations of the Committee on Foreign Relations, U.S. Senate (Washington, D.C., August 1975), p. 17.

9. Fajnzylber and Martínez Tarrago; Gary Gereffi, "Drug Firms and Dependency in Mexico: The Case of the Steroid Hormone Industry," Yale University & Harvard University Center for International Affairs mimeo., 1977; Bernardo Sepúlveda and Antonio Chumacero, *La inversion extranjera en Mexico* (Mexico: Fondo de Cultura Económica, 1973).

10. Fajnzylber and Martínez Tarrago, p. 7.

11. Cynthia Hewitt de Alcántara, *La modernización de la agricultura mexicana, 1940–1970* (Mexico: Siglo XXI, 1978), pp. 300–301.

12. Cockcroft, *Mexico*, pp. 205, 340–41.

13. Ibid., p. 245; *New York Times*, September 10, 13, November 24, 1984, and March 10, April 21, 1985.

14. Edward Kelly, "Industrial Exodus: Public Strategies for Control of Corporate Relocation," paper presented at Ohio Public Interest Campaign Conference—Alternative State and Local Policies, October 1977.

15. James D. Cockcroft, "Mexicali: Vortex of Political Problems," *Hispanic American Report* 15, no. 11 (November 1962): 989–92. For more on border pollution, see Albert Uton, ed., *Pollution and International Boundaries* (Albuquerque: University of New Mexico Press, 1972).

16. Baird and McCaughan, pp. 138–40.

17. See D. W. Barraesen, *The Border Industrialization Program of Mexico* (Lexington, Mass.: D. C. Heath, 1971); and Carlos F. Rico, "The Future of Mexican-US Relations and the Limits of the Rhetoric of 'Interdependence,' " in Carlos Vásquez and Manuel García y Griego, eds., *Mexican-US Relations: Conflict and Convergence* (Los Angeles: UCLA Chicano Studies Research Center, 1983), pp. 127–74.

18. Cited in NACLA, *Mexico 1968* (New York: NACLA, 1968), p. 37. See also María Patricia Fernández, "Maquiladoras, desarrollo e inversión transnacional," *Revista 'A'* 4, no. 8 (January–April 1983): 158.

19. For a good overview, consult *Punto Crítico* no. 142 (November 1984): 39–48; Jorge Carrillo and Alberto Hernandez, "Sindicatos y control obrero en las plantas maquiladoras fronterizas," *Revista Investigación Económica* no. 161 (July–September 1982); Peter F. Drucker, "The Rise of Production Sharing," *Wall Street Journal*, March 15, 1977; *Revista 'A'* 4, no. 8 (January–April 1983); and Rico.

20. Particularly insightful on this subject is María Patricia Fernández, op. cit., and her book *For We Are Sold, I and My People: Women and Industry in Mexico's Frontier* (Albany: State University of New York Press, 1983).

21. Calvin P. Blair, "Mexico: Some Recent Developments and the Interdependence Relationship with the United States," in *Recent Developments in Mexico and Their Economic Implications for the United States: Hearings before the Subcommittee on Inter-American Economic Relationships of the Joint Economic Committee* (Washington, D.C.: GPO, 1977), p, 357.

22. Fernández, "Maquiladoras," pp. 173–74.

23. As reported in the *Los Angeles Times*, September 27, 1982.

24. Quoted in the *New York Times*, September 20, 1982.

25. A good summary is Edmundo Jacobo Molina, "El dilema de la integración de la frontera norte," *Revista 'A'* 4, no. 8 (January–April 1983): 127–52. See also note 19 above.

26. Ibid.

CHAPTER 5

1. Many recent books substantiate the findings about the economic crisis described here. A good summary may be found in Gar Alperovitz and Jeff Faux, *Rebuilding America* (New York: Pantheon Books, 1984), pp. 21–43. See also Barry Bluestone and Bennett Harrison, *The Deindustrialization of America* (New York: Basic Books, 1982); Samuel Bowles, David M. Gordon, and Thomas E. Weisskopf,

Beyond the Waste Land (New York: Anchor Books, 1984); Manuel Castells, *The Economic Crisis and American Society* (Princeton: Princeton University Press, 1980); James O'Connor, *Accumulation Crisis* (New York: Basil Blackwell, 1984); *New York Times*, November 18, December 2, 1984; Howard Sherman, *Stagflation: A Radical Theory of Unemployment and Inflation* (New York: Harper & Row, 1976); Kari Stallard, Barbara Ehrenreich, and Holly Sklar, *Poverty in the American Dream* (Boston: South End Press, 1983); Union for Radical Political Economics (URPE), *US Capitalism in Crisis* (New York: URPE, 1978); and Alan Wolfe, *America's Impasse* (New York: Pantheon Books, 1981).

2. Alperovitz and Faux, p. 129 (cf. pp. 4, 34, 59, 98). See also Bowles et al., pp. 58, 113, 133; and James D. Cockcroft, *Mexico* (New York: Monthly Review Press, 1983), p. 256, 309.

3. *Business Week*, September 15, 1980, cited in *Monthly Review*, April 1984, p. 11.

4. *New York Times*, May 16, 1984; March 31, 1985.

5. Ibid., July 9, October 21, 1984; April 18, May 22, June 15, 1985.

6. Ibid., March 14, 1982.

7. Bowles et al., p. 95. "Tobin's Q" is the ratio of the stock market value to the current net replacement cost of capital goods. It roughly measures the amount one would have to pay to buy the average corporation on the stock market relative to the amount it would cost to build the firm anew. This is considered a good indicator of profit expectations.

8. Ibid., pp. 95–97. See also note 23, Chapter 2.

9. For more complete elaboration, consult Cockcroft, *Mexico*, pp. 145–317.

10. Ibid.; James D. Cockcroft, "Immiseration, Not Marginalization," *Latin American Perspectives* 10, nos. 2 and 3 (Spring–Summer 1983): 86–107.

11. Ibid.

12. Cited in Cheryl Payer, "The World Bank and the Small Farmer," *Monthly Review*, November 1980, p. 35.

13. The urban component of the World Bank's "investment in the poor" strategy is further analyzed in Cheryl Payer, *The World Bank: A Critical Analysis* (New York: Monthly Review Press, 1982).

14. US Delegation to the AID World Conference on Agrarian Reform and Rural Development, Rome, July 12–21, 1979, "Integration of Women in Development" (mimeo., May 24, 1979). More than likely, the control over reproduction really envisioned by AID is birth control (or sterilization, so often financed by AID) and *not* control over the means of production and reproduction as such. Indeed, AID is a major funder in Mexico of birth control injections of Depo-Provera (a synthetic form of the hormone progesterone banned by the FDA). The injection inhibits ovulation for three to six months. Experiments on animals have shown that it leads to cancer and other fatal side effects.

15. Cockcroft, *Mexico*, pp. 189, 222.

16. *Wall Street Journal*, June 18, 1976.

17. Gina Allen, "Across the River," *Humanist*, November–December 1981; Jorge A. Bustamante and James D. Cockcroft, "Unequal Exchange in the Binational Relationship: The Case of Immigrant Labor," in Carlos Vásquez and Man-

uel García y Griego, eds., *Mexican-US Relations Conflict and Convergence* (Los Angeles: UCLA Chicano Studies Research Center, 1983).

18. Released in 1984 by the Urban Institute in Washington, D.C.

19. *Hispanic Monitor*, May 1984; Allen; *San Diego Union*, October 14, 1980; and Bustamante and Cockcroft. See also Chapter 4.

20. Celestino Fernandez, "The Border Patrol and News Media Coverage of Undocumented Mexican Immigration During the 1970s: A Quantitative Content Analysis in the Sociology of Knowledge," *California Sociologist* 5 (1982).

21. *New York Times*, August 2, 1980.

22. Allen; M. Vic Villalpando et al., *A Study of the Socioeconomic Impact of Illegal Aliens on the County of San Diego* (San Diego: Human Resources Agency, County of San Diego, 1977); James D. Cockcroft and UAM-Azcapotzalco Migration Research Team, *Trabajadores de Michoacán: Historia de un pueblo migrante* (Mexico: imisac, Ediciones Contraste, 1982).

23. Ford Foundation, *Hispanics: Challenges and Opportunities* (New York, June 1984), p. 20.

24. Martin Oppenheimer, *White Collar Politics* (New York: Monthly Review Press, 1985), p. 87.

25. US Department of Health, Education, and Welfare, *Work in America* (Cambridge, Mass.: MIT Press, 1973), p. 38; Oppenheimer, p. 91.

26. Oppenheimer, p. 93.

27. John Naisbitt, *Megatrends* (New York: Warner Books, 1982); John Naisbitt and Patricia Aburdene, *Re-inventing the Corporation: Transforming Your Job and Your Company for the New Information Society* (New York: Warner Books, 1985).

28. *International Report*, July 1983; Alperovitz and Faux, p. 59. For more examples of runaway "high-tech" shops, see Oppenheimer.

29. *New York Times*, May 22, 1984; June 15, 1985.

30. Naisbitt, p. 24; Naisbitt and Aburdene, Chapter 3.

31. *New York Times*, October 14, 1984.

32. Michael Moritz, *The Little Kingdom: The Private Story of Apple Computer* (New York: William Morrow & Co., 1984).

33. James D. Cockcroft, interviews with workers and employers at Electrosound and Tigart, 1981.

34. *New York Times*, June 19, September 9, 1984, and January 20, 1985; Oppenheimer, Chapter 5.

35. *New York Times*, October 21, 1984.

36. *In These Times*, December 5–11, 1984; *New York Times*, January 20, 1985; *Guardian*, September 26, 1979; *Monthly Review*, April 1984.

37. *New York Times*, June 19, October 31, 1984; May 23, 1985.

38. Ibid., October 9, 31, 1984; New York City Urban League report, CBS News, November 1, 1984; *Hispanic Monitor*, January and April, 1985; US Commission on Civil Rights, *Social Indicators of Equality for Minorities and Women* (August 1978); Ford Foundation, p. 6; National Hispanic Center for Advanced Studies and Policy Analysis, *The State of Hispanic America*, vol. 2 (Oakland, Calif., 1982).

39. *New York Times*, June 27, 1980, cited in Alperovitz and Faux, p. 63.

40. *The Nation*, October 20, 1984; Jeremy Brecher, "Crisis Economy: Born-Again Labor Movement?," *Monthly Review*, March 1984.

41. Alperovitz and Faux, p. 62.

42. Brecher, pp. 8–9.

43. *New York Times*, October 18, 1979, cited in Alperovitz and Faux, p. 60.

44. *Business Week*, June 30, 1980; Alperovitz and Faux, pp. 46, 57–58.

45. *International Report*, July 1983.

46. Clark W. Reynolds, "Labor Market Projections for the United States and Mexico and Their Relevance to Current Migration Controversies," in Vásquez and García y Griego, pp. 326–55.

47. Cited by Copley News Service, September 27, 1981.

CHAPTER 6

1. *Latin American Weekly Report*, November 16, 1979; *International Herald Tribune*, April 20, 1980.

2. For useful background on "dominoes" and US foreign policy, consult Richard J. Barnet, *Intervention and Revolution: The United States in the Third World* (New York: World Publishing Company, 1968); James D. Cockcroft, "The Democratic Humanitarian Mythos in US Foreign Policy," in Anton-Andreas Guha and Sven Papcke, eds., *Amerika—Der Riskante Partner* (Berlin: Athenaum, 1984); and various issues of *NACLA Report on the Americas*.

3. Cited in Cockcroft, "Democratic Humanitarian Mythos," p. 14.

4. NACLA Report on the Americas, January–February 1978. See also the following issues of the same journal: July–August 1976; January 1977; March 1977; July–August 1977; September–October 1977; March–April 1978; May–June 1978; and September–October 1978. The author gratefully acknowledges the assistance of Professor Sheldon Liss of the University of Akron's History Department for compilation of much of this material. The *New York Times* reported on November 22, 1977, that the FBI "conducted extensive operations in Mexico to undermine Communist groups there that it said might filter across the border." More than a hundred pages of material released under the Freedom of Information Act are available for consultation at FBI headquarters in Washington.

5. James D. Cockcroft, unpublished field notes, 1964; Cockcroft, *Mexico* (New York: Monthly Review Press, 1983), pp. 261–64.

6. Cockcroft, *Mexico*, pp. 266, 296.

7. The phrasing is that of Professor John J. Johnson, then of Stanford University, as quoted by *Newsweek* August 23, 1965—and the message is carried through a panoply of US military training institutions from Panama to Puerto Rico that have provided instruction for most of Latin America's dictators and military presidents in recent decades.

8. *New York Times*, November 11, 1984.

9. *New York Times*, February 27, 1984.

10. For further elaboration, consult Cockcroft, "Democratic Humanitarian Mythos."

11. Ibid. The story of Guazapa is told in the 1984 film *In the Name of the People*, distributed by Cinewest in Los Angeles. The existence of America's secret

army in Nicaragua has been reported by the *Philadelphia Inquirer* (December 16, 1984) and other newspapers, as well as confirmed by soldiers serving in it.

12. *New York Times*, September 24, 1984.

13. Quoted in *Proceso*, November 9, 1981.

14. Cockcroft, *Mexico*, pp. 269–72, 308–11; *New York Times*, September 8 and 26, 1984 and January 18, 1985; Holly Sklar, ed., *Trilateralism: The Trilateral Commission and Elite Planning for World Management* (Boston: South End Press, 1980).

15. *The Nation*, May 19, September 8, 1984; Cockcroft, *Mexico*, pp. 201, 269–70.

16. *The Nation*, September 8, 1984.

CHAPTER 7

1. For further background, consult, among others, Rodolfo Acuña, *Occupied America: A History of Chicanos* (New York: Harper & Row, 1981); Doug Adair, "Texas Strike," *Liberation*, August 1967; Vernon M. Briggs, Jr., Walter Fogel, and Fred H. Schmidt, *The Chicano Worker* (Austin: University of Texas Press, 1977); Tony Castro, *Chicano Power* (New York: Sutton, 1974); Chicano Communications Center, *450 Años del Pueblo Chicano: 450 Years of Chicano History in Pictures* (Albuquerque: Chicano Communications Center, 1976); Jeff Coplon, "Cesar Chavez's Fall from Grace," *Village Voice*, August 14, 1984; Carlos E. Cortes, *Mexican Labor in the US* (New York: Arno Press, 1974); Mark Day, *Forty Acres: Cesar Chavez and the Farm Workers* (New York: Praeger, 1971); Chris J. Garcia, *La Causa Politica: The Chicano Political Experience* (Notre Dame, Ind.: University of Notre Dame Press, 1974); Leo Grebler, *The Mexican-American People* (New York: Free Press, 1970); Ray Martin, "La Huelga: The Desperate Cry along the Rio Grande," *UAW Solidarity*, March 1967; Matt S. Meier, *The Chicanos* (New York: Hill and Wang, 1972); Alfredo Mirande and Evangelina Enriquez, *La Chicana: The Mexican-American Woman* (Chicago: University of Chicago Press, 1979); Magdalena Mora and Adelaida R. del Castillo, eds., *Mexican Women in the United States: Struggles Past and Present* (Los Angeles: UCLA Chicano Studies Research Center, 1980); Antonio Ríos-Bustamante, ed., *Mexican Immigrant Workers in the US* (Los Angeles: UCLA Chicano Studies Research Center, 1981); Fred E. Romero, *Chicano Workers: Their Utilization and Development* (Los Angeles: UCLA Chicano Studies Research Center, 1979); Stephen H. Sosnick, *Hired Hands: Seasonal Farm Workers in the United States* (Santa Barbara: McNally & Loftin, 1978); Ronald B. Taylor, *Sweatshops in the Sun* (Boston: Beacon Press, 1973) and *Chavez and the Farm Workers* (Boston: Beacon Press, 1975); and various issues of *Aztlan* and *Southwest Economy & Society*.

2. To be sure, the social movements of Mexican workers and Americans of Mexican descent include their share of "Uncle Toms," or *tíos tacos* as those who ape "anglo" ways are pejoratively labeled. As in any social movement, there are opportunists and people who give up when faced with repeated failures. Yet a significant number have kept up the political struggle for *la raza* and remain active today. The long, often repetitive history of these movements for recognition and fairness among America's Mexican population is particularly relevant. Ever since their

incorporation into the United States after the 1848 US conquest of almost half of Mexico's territory, Mexicans in the Southwest have experienced an extreme racism second only to that suffered by Indians in the region. Swindled out of their properties, robbed, attacked, lynched, and abused without fair judicial recourse, they and their descendants (supposedly protected under the Treaty of Guadalupe Hidalgo) have put up a stiff though often futile resistance. In New Mexico the movement to reclaim stolen lands took on a new militance in the 1960s under the initial leadership of Reies López Tijerina. This rural movement made contact with other civil rights and progressive groups in the United States. Thus a wider public came to know of the land and cultural claims of these Mexican descendants and also of the decades of repression they have suffered, the endless legal charges and harassments, and the vigilante arson and assaults that still take place with official complacency or complicity today. Two particularly strong presentations of the history are Acuña's *Occupied America* and Roxanne Dunbar Ortiz, *Roots of Resistance: Land Tenure in New Mexico, 1680–1980* (Los Angeles: UCLA Chicano Studies Research Center, 1980).

3. Interview with Peter Schey, December 23, 1981.

4. David Montgomery, "Making History but Not Under Circumstances Chosen by Ourselves," *Monthly Review*, March 1984, p. 21.

5. *The Post-Star* (Glens Falls, N.Y.), September 17, 1983.

6. *Economic Indicators*, January 1980, April 1984; *BLS Monthly Labor Review*, May 1984; *Guardian*, October 10, 1984; Jane Slaughter, *Concessions and How to Beat Them* (Detroit: Labor Education and Research Project, 1982).

7. For further elaboration, consult Rebecca Morales, "Unions and Undocumented Workers," *Our Socialism* 1, no. 2 (April 1983): 33–37.

8. Guadalupe L. Sánchez and Jesús Romo, *Organizing Mexican Undocumented Farm Workers on Both Sides of the Border*, University of California Program in United States–Mexican Studies Working Paper No. 27 (San Diego, 1981), p. 6.

9. Ibid., p. 7.

10. Ibid., p. 12.

11. *Hispanic Monitor*, March 1984.

12. *New York Times*, July 9, 1985.

13. For these and other survey results, see James D. Cockcroft and UAM-Azcapotzalco Migration Research Team, *Trabajadores de Michoacán: Historia de un pueblo migrante* (Mexico: imisac, Ediciones Contraste, 1982).

14. *New York Times*, March 21, 1982.

15. See Fred Hirsch, *An Analysis of Our AFL-CIO Role in Latin America, or Under the Covers with the CIA* (San Jose, Calif., 1974); and Jack Scott, *Yankee Unions, Go Home! How the AFL Helped the U.S. Build an Empire in Latin America* (Vancouver, B.C.: New Star Books, 1978).

16. Quoted in the *Guardian*, June 20, 1984.

CHAPTER 8

1. *Guardian*, September 12, 1984.

2. US House of Representatives Doc. 520, 82nd Cong. (2nd sess.), June 25, 1952, p. 5. Cited in Joyce Vialet, "A Brief History of US Immigration Policy," Report No. 80–223EPW, Congressional Research Service (Washington, D.C.: Library of Congress, December 22, 1980), p. 21.

3. Examples abound in the daily press. See, for example, *New York Times*, September 4, November 26, 1984 (on violence against Mexicans), and August 31, 1985 ("Violent Incidents Against Asian-Americans Seen as Part of Racist Pattern").

4. Committee on Chicano Rights (CCR), *A Chicano Perspective on the President's Immigration Proposals* (National City, Calif.: CCR, 1981).

5. William Safire, *New York Times*, November 26, 1984.

6. See Celestino Fernandez, "The Border Patrol and News Media Coverage of Undocumented Mexican Immigration During the 1970s: A Quantitative Content Analysis in the Sociology of Knowledge," *California Sociologist* 5 (1982).

7. Cited in *Colombia Report* 3, no. 1 (November 1981).

8. Committee on Chicano Rights press release, April 24, 1984.

9. *New York Times*, July 21, 1984.

10. Copley News Service, August 3, 1983.

11. Committee on Chicano Rights, *A Chicano Perspective*.

12. *Hispanic Monitor*, February 1984.

13. US General Accounting Office, *Information on the Enforcement of Laws Regarding Employment of Aliens in Selected Countries* (Washington, D.C., August 31, 1982), cited by Wayne A. Cornelius, "Simpson-Mazzoli vs. the Realities of Mexican Immigration," in Wayne A. Cornelius and Ricardo Anzaldua Montoya, eds., *America's New Immigration Law: Origins, Rationales, and Potential Consequences*, University of California–San Diego Center for US-Mexican Studies Monograph Series, no. 11 (La Jolla, 1983), p. 143. For a summary of employer sanction laws and their nonenforcement, consult Kitty Calavita, "Employer Sanctions Legislation in the United States: Implications for Immigration Policy," in Cornelius and Anzaldua Montoya, pp. 73–81; and Calavita, *California's "Employer Sanctions": The Case of the Disappearing Law*, University of California–San Diego Center for US-Mexican Studies Research Report Series, no. 39 (La Jolla, 1982). See also Calavita's pathbreaking *United States Immigration Law and the Control of Labor: 1820–1924* (Orlando: Academic Press, 1984).

14. Calavita, "Employer Sanctions Legislation," p. 80.

15. M. Vic Villalpando et al., *A Study of the Socioeconomic Impact of Illegal Aliens on the County of San Diego* (San Diego: County of San Diego Human Resources Agency, January 1977); *Torch*, July 15–August 14, 1984.

16. *New York Times*, October 17, 1984.

17. Committee on Chicano Rights press release, April 13, 1981.

18. Copley News Service, April 18, 1984.

19. See, for example, "Académicos se pronuncian ante la revocación de la Carta Silva," *Uno más Uno* (Mexico City), January 13, 1982; and press reports on international press conference held by Jorge Bustamante, Herman Baca, and James Cockcroft in San Ysidro, California, January 27, 1982 (e.g., *San Diego Union* and *San Diego Tribune*, January 28, 1982).

20. *Hispanic Monitor*, January 1985.

CHAPTER 9

1. *New York Times*, November 12, 1984; April 17, 1985. See also "15 Years of the Burger Court," *The Nation*, September 19, 1984.

2. *New York Times*, December 5, 1984.

3. For background, consult Hedda Garza, *Watergate Investigation Index*, 2 vols. (Wilmington, Delaware: Scholarly Resources, 1982, 1985); Bertram Gross, *Friendly Fascism: The New Face of Power in America* (New York: M. Evans and Company, 1980); "Law and Order in the 1980s: The Rise of the Right," *Crime and Social Justice* 15 (1981); and Robert Lefcourt, ed., *Law Against the People* (New York: Vintage Books, 1971).

4. Ibid.; *Guardian*, May 2, 1984.

5. *Guardian*, March 14, 1984; *New York Times*, February 19, 1984.

6. *Newsweek*, February 1, 1982.

7. Task Force on Immigration and Refugee Policy, *Report to the President* (Washington, D.C.: GPO, July 1981).

8. Ibid.

9. *New York Times*, December 15, 1984; July 8, 1985.

10. Various press clippings, including reports on press conference held by Herman Baca, Jorge Bustamante, and James Cockcroft in San Ysidro, California, January 27, 1982 (*San Diego Union* and the *Tribune* of San Diego, January 28, 1982).

11. *New York Times*, June 4, 1985; *Working Class Opposition*, July 1985.

12. Compilation of federal court cases and decisions, including statistics and criticisms of the INS, is provided on a regular basis by the International Justice Fund for Immigrant and Refugee Assistance National Center for Immigrants' Rights, 256 S. Occidental Blvd., Los Angeles, CA 90057.

13. Ibid., *Los Angeles Times*, December 17, 1983.

14. Quoted in *New York Times*, September 24, 1984.

15. Quoted in ibid., March 6, 1984; *Guardian*, March 14, 1984.

16. *New York Times*, February 11, 1985.

17. Ibid., February 11, September 16, 1985.

18. Ibid., March 3, 1985.

19. Ibid., September 10, November 8, 1984; *Hispanic Monitor*, October 1984.

20. *Hispanic Monitor*, July 1984.

21. *Guardian*, June 20, 1984.

22. *New York Times*, November 26, 1984.

23. Ibid., and September 4, 1984; *Guardian*, March 14, 28, 1984. See also notes 8 and 10.

Important Notice to All Industrial Workers

KNOW YOUR RIGHTS

by the COMMITTEE IN DEFENSE OF MEXICAN WORKERS, Los Angeles, CA

IF YOU ARE ARRESTED BY THE POLICE, TAKE THE FOLLOWING PRECAUTIONS:

————DO NOT RESIST ARREST.

————ASK WHAT THE CHARGES ARE.

————WRITE DOWN THE NAME AND LICENSE NUMBER OR BADGE NUMBER OF THE OFFICER IF YOUR HOUSE OR CAR IS SEARCHED WITHOUT YOUR PERMISSION.

————DO NOT SIGN ANY CONFESSION.

————YOU HAVE THE RIGHT TO MAKE TWO TELEPHONE CALLS: ONE TO YOUR FAMILY OR YOUR LAWYER AND ONE TO A BAIL BONDSMAN.

————YOU CAN BE DETAINED FOR NO MORE THAN 48 HOURS WITHOUT A COURT HEARING. IF YOU DO NOT HAVE A LAWYER TO REPRESENT YOU, ASK THE COURT TO APPOINT ONE TO PRESENT YOUR DEFENSE.

IF YOU ARE ARRESTED BY THE IMMIGRATION DEPARTMENT (INS):

————DO NOT ACCEPT A VOLUNTARY DEPORTATION, NO MATTER WHAT THEY PROMISE OR HOW MUCH THEY THREATEN YOU.

————IF THE INS COMES TO YOUR PLACE OF WORK, DO NOT TRY TO RUN AWAY AND DO NOT HIDE IN UNSAFE PLACES. (*For example, areas near high voltage machinery, places where acids are kept or where there is a high concentration of poisonous gases, small places that have little ventilation, etc.*)

————IF YOU HAVE NO DOCUMENTS AND ARE ARRESTED, DEMAND YOUR RIGHT TO A DEPORTATION HEARING.

————NEVER GIVE NAMES OF FRIENDS, RELATIVES, NEIGHBORS, OR ANYONE YOU KNOW WHO DOESN'T HAVE DOCUMENTS. BY LAW, YOU ARE NOT OBLIGATED TO GIVE ANY SUCH INFORMATION.

————DO NOT SAY THAT YOU WERE BORN IN ANOTHER COUNTRY. DO NOT ADMIT THAT YOU ARE HERE WITHOUT PAPERS. DO NOT GIVE THE IMMIGRATION AGENTS ANY INFORMATION ABOUT HOW, WHEN, OR WHERE YOU ENTERED THE UNITED STATES.

————REMEMBER THAT YOU HAVE THE RIGHT TO REMAIN SILENT. THE ONLY THING YOU HAVE TO TELL THEM IS YOUR NAME AND ADDRESS. IF YOU GIVE THEM ANY MORE INFORMATION, IT WILL GIVE THE IMMIGRATION DEPARTMENT SUFFICIENT GROUNDS TO DEPORT YOU.

————REMEMBER THAT THE DEPORTATION HEARING IS A LONG PROCESS AND IS SUBJECT TO APPEAL. THE IMMIGRATION DEPARTMENT HAS TO PRESENT SUFFICIENT PROOF THAT YOU ARE IN THE COUNTRY ILLEGALLY.

OUR COMMITTEE HAS BEEN ACTIVELY WORKING IN THE DEFENSE OF WORKERS. WE FIRMLY BELIEVE THAT THE INS HAS NO RIGHT TO VIOLATE THE LABOR LAWS BY CONDUCTING RAIDS ON FACTORIES.

WE URGE ALL WORKERS TO UNITE IN THIS DEFENSE STRUGGLE AND ESTABLISH WORKERS' ADVISORY COUNCILS IN THE FACTORIES.

A todos los trabajadores Industriales

CONOZCA SUS DERECHOS

de COMITE EN DEFENSA DE
TRABAJADORES MEXICANOS, Los Angeles, CA

EN CASO DE QUE USTED SEA ARRESTADO POR LA POLICIA, TOME LAS SIGUIENTES PRECAUCIONES:

————NUNCA RESISTA FISICAMENTE EL SER ARRESTADO.

————PREGUNTE CUALES SON LOS CARGOS.

————RECUERDE EL NOMBRE Y NUMERO DE PLACA DEL OFICIAL SI LE ESCULCAN SU COCHE O SU CASA SIN SU CONSENTIMIENTO.

————NO FIRME NINGUNA CONFESION DE CULPABILIDAD.

————USTED TIENE EL DERECHO DE HACER DOS LLAMADAS TELEFONICAS: UNA A SU FAMILIA O ABOGADO Y OTRA A UN AGENTE DE FIANZAS.

————USTED PUEDE SER DETENIDO POR NO MAS DE 48 HORAS ANTE DE APARECER ANTE LA CORTE. SI NO TIENE UN ABOGADO QUE LO REPRESENTE, PIDA A LA CORTE QUE LE PROPORCIONEN UNO PARA QUE PRESENTE SU DEFENSA.

EN CASO DE QUE USTED SEA ARRESTADO POR AGENTES DE INMIGRACION (MIGRA):

———NO ACEPTE DEPORTACION VOLUNTARIA DEL PAIS, NO IMPORTA QUE TANTO LE PROMETAN O AMENACEN.

———SI LA MIGRA ENTRA A LA FABRICA DONDE USTED TRABAJA, NO CORRA O SE ESCONDA EN LUGARES PELIGROSOS. (*Por ejemplo, Departamentos con maquinaria de alto voltage, lugares donde se guardan ácidos o haya concentración de gases tóxicos, lugares reducidos que carezcan de ventilación, etc.*)

———SI USTED CARECE DE DOCUMENTOS Y ESTA ARRESTADO, INSISTA EN SU DERECHO DE TENER UN PROCESO DE AUDIENCIA DE DEPORTACION.

———NUNCA DE NOMBRES DE PERSONAS, AMIGOS, FAMILIARES O VECINOS QUE USTED CONOZCA Y LOS CUALES CARECEN DE DOCUMENTOS. LA LEY NO LE OBLIGA A DAR NINGUNA INFORMACION.

———NO DIGA QUE ES NACIDO EN OTRO PAIS O ADMITA QUE SE ENCUENTRA EN EL PAIS SIN DOCUMENTOS, NI LE DE INFORMACION DE COMO, CUANDO, O POR DONDE ENTRO A EEUU.

———RECUERDE QUE USTED TIENE EL DERECHO DE MANTENERSE SILENCIO Y UNICAMENTE DEBERA DARLES SU NOMBRE Y DIRECCION. SI USTED LES PROPORCIONA MAS INFORMACION, DARA CAUSA SUFICIENTE PARA QUE EL DEPARTAMENTO DE INMIGRACION LO DEPORTE DEL PAIS.

———RECUERDE QUE EL PROCESO DE AUDIENCIA DE DEPORTACION ES LARGO Y SUJETO A APELACION. EL DEPARTAMENTO DE INMIGRACION TIENE QUE PRESENTAR PRUEBAS SUFICIENTES DE QUE USTED SE ENCUENTRA EN EL PAIS ILEGALMENTE.

NUESTRO COMITE HA ESTADO ACTIVAMENTE TRABAJANDO EN LA DEFENSA DE OBREROS. CREEMOS FIRMEMENTE QUE LA MIGRA NO TIENE NINGUN DERECHO A VIOLAR LAS LEYES DE TRABAJO Y HACER REDADAS EN LAS FABRICAS.

ESTAMOS EXHORTANDO A TODOS LOS TRABAJADORES A UNIRSE EN ESTA LUCHA DE DEFENSA Y ESTABLECER CONSEJOS OBREROS DENTRO DE LAS FABRICAS.

The Immigration Bills: How They Compare

ENFORCEMENT PROVISIONS

SIMPSON	MAZZOLI	ROYBAL
Strengthens criminal penalties for transporting, harboring and bringing unauthorized aliens into the United States.	Similar to Senate for transporting aliens but with less severe penalties. Eliminates the "Texas proviso," which states employment shall not be deemed to constitute harboring.	Similar to Mazzoli but does not delete "Texas proviso."
Makes a statement showing that it is the sense of Congress to increase resources for border patrol and enforcement.	Similar to Senate regarding increased enforcement being "an essential element" of an immigration control and reform program.	Similar to Senate on two key elements. Calls for increase in border patrol and in INS service activities.
Permits attorney general to designate state officers to assist in enforcement.	No comparable provision.	Prohibits state and local law enforcement personnel from stopping suspected illegal aliens except as authorized by the Immigration and Nationality Act.
Prohibits warrantless INS entry on farms beyond 25 miles from the border.	Similar to Senate.	Same as Mazzoli version.
No comparable provision.	No comparable provision.	Requires attorney general and secretary of state to initiate discussions with Mexico and Canada to deal with problem of smuggling aliens and to create an anti-smuggling program.
No comparable provision.	No comparable provision.	Requires attorney general to take actions, including the training of INS officers, to safeguard the rights, safety and dignity of persons within the jurisdiction of the U.S.

274

| No comparable provision. | No comparable provision. | Expands the INS community outreach program to the district level to improve service and investigation of complaints. |

GUEST WORKER PROGRAMS

SIMPSON	MAZZOLI	ROYBAL
Creates provisions and procedures for an H-2 or guest worker program.	Similar to Senate.	No comparable provision until 1985 version calling for 3-year transitional "guest worker" program for agricultural interests.
No comparable provision.	States that the president should establish an advisory commission to consult with Mexico on the H-2 program.	No comparable provision.

IMMIGRATION COMMISSION

SIMPSON	MAZZOLI	ROYBAL
No comparable provision.	No comparable provision.	Creates a commission to further study the "push-pull" factors affecting illegal immigration and the incentives for employers to hire illegal workers.

EMPLOYMENT PROVISIONS

SIMPSON	MAZZOLI	ROYBAL
Unlawful to hire or recruit for fee an unauthorized alien.	Same as Senate but with added language "refer for consideration."	Amends the Fair Labor Standards Act by establishing a new civil penalty of up to $10,000 per violation of the Act's recordkeeping requirements.
All employers must check I.D. documents and those hiring four or more must attest under penalty of perjury that they have done so.	Employers of four or more must check I.D. documents and attest under penalty of perjury that they have done so. Compliance, however, is merely voluntary unless employer has been previously found to have employed unauthorized aliens.	Provides additional authorizations to the Labor Department and National Labor Relations Board for increased enforcement of the Fair Labor Standards Act, the Occupational Safety and Health Act and the National Labor Relations Act, insofar as violations of these laws involve undocumented workers. The additional authorizations are: $5 million for fiscal year 1984 (supplemental), $25 million for FY '85, $30 million for FY '86.

Creates affirmative defense for employers who have complied in good faith with verification requirements.	Same as Senate.	Directs secretary of labor to establish a program of labor law enforcement that would deter industry from hiring and exploiting unlawful residents.
Requires that within three years the president make changes necessary to create an I.D. system to determine employment eligibility. If the new system requires a card, it must be tamper proof and subject to congressional review before implementation.	Within three years the president must report to Congress on possible need for changes necessary for a secure I.D. system. It does not authorize creation of a national I.D. card.	No comparable provision.
Graduated penalty structure for hiring an unauthorized alien after a one-year phase-in: $1,000 civil fine for first offense, $2,000 fine for second offense, $1,000 fine and/or six month imprisonment for continued pattern of offenses.	Similar to Senate with a six-month phase-in period; Citation for first offense: $1,000 for second offense, $2,000 for third offense, $3,000 and/or one year imprisonment for fourth offense or continued pattern of offenses.	No comparable provision until 1985 version providing for employer sanctions.
Provides for General Accounting Office and Equal Employment Opportunity Commission review of discrimination by employers under this section.	Creates task force with heads of Labor Department, Justice Department and EEOC to monitor implementation and investigate discrimination complaints. Civil Rights Commission also to monitor possible discrimination resulting from employer sanctions.	No comparable provision. (Roybal's position is that his bill will not create a climate for discrimination. Special provisions, therefore, are unnecessary.)

NUMERICAL LIMITATIONS

SIMPSON	MAZZOLI	ROYBAL
Worldwide immigration ceiling set at 425,000, not including asylees, refugees and legalized aliens, immediate relatives and special immigrants— numerically unrestricted currently—are deducted from the ceiling.	Retains worldwide ceiling of 270,000, which does not include refugees, asylees, immediate relatives of U.S. citizens and special immigrants.	Same as Mazzoli.
Revises per-county limit applicable to Mexico and Canada to allow 40,000 visas each, with the numbers unused by either available to the other.	Similar to Senate but does not permit visas unused by one country to be used by another.	Same as Simpson.
No comparable provision.	No comparable provision.	Eliminates English requirements for naturalization applicants over 50 years old.

No comparable provision.

No comparable provision.

Reduces to four years residency requirements for naturalization. Eliminates six-month residency requirement in a state.

LEGALIZATION

SIMPSON

Grants permanent resident status to aliens who have resided continuously in the United States since Jan. 1, 1977. Grants temporary resident status to aliens who have resided continuously in the U.S. since Jan. 1, 1980. These aliens may adjust to permanent status after three years. Establishes requirements of minimal knowledge of English and U.S. system of government.

Those granted temporary status will be ineligible for federal assistance programs such as Medicaid or food stamps (except Cuban or Haitian entrants). Those with permanent status will be ineligible for federal benefits for three years. State and local governments are authorized to make such aliens ineligible for their programs.

Defines "resided continuously" for the permanent status requirement. Says an alien must not have been out of the U.S. for any one period of time in excess of 30 days or for an aggregate period of more than 180 days. Specifies proof to show continuous residency. The applicants need documentation of U.S. employment together with independent corroboration, except where inapplicable.

No comparable provision.

MAZZOLI

Similar to Senate but provides for a one-tier legalizaton program with a cutoff date of Jan. 1, 1982 for adjustment to permanent resident status.

Similar to Senate restrictions, but period of ineligibility is five years and certain types of aid, such as assistance to the aged, blind or disabled and emergency assistance, are not denied.

Leaves definition of "continuous residency" and requirement of proof up to attorney general, who will consult with congressional judiciary committees and designated organizations.

No comparable provision.

ROYBAL

Grants permanent resident status to those residing in the United States since Jan. 1, 1982. No language or knowledge of government requirements.

Restricts eligibility for federal benefits for those who have not been in the United States for five years.

Similar to Mazzoli but permits affidavits to show continuous residency and directs that special circumstances be considered. Says that absences of 45 days or less annually do not break continuous residency. Also provides waiver of requirement for undue hardship of the alien, his spouse, parent or child.

Protects confidentiality of data provided in any application for legalization. Prohibits disclosure of data without consent of alien, except as needed to carry out the legalization process.

| No comparable provision. | Protects aliens apprehended before application period from deportation. | Provides for transitional legal status for applicants. In other words, protects aliens from deportation while waiting decisions on their applications. |

ADJUDICATION AND ASYLUM

SIMPSON	MAZZOLI	ROYBAL
Creates separate U.S. Immigration Board with Justice Department to hear appeals on decisions made by administrative law judges (immigration judges). Board members and ALJs will be appointed by the attorney general.	Similar to Senate but the board is made an independent agency. Members are appointed by president and confirmed by Senate. ALJs are appointed by board chairperson.	Similar to Mazzoli.
No comparable provision.	No comparable provision.	Sets out procedures and safeguards for proper exercise of INS authority to conduct detentions, arrests, searches and interrogations.
No comparable provision.	No comparable provision.	Requires speedy bail determinations, advisement of rights in a language the person apprehended can understand. Also calls for prompt administrative and judicial determination, after arrest, of the sufficiency of evidence to initiate deportation.

Bill of Rights for the Undocumented Worker*

April 30, 1980

*FROM THE 1ST INTERNATIONAL CONFERENCE FOR THE FULL RIGHTS OF UNDOCUMENTED WORKERS

Article I:
Every immigrant worker shall have the right to establish legal residency by demonstrating a status as wage earner and taxpayer.

Article II:
Every immigrant worker shall have all of the Constitutional Rights guaranteed all persons in the U.S. This right shall include but not be limited to: the right to due process, and the right to be free in their persons and possessions from unreasonable searches and seizures; and such rights shall not be violated by raids in factories, residential areas and in public places and shall be free from deportations and other unconstitutional practices.

Article III:
Every immigrant worker shall have the right to be reunited with his or her family in country where he or she is a wage earner.

Article IV:
Every immigrant shall have the right to legalize and adjust their status within the U.S. without having to return to their country of origin.

Article V:
Every immigrant worker shall fully enjoy all the rights guaranteed to citizen workers including socio-economic and labor rights.

Article VI:
Every immigrant worker, particularly seasonal workers, shall be provided adequate housing, health and safety provisions.

Article VII:
Every immigrant worker shall be guaranteed the same rights enjoyed by U.S. citizens especially the right

279

of access to free and adequate social and health services, child-care, and other similar social benefits.

Article VIII:
Every immigrant person shall have the right to quality public education in his or her native language, utilizing English as a second language and shall not be restricted from fully practicing the culture of his or her country of origin.

Article IX:
Every immigrant worker shall have the right to receive disability insurance (partial or permanent), workers compensation, retirement and death benefits. In the event of a death, the cost of transporting the deceased to his or her country of origin shall be borne by the employer, and any corresponding benefits shall be delivered to the family of the deceased without regard to their place of residency.

Article X:
Every immigrant worker shall have the right to organize and to collective bargaining, including the right to join existing unions or form new ones, for the defense of their labor rights and for the improvement of their wage and living and working conditions.

A) The right to collective bargaining shall include agricultural and public service workers in order to protect their right to organize.

Article XI:
Every immigrant worker shall have the right to utilize his native language in all legal proceedings (i.e., to acquire citizenship, in judicial proceedings, etc.) and in all private or public contract agreements.

Article XII:
Every immigrant worker shall have the right to exercise their right to vote in their native country's federal elections. This right should be facilitated through consulates and all other places (union halls, schools, etc.) designated by competent authorities.

Article XIII:
Every immigrant worker shall have the right to vote in local and state elections from the moment of legalizing their immigration status without having to become citizens. The right is based on their status as taxpayers, workers and residents.

Por los Derechos Plenos de los Trabajadores Indocumentados (Conferencia Internacional)

30 de Abril de 1980

CARTA DE DERECHOS PARA LOS TRABAJADORES MIGRATORIOS

Artículo Primero:
Los trabajadores migratorios tendrán derecho a la residencia legal, demonstrando simplemente su calidad de trabajador y contribuyente, para lo que se les otorgará su visa de residentes permanentes.

Artículo Segundo:
Derecho a un procedimiento justo y legal que garantice la inviolabilidad de su domicilio y la privacidad de su persona y otros derechos civiles para el trabajador y su familia, suspendiéndose totalmente las redadas fabriles, domiciliarias y en lugares públicos, así como todo tipo de deportaciones y prácticas anticonstitucionales.

Artículo Tercero:
Derecho a la reunificación de las familias para todo trabajador con o sin documentos que así lo desee. Se podrá trasladar al cónyuge, hijos y padres sin más trámites que demostrar su calidad de trabajador y contribuyente en la sociedad norteamericana.

Artículo Cuarto:
Derecho automático a legalizar su residencia sin tener que regresar a su lugar de origen, como lo exige actualmente la Ley de Inmigración de los Estados Unidos.

Artículo Quinto:
Gozarán plenamente de los derechos sindicales, sociales y económicos que disfrutan el resto de los trabajadores ciudadanos.

Artículo Sexto:
Derecho a la vivienda en condiciones de higiene y seguridad adecuadas para todo trabajador cíclico o por obra determinada.

Artículo Séptimo:
Derecho a los servicios de salud y

atención médica gratuita y adecuada; guarderías y demás beneficios en las mismas condiciones que los recibe cualquier ciudadano norteamericano.

Artículo Octavo:
Derecho a recibir educación pública adecuada en el idioma materno, utilizando el inglés como segunda lengua y acceso sin restricciones a la cultura de su país de origen.

Artículo Noveno:
Derecho a disfrutar de los seguros de incapacidad (parcial o permanente), por accidente de trabajo, enfermedad profesional, vejez o muerte. En caso de fallecimiento, los gastos correrán a cargo del Patrón, y los beneficios de los seguros correspondientes serán entregados a los familiares, no importando su lugar de residencia.

Artículo Décimo:
Derecho a la organización sindical, ya sea ingresando a sindicatos ya existentes o formando nuevos, para la defensa de sus derechos laborales y el mejoramiento de sus salarios y condiciones de vida y de trabajo.

(A) Derecho a las Negociaciones Colectivas para los trabajadores agrícolas y trabajadores públicos que garanticen su derecho a la organización sindical.

Artículo Onceavo:
Derecho al uso de la lengua materna en los tribunales cualquiera que sea el carácter de estos, para adquirir la ciudadanía, en procesos judiciales y en todo arreglo contractual público o privado.

Artículo Doceavo:
Derecho a que se le otorguen plenas facilidades para el ejercicio del voto en elecciones federales de su país de origen. Este derecho se ejercerá a través de consulados y todo lugar (sindicatos, escuelas, demás) designados por autoridades competentes.

Artículo Treceavo:
Derecho desde el momento de legalizar su residencia y sin necesidad de adquirir la ciudadanía norteamericana de ejercer el voto en las elecciones locales y estatales en Estados Unidos. Este Derecho nace de su condición de contribuyente, de trabajador y de residente.

Esta CARTA DE DERECHOS PARA LOS TRABAJADORES MIGRATORIOS fue aprobada por unanimidad en la PRIMERA CONFERENCIA INTERNACIONAL POR LOS DERECHOS PLENOS DE LOS TRABAJADORES MIGRATORIOS, CELEBRADA EN LA CIUDAD DE MEXICO, el pasado 28, 29 y 30 de Abril de 1980.

COMISION INTERNACIONAL COORDINADORA

"Guest-worker" provision of the Immigration Reform and Control Act of 1982 (Simpson-Mazzoli bill)

Section II-B. Nonimmigrants. Special procedure established for H-2 seasonal workers in agriculture. The employer need not apply more than 80 days in advance of need. The Secretary of Labor must provide a decision on the certification no later than 20 days in advance of need (otherwise the application for certification is deemed approved). If the Secretary of Labor determines that a certain number of qualified U.S. workers will be available at the time needed, but at the determined time those workers are not qualified and available, an expedited 7-day procedure to determine continued need would be available. After the INS has implemented an automatic data processing system to properly track the entry and exit of nonimmigrants, the State Department may establish a pilot visa waiver program for 5 countries which provide a similar benefit to the U.S. if the visa refusal and visa abuse rates for the nationals of such countries are minimal, and if the visitor has a nonrefundable roundtrip ticket.

IMMIGRATION
CHRONOLOGY

1798 Alien and Sedition Acts, making possible the expulsion of "aliens" who represent "a danger to the peace and security" of the nation.

1830s–40s Attacks against Catholic, German, and Irish immigrants; formation by mid-century of the nativist Know-Nothing movement.

1846 US invasion of Mexico.

1848 Treaty of Guadalupe Hidalgo, ending the Mexico War and protecting cultural and property rights of Mexicans choosing to become US citizens and to remain within the expanded borders of United States (treaty basis for bilingual education and ballots).

1860s–70s Attacks against newly arriving immigrants, especially Chinese and Irish; most US-citizen Mexicans stripped of their lands and rights, some lynched.

1875 Barring of entry of convicts and prostitutes.

1882 Chinese Exclusion Act, barring entry of Chinese laborers; increase in flow of Mexican immigrant workers; Immigration Act, removing states' power to regulate immigration.

Mid-1880s Contract labor laws prohibiting importation of foreign labor under contract.

1891 Legislation prohibiting entry of the mentally retarded, polygamists, the ill, and others.

1900–33 As demand for Mexican labor continues to grow, an estimated one-eighth of Mexico's population moves to US.

1903 Legislation excluding people professing anarchist ideas or the violent overthrow of the government.

1907 Economic depression; President Teddy Roosevelt's "Gentleman's Agreement" barring entry of Japanese laborers; legislation authorizing deportation of "aliens" who have become prostitutes or "public charges" (paupers).

1909 US-Mexico treaty for importation of Mexican laborers to harvest sugarbeet fields of California.

1917 Importation of Mexican workers again legalized in face of labor shortages caused by US entry into World War I; Immigration Act establishing Asiatic Barred Zone, further restricting entry of Asians and introducing literacy requirements and $8 head tax for entry; foreigners sentenced to jail for acts of "moral dishonesty" subjected to exclusion or deportation.

1918 Legislation adding to list of "undesirable aliens" subject to deportation "aliens" joining anarchist organizations or any organization seeking the violent overthrow of the government.

1919 "Palmer Raids," rounding up and deporting, without due process, "aliens," "anarchists," and "communists," especially those from southern Europe and Latin America influential in organizing America's labor unions.

1920 List of "undesirable aliens" expanded to include "aliens" committing acts of espionage or sabotage or dealing with "enemy" powers.

1920s "Box laws" proposed in Congress to place a ceiling on number of Mexican immigrants.

1921 Temporary Quota Act, adding quantitative regulations to immigration law—the first step toward quotas.

1924 Immigration Act, making official the quota system that lasts until 1952, establishing the country's only national police force, the US Border Patrol, and providing for deportation of those who become public charges, violate US law, or engage in alleged anarchist or seditionist acts.

1929 Legislation fixing the quota system according to a complex formula guaranteeing the numerical predominance of white people in the population and making it a crime for a previously deported "alien" to try to enter the country again.

1930s Hundreds of thousands of Mexicans rounded up and deported during "Mexican scare" in early years of Great Depression.

1940s Tens of thousands of US-citizen Japanese stripped of properties and thrown into concentration camps; tens of thousands of Jewish refugees refused permission to enter US.

1942 Bilateral bracero program introduced, providing 5 million Mexican laborers for US employers during next two decades.

1943 Repeal of Chinese Exclusion Act; "Zoot-Suit Riots" in California sparked by racist attacks on Mexicans.

1947 Taft-Hartley Act, limiting labor's rights.

1948 Displaced Persons Act, first US refugee legislation.

1950 McCarran Internal Security Act, excluding communists and authorizing construction of "emergency" concentration camps (6 built by 1952).

1951 Public Law 78 (PL78), extending bracero program and granting secretary of labor power to set wages for Mexican workers.

1952 Immigration and Nationality Act (McCarran-Walter Act), excluding communists and allowing "denaturalizing" of naturalized citizens on political grounds, providing for family reunification, eliminating race as a bar to citizenship, prohibiting citizens' arrests of "wetbacks," and allowing employment of "aliens" (Texas Proviso).

1953 End of Korean War, onset of recession.

1954 "Operation Wetback," deporting 1.1 million or more Mexicans.

1956 Use of Public Law 414 to import Japanese and Filipino farmworkers.

1960s Independent unionizing drive undertaken by Cesar Chavez's United Farm Workers (UFW); lettuce, melon, and grape boycotts.

1963–64 Legislation providing for termination of bracero program.

1965 Civil rights legislation amending 1952 McCarran-Walter Act to repeal national origins quota system and replace it with one based on family reunification, needed skills, and political refuge.

1966 Incorporation of Chavez's UFW into AFL-CIO.

1969 First of recessions of prolonged economic crisis (next ones in 1973–75 and 1979–83).

1970s Rising tide of independent union organizing among "illegals," especially Mexicans; AFL-CIO also begins to organize among migrant workforce.

1976 Legislation placing 20,000 annual ceiling on each Western Hemisphere country, *including Mexico* (first numerical restriction on legal Mexican immigration).

1977 President Carter proposes amnesty for those in the country since 1970, prohibition of hiring of "illegals," and construction of fence ("tortilla curtain") along US-Mexico border.

1978 Congress establishes Select Commission on Immigration and Refugee Policy (Hesburgh commission), in effect defining issue as a national security one rather than an economic one of labor recruitment.

1980s Nativist attacks reminiscent of 19th century, focusing on Mexicans as well as other Latinos, Asians, and Middle Eastern peoples; admission of 125,000 Cuban "boat people"; US Coast Guard "interdictions" of Haitians on international waters; "concentration camps" holding Haitians exposed. Border Patrol detentions surpass a million per year, many of them repeat entries from Mexico. Some 50,000 activists participate in religious-oriented "sanctuary movement" for political refugees from Central America.

1980 Refugee Act, redefining "refugee" to conform with United Nations criteria; Bill of Rights for the Undocumented Worker (see Appendix III).

1981 Hesburgh commission report recommending a modified amnesty and increased legal immigration, with a possible guest worker program; President Reagan's proposal for a guest worker program and order to stop paroling of "aliens" whose hearings are still pending; Reagan's Task Force on Immigration and Refugee Policy recommends legislation "to establish an emergency mass migration fund for domestic crises" and development of permanent "detention centers."

1982 "Silva letter" holders (100,000 Mexicans holding temporary visas) threatened with immediate deportation; Supreme Court ruling that "aliens" are " 'persons' guaranteed due process of law"; various federal court rulings against INS factory raids, which increase as cases are appealed. Simpson-Mazzoli bill (see Appendix IV) introduced as Immigration Reform and Control Act of 1982. Passed by Senate, the bill dies in House.

1983 Simpson-Mazzoli bill passed by Senate.

1984 New grape and lettuce boycotts launched by Chavez's UFW. Roybal bill (see Appendix) introduced; Simpson-Mazzoli bill passed by House and sent to joint Senate-House committee; Hispanic delegates to Democratic Party national convention threaten to boycott first presidential nomination ballot in protest of Simpson-Mazzoli bill, which barely fails to pass Congress that fall. Supreme Court rulings that INS may conduct unannounced raids on factories and that "illegal aliens" are entitled to protections of federal labor law; National Security Decision Directive 138 allowing US military forces and intelligence agents to use force against persons or groups thought to be planning operations against US targets at home or abroad.

1985 INS implementation of "Operation Co-operation," continuing traditional cooperation with employers; Border Patrol activation of elite "SWAT team" known as Border Patrol Tactical Team (BORTAC). Revised Roybal bill introduced; Simpson-Mazzoli bill, more conservative than earlier versions, introduced with backing of influential liberal congressman Rodino; DeConcini-Moakley bill introduced to delay deportation hearings against Salvadoran "illegals"; Simpson-Mazzoli bill passed by Senate. First national day of protest on behalf of the "undocumented," October 12.

SELECTED BIBLIOGRAPHY

I. BOOKS, ARTICLES, AND DISSERTATIONS

Acuña, Rodolfo. *Occupied America: A History of Chicanos*. New York: Harper & Row, 1981.

Alperovitz, Gar, and Jeff Faux. *Rebuilding America*. New York: Pantheon Books, 1984.

American Enterprise Institute for Public Policy Research. *The Gateway: US Immigration Issues and Policies*. Washington, D.C.: AEI, 1982.

Aronowitz, Stanley. *Working Class Hero: A New Strategy for Labor*. New York: Pilgrim Press, 1983.

Bach, Robert L., Jorge A. Bustamante, et al. "Politics of Labor Migration." *Journal of International Affairs* 33, no. 2 (Fall–Winter 1979).

Bach, Robert, and Alejandro Portes. *Latin Journey*. Berkeley: University of California Press, 1984.

Baerresen, Donald W. *The Border Industrialization Program of Mexico*. Lexington, Mass.: D. C. Heath & Co., 1971.

Baird, Peter, and Ed McCaughan, eds. *Beyond the Border: Mexico and the United States Today*. New York: North American Congress on Latin America, 1979.

Balan, Jorge, and H. Browning. *Migration of Males to Monterrey*. Austin: University of Texas Press, 1974.

Barrera, Mario. *Race and Class in the Southwest: A Theory of Racial Inequality*. Notre Dame, Ind.: University of Notre Dame Press, 1979.

Barrera Bassols, Delia. "Condiciones de vida de la población trabajadora en la franja fronteriza norte." Mexico: UNAM Economics Thesis, 1980.

Barrio, Raymond. *The Plum Pickers*. Binghamton, N.Y.: Bilingual Review/Press, 1969.

Bennett, Marion T. *American Immigration Policies: A History*. Washington, D.C.: Public Affairs Press, 1963.

Bluestone, Barry, and Bennett Harrison. *The Deindustrialization of America*. New York: Basic Books, 1982.

Bortz, Jeffrey. "Industrial Wages in Mexico City, 1939–1975." Ph.D. diss., UCLA, 1982.

Bowles, Samuel; David M. Gordon; and Thomas E. Weisskopf. *Beyond the Wasteland*. New York: Anchor Books, 1984.

Braverman, Harry. *Labor and Monopoly Capital*. New York: Monthly Review Press, 1974.

Briggs, Vernon M. Jr. *Immigration Policy and the American Labor Force*. Baltimore: Johns Hopkins University Press, 1984.

Briggs, Vernon M., Jr.; Walter Fogel; and William H. Schmidt. *The Chicano Worker*. Austin: University of Texas Press, 1977.

Bryce-Laporte, R., ed. *Sourcebook on the New Immigration*. New Brunswick, N.J.: Transaction Books, 1980.

Buelna (Universidad Autónoma de Sinaloa). "Problemas fronterizos y migración," II:7 (October 1980).

Bustamante, Jorge A. Various articles in the Mexico City daily *Uno Màs Uno*, 1970s, 1980s.

Bustamante, Jorge A., and James D. Cockcroft. "One More Time: The 'Undocumented.' " *Radical America* 15, no. 6 (November–December 1981).

Bustamante, Jorge A., et al. *Estudios Fronterizos México–Estados Unidos: Directorio General de Investigadores, 1984*. Tijuana: Centro de Estudios Fronterizos del Norte de México, 1984.

Calavita, Kitty. *U.S. Immigration Law and the Control of Labor: 1820–1924*. Orlando: Academic Press, 1984.

California State Senate Hearings (SB 1494). *Plant Closures: Runaway Plants— Mexico*. Vols. 1 and 2. 1980.

Camara, F., and R. Van Kemper, eds. *Migration Across Frontiers: Mexico and the United States*. Albany: Institute for Mesoamerican Studies, State University of New York, 1979.

Camarillo, Albert. *Chicanos in a Changing Society*. Cambridge, Mass.: Harvard University Press, 1979.

Cardenas, Gilbert, and Charles Ellard. *The Economics of the US-Mexico Border: Growth, Problems and Prospects*. Edinburg, Texas: Pan American University, 1982.

Cárdenas, Gilberto; Rodolfo O. de la Garza; and Niles Hansen. *Economic Impact of Mexican Immigration on Mexican Americans*. Austin: University of Texas, Mexican American Studies Center, 1984.

Cardoso, Lawrence A. *Mexican Emigration to the United States, 1897–1931: Socio-Economic Patterns*. Tucson: University of Arizona Press, 1980.

Carliner, David. *The Rights of Aliens: The Basic ACLU Guide to an Alien's Rights*. New York: Avon Books, 1977.

Castellanos Guerrero, Alicia. *Ciudad Juárez: La vida fronteriza*. Mexico: Ediciones Nuestro Tiempo, 1981.

Castells, Manuel. *The Economic Crisis and American Society*. Princeton: Princeton University Press, 1980.

———. "Trabajadores inmigrantes y lucha de clases." *Cuadernos Políticos* 18 (October–December 1978).

Castles, Stephen, and Godula Kosack. *Immigrant Workers and Class Structure in Western Europe*. London: Oxford University Press, 1973.

CENIET. *Trabajadores Mexicanos en Estados Unidos: Encuesta Nacional de Emigración*. Mexico: CENIET, 1979–80.

Centro de Estudios Internacionales. *Los indocumentados: Mitos y realidades*. Mexico: El Colegio de México, 1979.

Chicano Communications Center. *450 Años del Pueblo Chicano: 450 Years of Chicano History in Pictures*. Albuquerque: Chicano Communications Center, 1976.

Chiswick, Barry R. (ed.). *The Gateway: U.S. Immigration Issues and Policies*. Washington: American Enterprise Institute, 1982.

Citizens Labor Committee on Plant Closures (CLCPC). *Stop Runaway Shops*. Los Angeles: CLCPC, 1980.

Coalson, George O. *The Development of the Migratory Farm Labor System in Texas: 1900–1954*. San Francisco: R & E Research Assoc., 1977.

Cockcroft, James D. "Immiseration, Not Marginalization." *Latin American Perspectives* 10, nos. 2 and 3 (Spring and Summer 1983).

———. "Mexican Migration, Crisis and the Internationalization of Labor Struggle." *Contemporary Marxism* 5 (July 1982).

———. *Mexico*. New York: Monthly Review Press, 1983.

———. "Über alles in der Welt: Das amerikanische Sendungsbewuβtsein." In *Amerika—der riskante Partner*, edited by Anton-Andreas Guha and Sven Papcke. Berlin: Athenaum, 1984.

Cockcroft, James D., and Ross Gandy. "The Mexican Volcano." *Monthly Review* 33 (May 1981).

Cockcroft, James D., and UAM-Azcapotzalco Migration Research Team. *Trabajadores de Michoacán: Historia de un pueblo migrante*. Mexico: imisac, Ediciones Contraste, 1982.

———, eds. "Migración, problemas fronterizos y crisis." *Revista 'A'* 4, no. 8 (January–April 1983).

Coles, Robert. *Uprooted Children*. New York: Harper & Row, 1970.

Community Services Administration. *The Problem of the Undocumented Worker*. Washington, D.C.: Community Services Administration, 1980.

Congressional Research Service, Library of Congress. *Impact of Illegal Immigration and Background on Legalization*. Washington: GPO, November, 1985.

Cornelius, Wayne A. *Mexican and Caribbean Migration to the United States: A Report to the Ford Foundation*. San Diego: University of California, 1979.

Cortes, Carlos E. *Mexican Labor in the US*. New York: Arno Press, 1974.

Corwin, Arthur, ed. *Immigrants—and Immigrants: Perspectives on Mexican Labor Migrations to the US*. Westport, Ct.: Greenwood Press, 1978.

Craig, Richard B. *The Bracero Program*. Austin: University of Texas Press, 1971.

Crewdson, John. *The New Immigrants and the Transformation of America*. New York: New York Times Books, 1981.

Cross, Harry E., and James A. Sandos. *Rural Development in Mexico and Recent Migration to the United States*. Berkeley: Institute of Government Studies, University of California, 1982.

Daniel, Cletus E. *Bitter Harvest: A History of California Farmworkers, 1870–1941*. Ithaca, N.Y.: Cornell University Press, 1981.

Data Center. *Plant Shutdowns: Good Business, Bad News*. Oakland, Calif.: Data Center, 1982.

De Leon, Arnoldo. *They Called Them Greasers: Anglo Attitudes Towards Mexicans in Texas, 1821–1900*. Austin: University of Texas Press, 1983.

Dunbar Ortiz, Roxanne. *Roots of Resistance: Land Tenure in New Mexico, 1680–1980*. Los Angeles: UCLA Chicano Studies Research Center, 1980.

Edwards, Richard E. *Contested Terrain: The Transformation of the Workplace in the Twentieth Century*. New York: Basic Books, 1979.

Edwards, Richard E., et al., eds. *Labor Market Segmentation*. Lexington, Mass.: D. C. Heath & Co., 1975.

Ehrlich, Paul R. *The Golden Door: International Migration, Mexico and the United States*. New York: Ballantine Books, 1979.

Fallows, James. "Immigration: How It's Affecting Us." *Atlantic Monthly* 45 (1983).

Fernandez, Celestino. "The Border Patrol and News Media Coverage of Undocumented Mexican Immigration During the 1970s: A Quantitative Content Analysis in the Sociology of Knowledge." *California Sociologist* 5 (1982).

———. "The Mexican Immigration Experience and the Corrido Mexicano." *Studies in Latin American Popular Culture* 2 (1983).

Fernández, María Patricia. *For We Are Sold, I and My People: Women and Industry in Mexico's Frontier*. Albany: State University of New York Press, 1983.

Fernández, Raúl A. *La frontera México–Estados Unidos*. Mexico: Ediciones Terra Nova, 1980.

Flores, Ésteban T. "La circulación internacional del trabajo y la lucha de clases." *Historia y Sociedad* 20 (1978).

Ford Foundation. *Hispanics: Challenges and Opportunities*. New York: Ford Foundation, 1984.

Fox, Geoffrey. "Organizing the New Immigrants: The Hispanic Trade Unionists' Perspectives." New York University Center for Latin American and Caribbean Studies, Occasional Papers, no. 40, 1984.

Frisch, M. H., and D. J. Walkowitz, eds. *Working-Class America: Essays on Labor, Community, and American Society*. Urbana: University of Illinois Press, 1983.

Galarza, Ernesto. *Farm Workers and Agribusiness in California, 1947–1960*. Notre Dame: University of Notre Dame Press, 1977.

———. *Merchants of Labor: The Mexican Bracero Story*. Santa Barbara: McNally & Loftin, 1964.

————. Spiders in the House and Workers in the Field. Notre Dame, Ind.: University of Notre Dame Press, 1970.

Gambrill, Mónica-Claire. La fuerza de trabajo en las maquiladoras: resultados de una encuesta y algunas hipótesis interpretativas. Mexico: CEESTEM, 1980.

Gamio, Manuel. Mexican Immigration to the United States. New York: Dover Publications, 1971.

García, Juan Ramón. Operation Wetback: The Mass Deportation of Mexican Undocumented Workers in 1954. Westport, Ct.: Greenwood Press, 1980.

Garcia, Mario T. Desert Immigrants: The Mexicans of El Paso, 1880-1920. New Haven: Yale University Press, 1981.

García y Griego, Manuel. El volumen de la Migración de Mexicanos no Documentados a los Estados Unidos: Nuevas Hipótesis. Mexico: CENIET, 1980.

Georgakas, Dan. Solidarity Forever: The IWW Reconsidered. Chicago: Lakeview Press, 1985.

Geschwender, J. Class, Race and Worker Insurgency. New York: Cambridge University Press, 1977.

Gómez-Quiñones, Juan. Development of the Mexican Working Class North of the Río Bravo. Los Angeles: UCLA Chicano Studies Research Center, 1982.

————. "La política de exportación de capital e importación de mano de obra." Historia y Sociedad 20 (1978).

Gonzalez, Juan L., Jr. The Tertiary Labor Force and the Role of Undocumented Mexican Laborers in the American Economy. El Paso: Center for Inter-American and Border Studies, University of Texas, 1985.

González Salazar, Roque. La frontera del norte. Mexico: El Colegio de México, 1982.

Gordon, David M. The Working Poor: Towards a State Agenda. Washington, D.C.: Council of State Planning Agencies, 1979.

Halsell, Grace. The Illegals. New York: Stein & Day, 1978.

Hancock, Richard H. The Role of the Bracero in the Economic and Cultural Dynamics of Mexico. Stanford: Institute of Hispanic American and Luso-Brazilian Studies, Stanford University, 1959.

Handlin, Oscar. The Uprooted. Boston: Little, Brown & Co., 1951.

————, ed. Immigration as a Factor in American History. Englewood Cliffs, N.J.: Prentice-Hall, 1959.

Harrison, Bennett, and Barry Bluestone. Capital and Communities: The Causes and Consequences of Private Disinvestment. Washington, D.C.: Progressive Alliance, 1980.

Higham, John. Strangers in the Land: Patterns of American Nativism, 1860-1925. New Brunswick, N.J.: Rutgers University Press, 1965.

Hinds, Lennox S. Illusions of Justice: Human Rights Violations in the United States. Iowa City: University of Iowa School of Social Work, 1979.

Hintz, Joy. Poverty, Prejudice, Power, Politics: Migrants Speak About Their Lives. Columbus: Avonelle Associates Publishers, 1981.

History Task Force of the Center for Puerto Rican Studies. Labor Migration Under Capitalism: The Puerto Rican Experience. New York: Monthly Review Press, 1979.

Hoffman, Abraham. *Unwanted Mexican Americans in the Great Depression*. Tucson: University of Arizona Press, 1974.

House, John W. *Frontier on the Río Grande: A Political Geography of Development and Social Deprivation*. New York: Oxford University Press, 1984.

Jaffe, A. J.; Cullen, R. M.; and Boswell, T. D. *The Changing Demography of Spanish Americans*. New York: Academic Press, 1980.

Jamail, Milton H. *United States–Mexico Border: A Guide to Institutions, Organizations, and Scholars*. Tucson: University of Arizona Latin American Area Center, 1980.

Jones, Maldwyn. *American Immigration*. Chicago: University of Chicago Press, 1960.

Justice Ministries. *Immigration, the Church's Response*. Chicago: ICUIS, 1981.

Keely, Charles B. *US Immigration: A Policy Analysis*. New York: Population Council, 1979.

King, Allan C. "El efecto de los inmigrantes ilegales sobre el desempleo en Estados Unidos." *Revista Mexicana de Sociología* 41, no. 4 (October–December 1979).

Kiser, George C., and Martha Woody Kiser. *Mexican Workers in the United States: Historical and Political Perspectives*. Albuquerque: University of New Mexico Press, 1979.

Kritz, Mary M. (ed.). *US Immigration and Refugee Policy: Global and Domestic Issues*. Lexington: D.C. Heath and Co., 1983.

Landmann, Robert S., ed. *The Problem of the Undocumented Worker*. Santa Fe: University of New Mexico Latin American Institute, 1979.

Lewis, Sasha G. *Slave Trade Today: American Exploitation of Illegal Aliens*. Boston: Beacon Press, 1979.

London, Joan, and Henry Anderson, *So Shall Ye Reap*. New York: Harper & Row, 1972.

Loyo Camacho, Marta, and Javier Rodríguez Piña. *Historia de la migración mexicana a los Estados Unidos*. UAM–Azcapotzalco Reporte de Investigación, no. 82, 1982.

McWilliams, Carey. *Factories in the Field: The Story of Migratory Farm Labor in California*. Boston: Little, Brown & Co., 1939.

———. *Ill Fares the Land: Migrants and Migratory Labor in the United States*. New York: Ayer Co., 1942.

———. *North from Mexico*. New York: Greenwood Press, 1968.

Madrigal, Sergio. "Racial/Ethnic/Gender Wage Differentials in the Early Labor Career: The Case of Hispanic, Black, and White Youth." Ph.D. diss., University of Notre Dame, 1983.

Maram, Sheldon L. *Hispanic Workers in the Garment and Restaurant Industries in Los Angeles County: A Social and Economic Profile*. Fullerton: California State University, 1980.

Martinez, Oscar J. *Border Boom Town: Ciudad Juárez Since 1848*. Austin: University of Texas Press, 1978.

Melville, Margarita B., ed. *Twice a Minority: Mexican American Women*. St. Louis: C. V. Mosby Co., 1980.

Méndez González, Rosalinda. "Capital Accumulation and Mexican Immigration to the United States." Ph.D. diss., University of California–Irvine, 1981.

Méndez González, Rosalinda, and Raúl A. Fernández. "US Imperialism and Migration: The Effects on Mexican Women and Families." *Review of Radical Political Economics* (Winter 1980).

Moore, Joan, and Harry Pachon. *Hispanics in the United States.* Englewood Cliffs, N.J.: Prentice-Hall, 1985.

Mora, Magdalena, and Adelaida R. del Castillo, eds. *Mexican Women in the United States: Struggles Past and Present.* Los Angeles: UCLA Chicano Studies Research Center, 1980.

Morales, Patricia. *Indocumentados mexicanos.* Mexico: Editorial Grijalbo, 1982.

Murray, Robert K. *Red Scare: A Study in National Hysteria, 1919–1920.* Minneapolis: University of Minnesota Press, 1955.

Nafzieger, James A. R. "A Policy Framework for Regulating the Flow of Undocumented Mexican Aliens into the United States." *Oregon Law Review* 56, no. 1 (1977).

Nalven, Joseph, and Craig Frederickson. *The Employer's View: Is There a Need for a Guest-Worker Program?* San Diego-Community Research Associates, 1982.

National Association for Chicano Studies. *The Chicano Struggle: Analyses of Past and Present Efforts.* Binghamton: Bilingual Review/Press, 1985.

———. *History, Culture and Society: Chicano Studies in the 1980s.* Ypsilanti, Mich.: Bilingual Press, 1983.

National Center for Immigrants' Rights (NCIR). *Immigration-Deportation Skills Manual.* Los Angeles, NCIR, 1982.

———. *Paralegal Immigration Defense Manual.* Los Angeles: NCIR, 1982.

National Commission on Working Women (NCWW). *Survey.* Washington, D.C.: NCWW, 1978.

National Council on Employment Policy. *Illegal Aliens: An Assessment of Issues.* Washington, D.C., 1976.

National Council of La Raza. *Parent Power in the Migrant Education Program.* New York, 1980.

National Education Association. *Neglect in the Education of Migrant Children.* Philadelphia, 1969.

National Hispanic Center for Advanced Studies and Policy Analysis, and National Hispanic University. *The State of Hispanic America.* 5 vols. Oakland: National Hispanic Center/BABEL, 1981–85.

National Lawyers Guild. *Immigration Law and Defense.* New York: Clark Boardman Co., 1982.

Nelson, Eugene. *Pablo Cruz and the American Dream: The Experience of an Undocumented Immigrant from Mexico.* Salt Lake City: Peregrine Smith, 1975.

New Scholar. Special issue on US-Mexico border (Fall 1981).

North, David S. *The Border Crossers.* Washington, D.C.: TransCentury, 1970.

North, David S., and Marion F. Houston. *The Characteristics and Role of Illegal Aliens in the US Labor Market: An Exploratory Study.* Washington, D.C.: Linton & Co., 1976.

North American Congress on Latin America (NACLA). "Hit and Run: US Runaway Shops on the Mexican Border." *NACLA Latin America and Empire Report* 9, no. 5 (1975).
————. *Immigration, Facts and Fallacies.* 1977.
Novotny, Ann. *Strangers at the Door.* New York: Bantam Books, 1971.

O'Connor, James. *Accumulation Crisis.* New York: Basil Blackwell, 1984.
Oppenheimer, Martin. *White Collar Politics.* New York: Monthly Review Press, 1985.

Panunzio, Constantine M. *The Deportation Cases of 1919–1920.* New York: Da Capo, 1970.
Piore, Michael J. *Birds of Passage: Migrant Labor and Industrial Societies.* New York: Cambridge University Press, 1979.
Portes, Alejandro. "La inmigración y el sistema internacional: Algunas características de los mexicanos recientemente emigrados a los Estados Unidos." *Revista Mexicana de Sociología* 41, no. 4 (October–December 1978).
————. "Migration and Underdevelopment." *Politics and Society* 8, no. 1 (1978).
Portes, Alejandro, and John Walton. *Labor, Class and the International System.* New York: Academic Press, 1981.
Power, Jonathan. *Migrant Workers in Western Europe and the United States.* London: Pergamon Press, 1979.
Preston, Julia; Americo Badillo-Veiga; and Josh DeWind. "Undocumented Immigrant Workers in New York City." *NACLA* 12, no. 6 (1979).
Preston, William, Jr. *Aliens and Dissenters: Federal Suppression of Radicals, 1903–1933.* Cambridge: Harvard University Press, 1963.
Program in United States–Mexican Studies, University of California, San Diego. Monograph, Research Report, and Working Papers Series (various through 1985).

Rand Corporation. *Mexican Immigration into California: Current and Future Effects.* Santa Monica: 1985.
Reavis, Dick. *Without Documents.* Austin: Condor Publishing Co., 1978.
Reimers, David. *Still the Golden Door: The Third World Comes to America.* New York: Columbia University Press, 1985.
Reisler, Mark. *By the Sweat of Their Brow: Mexican Immigrant Labor in the United States, 1900–1940.* Westport, Ct.: Greenwood Press, 1976.
Ríos-Bustamante, Antonio, ed. *Immigration and Public Policy: Human Rights for Undocumented Workers and Their Families.* Los Angeles: UCLA Chicano Studies Research Center, 1977.
————. *Mexican Immigrant Workers in the US.* Los Angeles: UCLA Chicano Studies Research Center, 1981.
Rist, Ray. *Guestworkers in Germany: The Prospects for Pluralism.* New York: Praeger, 1977.
Roberts, Kenneth D. *Agrarian Structure and Labor Migration in Rural Mexico: The Case of Circular Migration of Undocumented Workers to the US.* Austin: University of Texas Institute of Latin American Studies, 1980.
Rogers, Everett M., and Judith K. Larsen. *Silicon Valley: Fever Growth of High-Technology Culture.* New York: Basic Books, 1984.

Romero, Fred E. *Chicano Workers: Their Utilization and Development.* Los Angeles: UCLA Chicano Studies Research Center, 1979.

Rosenbaum, Robert J. *Mexicano Resistance in the Southwest.* Austin: University of Texas Press, 1981.

Rosenblum, Gerald. *Immigrant Workers.* New York: Basic Books, 1973.

Ross, Stanley R., ed. *Views Across the Border: The US and Mexico.* Albuquerque: University of New Mexico Press, 1978.

Samora, Julian. *Los Mojados: The Wetback Story.* Notre Dame, Ind.: University of Notre Dame Press, 1971.

Samora, Julian; Joe J. Bernal; and Albert Peña. *Gunpowder Justice: A Reassessment of the Texas Rangers.* Notre Dame, Ind.: University of Notre Dame Press, 1979.

Schey, Peter A. "Supply-Side Immigration Theory: Analysis of the Simpson-Mazzoli Legislation." Los Angeles: National Center for Immigrants' Rights, 1983.

Secretaría de Trabajo, Mexico. Various publications.

Selby, Henry A., and Arthur D. Murphy. "The Role of the Mexican Urban Household in Decisions About Migration to the United States." Austin: University of Texas Department of Anthropology, 1980.

Shelp, Ronald K. *Beyond Industrialization.* New York: Praeger, 1981.

Sheppard, C. Stewart, and Donald C. Carroll, eds. *Working in the 21st Century.* New York: John Wiley & Sons, 1980.

Slaughter, Jane. *Concessions and How to Beat Them.* Detroit: Labor Education and Research Project, 1982.

Sosnick, Stephen H. *Hired Hands: Seasonal Farm Workers in the United States.* Santa Barbara: McNally & Loftin, 1978.

Special Study Group on Illegal Immigrants from Mexico. *A Program for Effective and Humane Action on Illegal Mexican Immigrants: Final Report to the President.* Mimeo. Washington, D.C., January 15, 1973.

Stallard, Karin; Barbara Ehrenreich; and Holly Sklar. *Poverty in the American Dream.* Boston: South End Press, 1983.

Stanford Center for Chicano Research. *Chicano Urban Studies Research Bibliography.* Stanford, 1984.

Stoddard, Ellwyn. "A Conceptual Analysis of the 'Alien Invasion'—Mexico." *International Migration Review* 1, no. 2 (1976).

Strickland, Barbara. *Análisis de la ley y los procedimientos de inmigración en los Estados Unidos.* Mexico: CENIET, 1978.

Swanson, Jon. "The Consequences of Immigration for Economic Development: A Review of the Literature." *Papers in Anthropology* 20 (1979).

Task Force on Immigration and Refugee Policy. *Report to the President.* Washington, D.C.: Government Printing Office, July 1981.

Teitelbaum, Michael. *Latin Migration North.* New York: Council on Foreign Relations, 1985.

Tienda, Marta, and George Borjas, eds. *Hispanics in the US Economy.* New York: Academic Press, 1983.

Union for Radical Political Economics (URPE). *US Capitalism in Crisis.* New York: URPE, 1978.

United Nations. *Trends and Characteristics of International Migration Since 1950.* New York, 1979.

US Bureau of Labor Statistics. *Immigrant Workers in the United States.* Washington, D.C., 1982.

———. *Labor Force and Employment in the States by Race, 1980 Annual Average.* Washington, D.C., March 1981.

———. "Workers of Spanish Origin: A Chartbook." 1979.

US Department of Health, Education, and Welfare. *To Improve the Living Conditions of Migrant and Other Seasonal Farmworkers.* Washington, D.C.: US Comptroller General, 1973.

———. *Work in America.* Cambridge, Mass.: MIT Press, 1973.

US Departments of Agriculture and Labor. Various publications.

US House of Representatives, Committee on the Judiciary. *Immigration Reform and Control Act of 1983, Report.* Washington, D.C.: Government Printing Office, 1983.

US Select Commission on Immigration and Refugee Policy. *US Immigration Policy and the National Interest. Final Report.* Washington, D.C.: Government Printing Office, 1981.

US Senate, Committee on Foreign Relations and Joint Economic Committee. *Mexico's Oil and Gas Policy: An Analysis.* Washington, D.C., December 1978.

US Senate, Committee on the Judiciary. *Immigration Reform and Control.* Washington, D.C.: Government Printing Office, 1983.

US Senate, Subcommittee on Immigration and Refugee Policy. *Hearings.* Washington, D.C., November 1981.

Various authors. *Our Badge of Infamy: A Petition to the UN on the Treatment of the Mexican Immigrant.* New York: American Committee for the Protection of the Foreign Born, 1959.

Vásquez, Carlos, and Manuel García y Griego, eds. *Mexican-US Relations: Conflict and Convergence.* Los Angeles: UCLA Chicano Studies Research Center, 1983.

Villalpando, M. Vic, et al. *A Study of the Socioeconomic Impact of Illegal Aliens on the County of San Diego.* San Diego: County of San Diego Human Resources Agency, January 1977.

Waldinger, Roger. *The Case Against Employer's Sanctions.* Cambridge: Joint Center for Urban Studies of MIT & Harvard University, March 1980.

Weaver, Thomas, and Theodore E. Downing, eds. *Mexican Migration.* Tucson: University of Arizona Press, 1976.

Wilson, Michael. *Salt of the Earth: A Screenplay.* Old Westbury, N.Y.: Feminist Press, 1978.

Wolfe, Alan. *America's Impasse.* New York: Pantheon Books, 1981.

Zimbalist, Andrew, ed. *Case Studies in the Labor Process.* New York: Monthly Review Press, 1979.

II. JOURNALS, BULLETINS, NEWSLETTERS, AND PERIODICALS

AFL-CIO American Federationist; American Friends Service Committee (Philadelphia, occasional papers); *American Labor* (Washington, D.C.: American Labor Education Center); *Aztlan*; *Basta Ya!*; *La Causa*; *La Cosecha* (El Mirage, Arizona: Centro Adelante Campesino); *Chicano Times*; Clergy and Laity Concerned (New York, occasional papers); *Comercio Exterior*; *Cuadernos Políticos*; *Economic Notes* (New York: Labor Research Association); *Foreign Affairs*; *El Foro del Pueblo*; *El Gallo*; *El Grito del Norte*; *La Guardia* (Milwaukee); *The Guardian*; *Hispanic American Report*; *Hispanic Monitor*; Human Rights Education Project (Washington, D.C., occasional papers); *Human Rights Perspectives* (National Council of Churches); *Immigration Law Bulletin* (Los Angeles: National Center for Immigrants' Rights); *Industrial and Labor Relations Review*; *International Labor Review*; *International Migration Review*; *Justice to Immigrants* (Interfaith Coalition); *Labor History*; *Labor Today*; *Lado*; *Latin American Perspectives*; *Latin American Research Review*; *Lider* (The Latino Institute, Chicago); *El Malcriado*; *Migraciones* (Mexico); *Migration today*; *Monthly Labor Review*; *Monthly Review*; *Monthly Review of ILO*; *NACLA*; *The Nation*; *Nuestro Business Review*; *La Opinión*; *Punto Crítico*; *La Raza*; *Relaciones Internacionales* (UNAM); *Revista del Centro de Investigación y Docencia Económicas* (CIDE); *Revista Mexicana de Sociología*; *Revista Nuestro Siglo* (Mexico); *El Sentimiento del Pueblo* (Riverside, Ca.); *Sin Fronteras* (Chicago); *Southwest Economy and Society*; *Studies in Latin American Popular Culture*; *Survey of Current Business*; *La Verdad*; *Voice of the ICC* (El Paso, Tex.: International Coordinating Committee); *Voz Fronteriza* (University of California–San Diego).

INDEX

GROVE PRESS BOOKS ON LATIN AMERICA

Barnes, John / EVITA—FIRST LADY: A biography of Eva Peron / The first major biography of the beautiful and strong-willed leader of the impoverished Argentina of the 1940's. / $4.95 / 17087-3

Barry, Tom, Wood, Beth, and Preusch, Deb / DOLLARS AND DICTATORS: A Guide to Central America / ''A thorough and comprehensive study of the effect the ubiquitous corporate presence in the region has had on its politics and on American foreign policy.''—*The Progressive* / $6.95q62485-8

Borges, Jorge Luis / FICCIONES (ed. and intro. by Anthony Kerrigan) / A collection of short fictional pieces from the man whom *Time* has called ''the greatest living writer in the Spanish language today.'' / $6.95 / 17244-2

Borges, Jorge Luis / A PERSONAL ANTHOLOGY (ed. and frwd. by Antony Kerrigan) / Borges' personal selections of his work, including ''The Circular Ruins,'' ''Death and the Compass,'' and ''A New Refutation of Time.'' / $6.95 / 17270-1

Fried, Jonathan, et. al., eds. / GUATEMALA IN REBELLION: Unfinished History / A sourcebook on the history of Guatemala and its current crisis. / $8.95 / 62455-6

Gettleman, Marvin, et. al., eds. / EL SALVADOR: Central America in the New Cold War / A collection of essays, articles, and eye-witness reports on the conflict in El Salvador. ''Highly recommended for students, scholars, and policy-makers.''—*Library Journal* / $9.95 / 17956-0

Neruda, Pablo / FIVE DECADES: POEMS, 1925-1970 (Bilingual ed. tr. by Ben Belitt) / A collection of more than 200 poems by the Nobel Prize-winning Chilean poet. / $12.50 / 17869-6

Neruda, Pablo / NEW DECADE: POEMS, 1958-1967 (Bilingual ed. tr. by Ben Belitt and Alastair Reid) / $5.95 / 17275-2

Neruda, Pablo / NEW POEMS (1968-1970) (Bilingual ed. tr. and intro. by Ben Belitt) / $8.95 / 17793-2

Neruda, Pablo / SELECTED POEMS (Bilingual ed. tr. by Ben Belitt) / A selection of Neruda's finest work. Intro. by Luis Monguio. / $5.95 / 17243-4

Paz, Octavio / THE LABYRINTH OF SOLITUDE, THE OTHER MEXICO, AND OTHER ESSAYS (New preface by the author. Tr. by Lysander Kemp, Yara Milos and Rachel Phillips Belash) / A collection of Paz's best-known works and six new essays, one especially written for this volume. / $9.95 / 17992-7

Paz, Octavio / THE OTHER MEXICO: Critique of the Pyramid (tr. by Lysander Kemp) / Paz defined the character and culture of Mexico in what has now become a modern classic of critical interpretation. / $2.45 / 17773-8

Rosset, Peter and Vandermeer, John / THE NICARAGUA READER: Documents of a Revolution Under Fire / A sourcebook of articles on the Nicaraguan revolution and U.S. intervention / $8.95 / 62498-X

Rulfo, Juan / PEDRO PARAMO: A Novel of Mexico (tr. by Lysander Kemp) By the Mexican author whom the *New York Times* says will "rank among the immortals." / $3.95 / 17446-1

Thelwell, Michael / THE HARDER THEY COME / The "masterly achieved novel" (Harold Bloom) by Jamaica's finest novelist. Inspired by the now-classic film by Perry Henzell, starring Jimmy Cliff, it tells the story of a legendary gunman and folk hero who lived in Kingston in the late 1950's. / $7.95 / 17599-9

Books may be ordered directly from Grove Press. Add $1.50 per book postage and handling and send check or money order to: Order Dept., Grove Press, Inc., 196 West Houston Street, New York, N.Y. 10014.